AUTHOR OF THE TOP-SEL
HOW TO KILL A NARC......

HOW TO
BURY
A NARCISSIST

FOREVER END THE
NARCISSISM CYCLE
AND FIND A NEW BEGINNING
AFTER NARCISSISTIC ABUSE

JH SIMON

This book is not intended as a substitute for legal, medical or mental health advice. The intent of this book is to provide general advice on the topic matter covered. If professional advice or expert assistance is required, it should be sought out.

Previously published under 'Narcissism To Rebirth.'

Second edition.

ISBN: 9798846387812

Contents

Contents

Contents

Contents

Contents

Contents

Contents

Contents

Answering the call

Show me a hero, and I'll write you a tragedy.

- F. Scott Fitzgerald

Like waking from a years-long coma, to escape narcissistic abuse is to be resurrected. The spell breaks, and you see the world with new eyes. Life regains its vibrancy, hope seeps back into your heart, and for the first time in a long time, you dare to dream of a better future.

Then the honeymoon ends, and the night sets in. You find yourself in a world that has moved on without you, while the aftershocks of your ordeal rise to the surface. Waves of emotion, nightmares, even panic attacks seem to come from nowhere. For a time you struggle with recovery, having good days and bad, occasionally reaching a point of clarity and focus. Other times you find yourself thrust into the fog of despair and confusion. The crushing loneliness feels like it will never end.

As you progress with recovery, you start having more good days, and the flashbacks taper off. It seems like the worst is over. This is a time to reflect, to understand what happened. You draw comfort from the fact that your efforts are paying off. You are growing, and you are healing. You look ahead with newfound clarity, and the realisations hit you one by one. You find that your earlier innocence has given way to an emerging awareness and wisdom. You are maturing and discovering confronting truths about your world. Your eyes are opening.

Something new is also surfacing inside you, having appeared soon after the spell broke. You grow curious about this 'strange other,' but also unsettled. It trembles your foundations and brings with it an ominous warning. You get a sense that nothing will be the same again, that you are standing on a precipice. Far from fleeing, however, you find yourself drawn within, toward a boundless realm filled with opportunity. You eventually get on with your life, but you cannot help occasionally peeping inside the dark, mysterious cave. It whispers to you, sends ripples through you, and draws you in with its allure. If you go too far inside, however, you quickly feel unnerved and return your focus to the outer world of distraction.

What you may have realised by now is that you are being called to undertake a journey; one that you were born to embark on before narcissism corrupted your world. Somewhere along the line, what began with promise and hope descended into a dystopian, claustrophobic maze without end. Yet you have re-emerged, ready to take the first step back toward your evolution. You look around, and notice that outside is a life not yet fully lived, while within you are the ashes and rubble of narcissistic abuse.

So far, you have exposed the narcissist while taking steps toward healing. That mysterious presence inside you is now pointing to the future, while deep down you know that the fight is not over. Something still feels unresolved. Will you answer the call? Perhaps you are already on the path without being conscious of it. Maybe you are wondering what this path is, and what form your journey is supposed to take.

Joseph Campbell called it the *hero's journey*. This tale of adventure has been told in countless forms, wherein a protagonist leaves home, overcomes numerous obstacles and challenges, and then returns transformed. From Hercules to Perseus, all the way to Luke Skywalker and Wonder Woman, there is no shortage of hero stories in our culture, and no sign of this phenomenon slowing down. Something about them resonates deep within us, and for good reason. That these stories are so ubiquitous can numb us to their significance and distract us from their purpose, which is to awaken the hero within ourselves. Yet why go on a journey, suffer, and then return transformed? What is the point? And how does this relate to modern life?

A common thread in all hero stories is adversity. Without it, there would be no need for heroism. In every version of this myth, something is wrong with the world. There is an evil that must be faced and conquered. Tyranny has gripped society, and the people face terrible hardship or even death; unless someone steps up and does something.

Enter the hero.

In most cases, the hero is thrust into their situation by chance, or is 'chosen.' They receive the call and know they must answer. The hero never feels ready to face the challenge, but knows instinctively that they have the potential to rise to the occasion — if they are prepared to suffer through adversity. Whether in fiction or the real world, answering the call always comes with potential danger. Heroes are not celebrated for nothing. They take real risks, and own the consequences.

For us, narcissism is the tyranny we must conquer. For reasons that we will explore later, it descended upon us and corrupted the natural order of our world. Overcoming it requires facing enormous challenges. The target of narcissism must shed their identity, descend into the belly of the beast, fight numerous demons, and then return ready to face the world from a higher state. A part of you may dread this, but another part may feel excited to rise to the occasion. That is your inner hero awakening.

Some humans were destined to take the unexplored path. In doing so, they test their potential and integrate the results so they can better serve the world. Routine, doctrine and ideology all distract from this. The hero inside us is the pioneer who leaps into the unknown and discovers riches that they can share with others. The hero's journey is an attempt at removing the training wheels, and with that, discovering one's strength. Without an outer journey, there can be no inner. The two are entwined.

Many people choose not to take the hero's journey, remaining in their routine, content to live out their lives simply. There is nothing wrong with this. Sometimes the sacrifice is not worth it, other times a hero's journey is not required. Some of us, however, are destined for more. The target of narcissism, much like a conventional hero, is thrust into the underworld against their wishes. Maybe they were 'chosen.' Who knows? In any case, tyranny found its way to their doorstep, and they have no choice but to undertake the difficult journey out of their predicament. Going 'no contact' is not enough; the target of narcissism has internalised the abuse, and must transform through and through if they are to truly thrive.

The hero's journey is there to guide us toward an actualised and purpose-filled life. There is no one size fits all. Everyone's path is unique, and must be adapted to their true nature. Breaking free of the narcissist is one thing, growing to your highest potential is another. The outer journey helps you carve out a life worth living, which is carried out in conjunction with an inner journey into the Self. This book supports that endeavour by providing you with a complete map of the journey, as well as the steps to get through it.

In 'PART I: THE ORIGINS OF SELFHOOD,' we start by mapping out the True Self, which reveals the building blocks required for an enriching life. This includes the blueprints which shape us and the energy forms that empower us. By sceing our inner gifts clearly, we come to know how power is lost, regained and expanded in our relationships. Above all, by integrating the True Self and its gifts, we can better weave an empowered reality. Ideally, this initial phase is managed by a good-enough parent, wherein the Self thrives as a result and we become captains of our own ship, proudly sailing toward actualisation. What begins as a divine Utopia during infancy leads to growth and prosperity in adulthood — unless the process is interrupted, of course.

'PART II: THE AGE OF NARCISSISM' details the fall from this garden, so to speak, where trauma lays waste to the soul. The natural flowering of the True Self abruptly stops, and a rigid personality emerges to compensate and defend from insanity. Meanwhile, the True Self remains buried deep within the rubble of the soul. During this dark period of tyranny, the narcissist enslaves anyone they can to gain supply, eventually taking this corrupted mindset into family life. Here we explore the roles and dynamics of the narcissistic family, along with how this blueprint manifests at all levels of society, including friendships, workplaces and spiritual communities. The kaleidoscope of the narcissist's many faces is also explored, including the cluster B personality disorders and psychopathy, allowing you to spot a narcissist in their infinite, hidden forms. Additionally, we will explore the narcissist's playbook of manipulation tactics, such as scapegoating, gaslighting and triangulation, which will further arm you against toxic abuse. Finally, you will be guided in seeing how this entire landscape shaped you. By knowing the scope of the problem, and having the courage to own your part in it, you can break the cycle of narcissistic abuse for good.

We find ourselves now having temporarily broken free of the narcissist's spell. Yet this moment is not the end of our journey, nor is it the beginning. Rather we are *resuming* an original journey by first freeing our True Self from the clutches of narcissism, and then going deep within ourselves to restore the five developmental forces of the Self: *security, vitality, tenacity, divinity and wisdom.* 'PART III: THE HERO'S JOURNEY' outlines the process of shedding the layers of narcissistic abuse and actively developing the five forces from our core.

Such an undertaking is not to be pursued lightly. It requires the heart of a hero, a person willing to venture to the edge of their faith — and then further. This modern-day spiritual journey requires that you travel away from home — i.e. your routine and comfort zone, and into the depths of your being. There you will encounter formidable opponents such as toxic shame, rage, despair, confusion, the inner critic, your abandonment wound and, of course, fear. Facing and moving through these 'demons' will be essential to your success. It is on this path that you will also meet with a mysterious figure; a certain someone who has been there the whole time, waiting for their saviour to arrive. You are that saviour, and you are the mysterious figure.

As you will soon discover, this enigmatic 'other' is your divine essence, which feeds your actualisation and growth. Tapping into it opens you to a world not only of torrential grief, but also abundant potential. For reasons beyond your control, this divine figure was imprisoned, left alone in the depths of your soul as the narcissist took control of your mind. It is this powerful being who you will bring back from your journey, and it is their superhuman qualities which you will integrate so that you can find wholeness. Only then can your evolution truly begin.

As it is with all heroes, inside you is the blueprint and resources to actualise into the person you were meant to be. Hero energy lies within all of us, having been gifted to us by our ancestors, who underwent their own journey into the soul in order to conquer the challenge of their day. We are here because they faced their demons and won. We are products of countless generations of successful evolution. What is needed from us now is the readiness to pay our ancestors homage by also taking on the mighty struggle. We must willingly be torn apart and put back together; to be pushed to our limits, and emerge anew. This is not wishful storytelling, but a genuine alchemical and psychological process. You should not take hero stories literally, they merely point toward a necessary human undertaking. This process leads to a cosmic expansion of your consciousness, the evolution of your mind, body and spirit, and the discovery of unimaginable wonders.

Every hero who ventures into the underworld will have help along the way. While this can and probably should take the form of a therapist, support group or good friend, assistance will also come from unexpected places. As you plunge into the depths of your Self, you will discover resources you thought only others possessed. You find that every courageous act brings with it unexpected rewards, as periods of pain and frustration lead to an eventual revelation or breakthrough. With each minor victory, you learn that your pain tolerance is great, and that inside you is an organism which is self-regulating, supportive and wise beyond imagination. The more you learn to trust this organism, the further you will progress.

As already stated, healing from narcissistic abuse is not a goal in itself; we do it so we can free our inner resources and channel them toward a higher purpose. It was narcissistic abuse which put us in this position, and it is the hero's journey which gets us back on course. Only when the road is sufficiently travelled will you truly know yourself. When all is said and done, you will return with 'the gold.' That is, you will be in possession of a fully-actualised Self that you can channel in incredible ways. What you choose to do with this powerful gift is the focus of 'PART IV: THE RETURN,' where you take what you have learned and gained, and apply it to your daily life, except this time on your terms. By living through your True Self, you will finally have a sense of meaning and purpose. That gnawing feeling of emptiness gradually fades, and your relationships cease to be dysfunctional and abusive.

Having returned from your hero's journey, you see your old world with new eyes. You take a sobering look at the part you played in the narcissistic dynamic, and undergo deep grief, as fantasy gives way to reality. Furthermore, you come to see the wounding behind every narcissist you meet while maintaining a safe distance. In doing so, the tyrannical grip of narcissism shatters forever, and an age of authenticity and hope can emerge.

The narcissist's dystopian world is perilous, yet you nonetheless possess the capacity to overcome it. Narcissists are everywhere, always seeking to dominate and control. Narcissism is a part of human nature, and as a consequence, so is malignant narcissism. Its sorcery is boundless.

Lucky for you, so is the power of your True Self.

PART I:
THE ORIGINS OF SELFHOOD

The birth of worship

Man, so long as he remains free, has no more constant and agonising anxiety than find as quickly as possible someone to worship.

- Fyodor Dostoevsky

Self-actualisation is an unfolding toward a higher state. We are hardwired to explore and learn about our surroundings as well as look for our place in society. How we actualise depends on our personality, our environment, our DNA, our influences, and what resonates with our True Self.

We pursue actualisation in countless ways, such as public service, research, literature, art, sports, philosophy, study, business or raising a family. Once something resonates with us, we immerse ourselves in it. This begins a process of deepening our relationship with the world, deepening our maturity, and most importantly, deepening our connection with our True Self. In doing so, we move into our spiritual centre and direct it toward a higher purpose, hence emulating all other life forms. From the single-celled organism to the mighty blue whale, life has a great deal to teach us, not only about physical growth, but also our actualisation.

Take a tree, for example, which we can characterise in three ways:

1. **Earth:** It is nurtured from beneath by rooting itself in the soil.
2. **Heaven:** It is sustained from above by photosynthesising and growing toward the sun.
3. **Divine Purpose:** It supports life by providing oxygen, food, shelter or even medicine.

Using the tree as an analogy, we see that humans are bound to this same process of development. We too must be supported by a source of nurture, must have a higher state to aspire toward, and so long as we are alive, must direct our life energy toward a creative purpose which contributes to our world. If any of these three elements are missing, we fall into ill-health and despair.

This dark, heavy state plagues us all on occasion, and lies at the core of every living being. Sigmund Freud, in his book 'Beyond the Pleasure Principle,' proposed that 'the goal of all life is death,' of which he is mostly correct. In reality, the goal of all life is death and *rebirth*. This is the endless cycle of the universe, where life is born, dies, and is replaced by new life forms. This process is balanced by opposing drives which constantly work together to achieve balance. Freud called one the *life instinct*, and the other the *death instinct*.

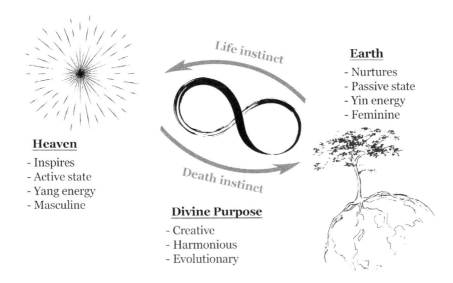

Figure 1: The actualisation of life. The tree, like any living organism, originates from a single point (Earth), growing from nothing to a higher state (Heaven), while playing out a divine purpose in its environment. Binding this process together are the opposing life and death instincts.

The life instinct compels us to survive, pursue pleasure, love and care for others, cooperate, reproduce, and self-actualise. The death instinct, in comparison, has a magnetic pull toward a desolate state which the life instinct must overcome. We all experience this when we struggle to get out of bed, or get caught in negative thinking, or procrastinate, or fall into apathy and depression. Behind these inhibiting acts of self-sabotage is the death instinct, continually working to return life to its original, inorganic state. However, so long as our basic needs for food, shelter and connection are met, and as long as we have a higher power to aspire toward, the life instinct can thrive — despite the pull of the death instinct. What Freud referred to as the 'pressure toward death' is then overcome, and our journey can progress. The only remaining concern we have is determining which direction this so-called life instinct should take.

Permission to grow

Our divine purpose is unique compared to other life forms, due to our ability to choose a higher power to model ourselves after, which we do through *worship*.

The definition of worship is: 'adoration for a deity.' Yet this does not fully capture it. Another way to define worship is: 'the act of channelling our actualisation through another person or entity.' This involves making ourselves completely vulnerable and defenceless, as well as identifying with someone or something which we believe can lead us to a higher state of being.

Furthermore, before we can begin the path toward Self-actualisation, we need to secure help. While a tree can anchor itself in the soil and grow toward the sun, humans need the support of other humans to grow to maturity. The world is complex and full of danger, and our True Self has infinite potential, while our body is limited — especially early in life. We start off helpless while overwhelmed with possibilities in an ever-expanding civilisation. Along with nurture, we need life presented to us in a structured way. We also need initiation into the world, which we gain by imitating specific role models within our 'tribe.' For this reason, we feel an instant pull toward people who we believe can show us the way forward; people of higher power who 'have it all worked out.'

The original higher power

Regardless of whether you are religious or not, you have already given yourself over to a higher power. The second you came out of the womb, you were a frightened, vulnerable baby, with a desperate need for care and security. From this precarious position, anyone who cared for you became larger than life. These family figures were flawed, of course. Yet from your infantile perspective, they were magical beings from a divine realm, possessing qualities and abilities that were beyond your comprehension.

Consider that your experience back then was immensely different from now. For one, you did not possess the mind you now take for granted. Logic and knowledge were non-existent. There was no analysing and making sense of the world. Instead, you experienced the world *energetically*. An example which demonstrates this mode is a superhero movie, or any movie with a compelling protagonist. These transcendental characters are portrayed as supremely gifted, and hence morph into someone other-worldly. An underdeveloped mind views its parents precisely this way. Relative to a baby, consider the herculean strength of your father as he picked you up without effort. Imagine for a second your mother's nurturing softness, and the intoxicating way her breast milk would have nourished your fledgling body. These paragons really would have been something to behold for a child.

When you reached your 'terrible twos,' you entered the narcissistic phase of childhood development, and your grandiosity peaked. You believed you were indestructible, and that the world revolved around you. Your vocabulary consisted mostly of 'I,' 'me' and 'mine.' You roamed your environment shamelessly, while there was always somebody taking care of your every need. Eventually, you hit barriers. As frustrating as it was, there was a gap between your perceived capabilities and your actual power. You realised that without someone to support you and cater to your needs, you would get nowhere. Due to your lack of real-world ability, you had no choice but to delegate power to your guardians. You noticed that food, clothing and toys appeared like magic, and you took for granted that they would keep coming. Where things came from and who made them did not cross your mind, nor did the thought that you would one day have to provide for yourself. Personal power would come later in life as you grew and developed. Meanwhile, your guardians reigned over your life. You allowed them to feed you, shelter you, clothe you, help you go to the bathroom, manage your bedtime, and tell you where it was safe and unsafe to play. It was a given that they ran the show. This act of surrendering your personal power is called *infantilisation.*

Infantilisation is a state of helplessness, a survival mode in which a child entrusts their guardian to look after their well-being. It is like a warm blanket that slips over someone and sheds them of agency as soon as they are in the presence of any figure of perceived higher power. When infantilised, a person unconsciously hands over the wheel for their life. It is like being 'remote-controlled' by the mind of another person.

Here you have no agency except when the other person says so. In childhood, this is normal and expected. Whether the higher power is nurturing and loving, or neglectful and abusive, is irrelevant. The primary concern is survival, and therefore *any* higher power is better than none.

Infantilised and with no capacity to influence outcomes, the child reverts to using a crude psychological mechanism to establish a sense of control. Much like a binary switch, on one side is a state of absolute worship, and on the other, a total rejection of it.

Split to survive

Having no capacity to protect or care for oneself is terrifying. You will appreciate that for the child, abandonment equals death. This vulnerable position would have brought you face to face with the death instinct. When the death instinct arises, a child is gripped with terror. Life becomes black and white, meaning you lose the ability to see the nuances of a situation. Survival becomes your sole concern.

While some situations terrify more than others, the child can never feel entirely at ease. They remain acutely sensitive to stressors at all times. Also, at that age, the child cannot comprehend that their guardian might have stress in their life, have bad moods, or still be dealing with unresolved trauma. The child only knows that anger and neglect equate to danger.

To deal with the terror of being alive, we reverted to a binary view of the world. We abstracted our experiences to maintain tight psychological control, switching between a state of absolute loving, or pure loathing. We adored anything that we perceived as 'good' with all our heart, such as our family or favourite toy. On the other hand, we hated anything that we saw as 'bad' or that frightened us, which also included our family members when they were neglectful, unpredictable or abusive.

This polarised state can be represented on a continuum as follows:

Love/Loathing Continuum

Loathing	Neutrality	Love
"You are pure evil"	"You are human"	"You are divine"
"Get away from me"	"I see you"	"Come closer"
"Stop existing"	"I acknowledge you"	"Never change"

Figure 2: The love/loathing continuum. *Children, as well as adults polarised by fear, will alternate between two extremes to regain a sense of control. With loathing, one aims to psychologically annihilate a source of threat, whereas with love, they aim to merge themselves with a source of nurture and power.*

For a child, neutrality is not an option. Life is black and white, all or nothing. When your guardian mirrored you, catered to your needs and helped you feel safe, you loved them with all your heart. This would have brought you closer to the life instinct; that warm feeling of safety and confidence which propels you toward Self-actualisation. When your guardian became angry, cold or neglectful, your death instinct activated instead, and you directed your rage toward them. This polarised state is why babies and children can turn to anger so unexpectedly, and then be instantly appeased and made calm again.

What Melanie Klein referred to as *splitting* gave you somewhere to direct the intense emotions which you could not process in your under-developed mind. It was vital for you to create a *tyrant* figure and focus your rage toward them. You did this to preserve what came to be a *divine being*, a loving and perfect figure who would never abandon you. Furthermore, by having a perceived tyrant to rage against, you could 'empower' yourself against the terrifying prospect of abandonment or annihilation. In the child's mind, a person remains divine until they let the child down, after which they become the tyrant. In reality, your guardian was a person whom you experienced in polar opposite ways.

A word such as 'annihilation' might seem extreme to an adult, but in the child's mind, it is a real possibility. The more abusive or neglectful a guardian is, the more overwhelming the terror becomes, and the more a child must split to cope. When situations feel frightening, the child clings to any sign of the divine being, thus helping alleviate their dread. In the child's mind, this will protect them. In reality, the split is keeping the child sane.

The split is also why we are so strongly affected by heroes and villains in popular culture. By identifying with and worshipping the hero, we vicariously experience a sense of power, whereas the villain becomes the dumping ground for our negative emotions and fear of helplessness. The split is why we fantasise and project ideal situations and outcomes in our minds. It helps us cope with the unpleasantness of life. It also explains how parents often continue to hold tremendous sway over their children for decades, turning with one snide remark an otherwise independent and robust adult into a helpless infant.

The great parent

A fascinating effect of the split is the uncanny 'quality' it gives the people we project it on — above all our parents. Regardless of what we believe, nobody can deny that they have experienced this polarised state. We have all adored our heroes and role models to the point of obsession, or have found ourselves despising our loved ones or public figures to the point of utter disgust.

As already explained, a higher power is critical for our development. Losing it for even a second throws us into disarray. This is what gives parents such power. Like the soil nourishing a tree's roots, or the sun shining above, our guardians play a fundamental role in our growth which permeates the deepest corners of our psyche. Helping them with this tremendous, life-creating responsibility are a set of archetypal energies based on Heaven and Earth. One represents profound wisdom, the other embodies boundless abundance. One provides structure, guidance and purpose, the other demonstrates the art of life. These masculine and feminine energies manifest in the psyche in the form of two *archetypes* separated by gender; the *great father* and the *great mother*.

An archetype is a blueprint handed down from our ancestors, which contains a pool of traits, points of view, abilities and energy forms. An example of an archetype is the *warrior*, who is aggressively strong and competent in combat and warfare. Another is the *explorer*, a restless person who is naturally driven to challenge the status quo and pursue the unknown path. The hero is naturally an archetype, being the person who rises to meet a challenge in order to make meaningful change. In their purest form, archetypes hold enormous potential, and they are within us all. However, because we are human, embodying their potential is a lifelong challenge which we never get right. It is no different for the great father and mother, both of which posed enormous challenges for our ancestors trying to embody them. The immense capacity of these two archetypes to nurture and support life was passed on from one generation to the other, until it was time for our parents to embody them.

First of all, the great mother and father archetypes are not limited to a person of the corresponding sex. A man can embody the great mother, and a woman the great father. Fathers can be affectionate and nurturing, and mothers can provide guidance and wisdom. Secondly, no person can be perfect in their endeavour to live up to these God-like figures. Nonetheless, they exist in every human being as latent energy waiting to be released when duty calls. From the point of our conception, these archetypes looked to express themselves through our guardians. When a parent recollects the moment their first child was born, they tend to describe a momentous shift. This is, in fact, the great parent archetype awakening within them. They sense themselves presented with a significant responsibility which calls on them to leave youthful pretence behind, and transform into the formidable figure their child needs them to be.

At its best, the great parent brings out superhuman qualities in a person, along with the ability to create a safe container for the child to grow and actualise. The guardian becomes wise, calm and supportive, able to attune to the child's needs by drawing on the abundant powers coming from within. In the worst case, however, when the parent is traumatised, stressed or caught up in addiction, the great parent archetype transforms into the tyrant. The parent's posture stiffens, their face permanently hardens, and their gaze sharpens. They use a combination of anger, disapproving stares, emotional coldness and shamelessness to enforce the image of authority and control. Some parents alternate between the two extremes in a split moment, lovingly channelling the great parent, until frustration tips them over the edge, from which they grow rigid and angry, unconsciously channelling the tyrannical parent. Other times, we project the tyrant onto our parents regardless of whether it is justified, as captured in the teenager who screams "I hate you!" when they fail to get their way, or the three-year-old who throws a tantrum.

The split also works the other way when adults are overwhelmed and insecure. When you were angry and uncooperative, your guardians experienced you as the 'bad child,' and when you were cooperative and loving, they experienced you as the 'good child.' Many parents even call their children 'good girl/good boy' and 'bad girl/bad boy' depending on the child's behaviour, which is the parent's split in action.

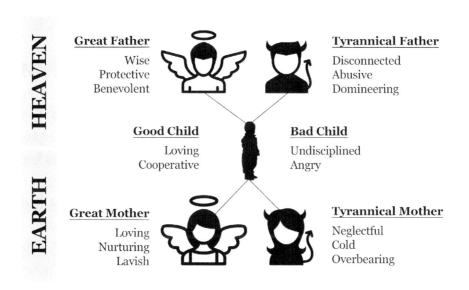

Figure 3: The split dynamic between a child and their guardian/s. *The figures which arise from the split are enigmas, uncanny 'spirits' from another realm. When the energy of the great or tyrannical parent expresses itself through our guardian, however, it becomes quite real. The great mother offers a source of nourishment for the True Self via the Earth realm. The great father is a north star or lighthouse who leads us to our Self-actualisation.*

In childhood, you looked to the great mother for *yin* energy, a passive force which regenerates and sustains the soul. The great mother held you safely in her womb, then nurtured you once you were born, caring for you and helping you feel secure. Through the yin energy of the great mother you were able to rest in being, and so align yourself with the harmonious flow of life energy. Later, you connected with the great father; a figure who could provide structure and protection. His role was to help you channel *yang* energy, an active force for penetrating and impacting the world.

These two enigmatic archetypes dominated your psyche, and you yearned for them as the figures who would shield you from the terror of life. Your later expectations of them depended on your experiences with your carers, which began with your guardians, then extended to older siblings, uncles and aunties, teachers and any other adult of perceived higher power. Each person contributed toward your idea of what the great mother and great father archetypes encapsulate. For example, if your father was short-tempered and angry, you would form a picture of men as being more tyrannical than benevolent. If your mother was emotionally closed off, you might see women as cold and difficult to please — a source of shame and rejection. Such experiences remain firmly planted in your psyche for the rest of your life as *paternal complexes*, which the Jung Lexicon defines as 'a group of emotionally charged images and ideas associated with the parents.' These are activated and projected onto anybody you perceive as more powerful than you, which helps explain why we often feel fear and uncertainty around people of high status or beauty. Their apparent perfection associates them in our minds with the frustration and pain of trying to obtain the love of the great parent. These deeply entrenched complexes can cripple us and render us helpless. They also influence our relationships moving forward, and as much as it can feel like it is the person who is triggering these emotions, it is in fact our split activating, along with flashbacks of past experiences with the great mother or father.

From splitting to worship

Due to your precarious position, you had no choice but to split and project onto your guardians the archetype of the great parent. The alternative was unthinkable; the tyrannical mother or father could annihilate you. As a result, you infantilised yourself and worshipped your guardians. In your developing mind you looked up to them, hoping they would use their power to support you, inspire you and mirror back your divine nature. When you ran out to explore the world, you looked back on occasion to make sure they were still there watching over you. In turn, you observed them and imitated their actions. You shared your smallest successes with them. Their approval was everything, and their disapproval crushed you.

Because they were 'perfect,' their word was gospel. Consequently, their anger and disapproval could never be their fault; it had to be someone else's. To blame the great parent would be to risk losing your source of nourishment and safety. So you focussed your rage and negative feelings toward the tyrannical parent instead. How your guardian handled their alternating position as the great parent and tyrant would play an enormous part in your growth and future relationships. Such is the power of the split. Such is the power of anyone we worship.

This early tendency to externalise our source of higher power gives others a license to set us free, or imprison and control us. Behind our surrender lies the enigmatic great parent, setting the stage for every future relationship, running deeper than we could ever imagine. Society feeds off our split in numerous ways. Celebrities project an image of perfection, and we unconsciously see them as a higher power. Monarchies maintained a firm grip over whole empires for centuries in the same way by projecting divinity. Dictators, through fear and cult of personality, also capitalise on this phenomenon. On a smaller scale, the split is responsible for the halo effect, which is when we exaggerate a person's goodness and wisdom based on their appearance and body language, becoming putty in their hands while doing our best to please them. A lesser-known but common form of the split is when we meet someone who reminds us of our parents in particular ways, wherein we feel ourselves unconsciously drawn to them in a child-like way.

Whoever can project the illusion of high status and grandeur can awaken our inner child and therefore hijack our personal power. The woman or man of stature, strength or undeniable beauty, the celebrity, the politician, the charmer, the social media influencer; anyone can activate our split and gain our worship, or at least our curiosity. It is easy to forget the intended purpose of the split, which is to maintain psychological health long enough for us to come of age. Easy to lose sight of is our divine purpose, which is Self-actualisation. The goal is not to forfeit our personal power to others, but rather to use worship as a launching pad for our growth, with the result being the constellation of a competent and fully-developed Self.

The making of an empowered Self

There is a vitality, a life force, an energy, a quickening, that is translated through you into action, and because there is only one of you in all time, this expression is unique.

- Martha Graham

We can only pursue actualisation when our core needs are sufficiently met, and it is the role of a higher power to provide a structure for those needs. The higher power is not the destination, but rather the lighthouse which guides us while we come of age. As children, our guardians are our higher power, while family is our vessel. The purpose of family is to love and empower us, and give us a sense of belonging. It is intended to remain in place until we are old enough to differentiate and follow our chosen path. The result of an ideal upbringing is a battle-tested, resourceful Self which can hold its own. Rather than relying purely on others, we draw on the Self as a source of yin and yang energy which sustains and guides us from within.

The five developmental forces of the Self

Who we are, how we should live, our limits, and how capable we are; these are a web of stories we pick up over a lifetime. Fuelling these stories, however, is a realm beyond the mind, where personality is shaped by energy. This comes in the form of five developmental forces; *security, vitality, tenacity, divinity* and *wisdom*.

Stage		Accompanying Traits	Governing Emotion
1	Security	- Sense of safety - Inner harmony - Feeling of being 'ok'	Fear
2	Vitality	- Capacity for bonding - Passion for life - Curiosity and spontaneity	Love
3	Tenacity	- Boundary setting - The will to act - Durability and perseverance	Hate
4	Divinity	- Self-esteem - Self-legitimacy - Radiance	Pride
5	Wisdom	- Knowledge and competence - Humility - Intuition	Shame

Figure 4: The five developmental forces of the Self.

The developmental forces emerge at various phases of early life, with each one accompanied by a governing emotion. *Fear* is the first to arise during the prenatal stage, where the child draws security from the womb and gauges the safety of the outside world via the mother. After birth, a push-pull dynamic of *love* and *hate* establishes itself as soon as the child identifies their loved ones i.e. the mother and father. When the parent meets the child's needs and is warm and attentive, the child loves them openly, and the bond can deepen. When the parents do not meet the child's needs or are cold and neglectful, the child's hate bubbles up in the form of rage to compel the parents to engage the child how it wants. *Pride* and *shame* arise next, coming into play when the child's ego emerges, where the child gains the ability to 'conceptualise' themselves as an individual in the world who has status, value and agency. The child begins to experiment with grandiosity, hungry to grow in social stature and to influence the people around them. Where they hit roadblocks, shame brings them down a peg and reminds them of their limits.

Developing the True Self is a dynamic process, where the foundational emotions flood our system and shape us in unique ways. Learning to work with these energies is critical to confident living, as is understanding how they can be turned against us. Anyone who has suffered narcissistic abuse knows that love can entrap you, or set you free. Shame can be a force which crushes you, or it can instil in you the humility and discipline to achieve your goals. Like Icarus, pride can be your downfall, or it can awaken your potential. When used to set boundaries, hate can free you from perpetual people-pleasing and resentment.

These five, interconnected forces are crucial for empowerment. If any of them is compromised, the remainder will suffer, and compensation strategies must come into play to rc-cstablish balance. For example, a lack of tenacity leaves a person in a passive state, making them reliant on the whims of others to get what they need. A lack of pride leaves a person doubtful about their place in the world, and shame seeps in to fill the void, halting progress behind a wall of self-doubt and despair. A lack of any of the five forces impacts not only a person's relationships, but also their belief system, their body, their capacity to assert themselves and connect with others, and their self-esteem. How these forces develop can be the difference between a life of perpetual suffering and frustration, or one of prosperity and abundance.

1. Security

Fear is the foundation of safety.

- Tertullian

The cortex of an unborn baby's brain develops around six months, making it highly likely that we were conscious before birth. While we may not have explicit memories of our time in the womb, what we experienced nonetheless remains deeply entrenched.

During these formative months, we adopt our mother's state, sensing much of what she experiences in the outside world. If our mother is overwhelmed, the stress hormones in her system will invade and put us on high alert. As a result, her anxiety becomes imprinted in us at a cellular level. We curl our hands and feet while tensing our tiny body to resist the fear seeping in. This 'armouring' of our bodies is a way of withstanding the stress of our environment, and it can remain with us indefinitely. The plus side is that we survive, the minus side being that we can never truly relax. This explains why some people can find it difficult simply to feel 'ok' in the world. They are still physiologically 'holding on,' haunted by the inescapable, prenatal imprints of fear.

After we are born, our mother uses non-verbal methods of communication to help us regulate our emotional state and feel calm and safe. The more secure she feels in herself, the more skilful she will be at helping us achieve the same. By emotionally and physically grounding ourselves in her, we can feel at home in our body. In dysfunctional or overstressed families, this becomes nearly impossible. The child tries to read the state of the distracted mother through her body language and facial expressions, looking for reassurance. Instead of being met with a calm and happy face, they see only anxiety, gloom and emotional distance. The result is a deep-seated feeling of terror and the surfacing of the death instinct.

Fear: The governing emotion of security

Meditation is the act of observing without judgement. This means letting go of the mind, and having the discipline to 'see' beyond your thoughts. It requires a willingness to embrace 'being,' to become a single point of focus — i.e. the observer.

Through the observer you become consciousness, and witness your thoughts without engaging them. You see them not as gospel, but as psychological form which comes and goes. As the observer, you can go even further, where you discover that your emotions are also just form; a set of sensations which come and go. Once this practice becomes clear to you, you can sink further into the Self, where you experience a temporary 'death.' Here the realm of energy reveals itself, making it easier to spot the patterns which form your being. Moreover, you can witness how emotions constellate predictably in response to how you perceive the world. Without these thoughts, sensations, emotions and patterns to create a 'Self' from, the psychological construct you believed to be 'you' collapses. All that is left is the witness, who comes to know that beyond all form is nothing. Emptiness. A void.

And yet, just as life grows from nothing and continuously evolves, you discover that within the void there is restless movement. Past the stillness, inside the black, you experience a torrent of energy rushing toward you. The more neutral and focussed you are, the more this energy flows out in its purest form. If you remain centred and cease to analyse the mental, emotional and sensual facets of yourself, you learn that behind all life energy there is one ingredient: *fear*.

One could argue that without fear, our lives would collapse. There would be nothing but emptiness. If we did not fear death, we would fall into the void and have no reason to come back out. Because of fear, a state of emptiness always results in its opposite: fullness. When we go beyond the mind, the void emerges. From within the void, fear flows. When fear peaks, we awaken fully.

Fear is the basic building block of our life, the core ingredient which forms the other emotional forces. Fear directs our attention away from the void and wills us toward fullness. However, it also needs to come in manageable doses — especially early in life. Children cannot withstand and act proactively in the face of fear. Their little bodies cannot handle it. They need to feel secure to combat the terror of being alive.

When life is structured and we feel supported, we stop experiencing fear as a raw, destabilising emotion. Instead, it converts to other forms which we can utilise for our evolution — i.e. love, hate, shame and pride. If life becomes unpredictable and threatening, however, then we revert to a fearful state to ensure our survival.

When security is disrupted

A child's capacity to contain fear is at first wholly determined by the mother's state. If the mother is calm, content and secure, then the baby will internalise that same state. When security is lacking, the child cannot remain present. The death instinct is a dark, intolerable apparition. The child therefore 'checks out' from reality, creating fantasies of security which remind them of the warmth of the womb. If this goes on long enough, the child cannot fully come into the world, psychologically speaking. They live life with one foot in the real world and the other in an alternate reality. They want to take part in and explore their environment, but are unable to shake free from their bone-deep anxiety. They continue to fear exposure while craving an elusive Utopia in their mind.

Every child is born with an intoxicating awareness of their divine nature, which pours out of the True Self. As the child grows, the outside world slowly consumes them, and they leave the energetic realm behind. The insecure child, on the other hand, with their 'one foot in the door' state of mind, maintains their bond with the 'other side.' They do this because, to them, reality cannot be trusted. We have all met such people. They are often dreamers and creative types, or otherwise seem 'not all there.' That is because they are not. They find it so easy to check out, they are usually in a state of fantasy and imagination. This occurs especially when they are anxious, fearful or overwhelmed, where they use dissociation and imagination to soothe themselves. They also tend to be intuitive, and where others get stuck on the details, they can see the world in an abstract manner.

Becoming stuck in security

Security is the foundation for actualisation. If a child can sufficiently ground themselves through the mother, feeling 'ok' stops being a concern for them. They take it for granted that everything will be fine, and turn their attention outwards. On the other hand, the insecure child remains stuck in between, held back from fully engaging the world by persistent, overwhelming fear. Instead, they cope by dreaming of a perfect, frictionless Utopia, an abstract concept which never arrives and which they can never let go of.

Unable to escape mortality, the mind compensates by creating the promise of security. Deep down, we all know that absolute security does not exist. Every living being is doing its best while constantly vulnerable to harm and death. For the ego, which is only interested in survival, this is an unacceptable reality. Instead, it manifests the illusion of being omnipotent, hence rendering it 'invulnerable' to outside harm. This is a useful coping mechanism, but nothing more. To be invincible and indestructible is a utopian dream which keeps a person stuck, and empowers them as much as an ostrich with its head in the sand. Real security only comes in one form, and that is the *offensive* strategy of finding the courage to enter into and engage the flow of life.

When security is established

While absolute security is a fantasy created by the mind, a sense of security can be obtained by *moving with* the flow of life. To achieve this, a person needs to experience *just* the right amount of fear. This spontaneous, open way of living generates security by encouraging the person to be at one with life. Someone engaged with the world is prepared to act when something goes wrong. For that they require a healthy amount of fear which comes from allowing life energy to flow. Anything less, and they descend into the formless void and lose motivation. Any more than they can handle, and they soon become overwhelmed and dissociated, growing tense to hold back the intensity and living in their head. Without a secure baseline, a person loses touch with their body, and their focus scatters. However, take a peak amount, and combine it with trust, and a state of ease and flow will emerge, giving a person the confidence to engage the world. Bonding with others becomes possible, and vitality awakens.

2. Vitality

Some people would claim that things like love, joy and beauty belong to a different category from science and can't be described in scientific terms, but I think they can now be explained by the theory of evolution.

- Stephen Hawking

Evolution has a restless force fuelling it, thrusting life toward ever higher states of being. When growing organisms collide, they adapt to each other in unprecedented ways. This same force is always looking to act through us, to move us toward creating bonds and evolving as actualised beings.

Vitality is characterised by curiosity, openness and joy. It gives you a sense that change is coming, and that you need to be there to meet it, lest you miss the ship and get left behind. Vitality excites you and simultaneously fills you with unease and dread. Like a double-edged sword, it promises endless wonders, while asking you to accept uncertainty and risk. As long as you remain fixed to routine and the status quo, vitality will never visit you. You will resist it at every turn, and in doing so, miss the opportunities it offers. Carl Jung called it the 'Anima,' which represents the feminine element of the psyche. To Jung, the Anima is a symbol of chaos, a call to adventure and reckless abandon. At the very least, it calls you to be open-hearted, willing to be forged by the fire of life. To have vitality is to be a river, always flowing and changing, alive and sensitive to the world around you.

The child is the quintessential example of vitality in motion. They tremble with overflowing vigour, curious about everything they see, their senses overloaded as they absorb the world at a rapid pace. Vitality is also the coveted 'supply' which narcissists seek. When the target exposes their True Self, vitality flows. Narcissists then sense the opportunity and brainwash their target into investing this energy into them. Because the narcissist lacks access to their True Self, it is always *through another person* that they experience vitality.

Vitality enables personal evolution, or it can be directed into a hierarchy or power structure and used to fuel that entity's growth instead. The narcissist exploits vitality much like this, colonising the target's mind before extracting supply. In this way, vitality is a resource worth more than gold, obtained when the target unwittingly surrenders their love.

Love: The governing emotion of vitality

Love is a component of the life instinct. It thrives when a person feels secure and connected; especially to sources of perceived higher power. Loving and being loved awakens and empowers the soul. It has a contagious vibrancy, enhancing a person's life force and activating their libido. This is not a reference to romantic love, but rather to a mutual space of openness and surrender where energy is shared. For a person to love, they need to make themselves vulnerable by exposing their True Self. In such a state, you *see* the person you love in their fullness — not just an abstraction. Their eyes stand out, and their energy penetrates as you both enter a state of mutual flow.

All creative acts depend on love. Making art, dance, giving a speech; these all require a state of flow and excitement for life, where the core ingredient is vitality. To be in flow is to forgo control, allowing the wisdom of life energy to lead you forward. You know this to be true during moments where things magically work out without you needing to control a situation. Overthinking, fear and self-doubt all thwart this process.

A relationship is a fascinating example of such creativity. It is at once incredibly complex yet has no physical form, existing only in the hearts and minds of those who partake. Think of two or more old friends bantering back and forth. Often this simple act of 'hanging out' contains something deeper than meets the eye, revealing an entire microcosm of inside jokes, shared knowledge and quirky behaviour which seamlessly builds on itself with each interaction. With a state of shared trust, flow opens between the friends, and vitality creates new threads which reinforce the friendship.

When trust is established between two or more people, love can grow, and the creative process begins, with no two relationships being the same. Each person develops through love, and as long as trust and mirroring remain, growth and actualisation are possible.

When vitality is disrupted

Vitality requires a witness. At birth, a child immediately seeks out a loved one; a person who can contain and mirror the outpouring of their life energy. Otherwise, they cannot cope.

If there is a lack of mirroring, the flow of vitality is interrupted, wherein the effects can vary from disruptive to downright devastating. When a guardian acknowledges the child some of the time and is emotionally or physically distant the rest of the time, the child pendulates between connection and abandonment. Because of their guardian's intermittent affection, the child becomes like a gambling addict, desperate to finally 'win' the jackpot and secure their parent's love. Much like a slot machine, the parent is unpredictable, and fear of abandonment becomes a fixture in the child's psyche. As a result, they grow needy and uptight, never feeling fully secure in their relationships.

Other children are actively abused and terrified by their loved ones. Such a person associates vitality with fear, and any excessive flow of life energy — especially in a social context — sends that person back to the level of security. They tighten their body, withdraw physically or check out mentally and drift into their imagination. To them, connection equates to unpredictable negative consequences, and they unconsciously sabotage their fledgling relationships.

Where a guardian is emotionally distant at all times, the child gives up outright, losing trust in relationships and refusing to be vulnerable.

Becoming stuck in vitality

A child who does not experience consistent connection and mirroring remains stuck at this stage of development, becoming preoccupied with obtaining and keeping love rather than moving on to the higher stages of development. For them, love ceases to be a means to an end, and instead becomes the focus of their life. They remain stuck, never able to fully trust love. Even when they obtain it, they remain preoccupied with the fear of losing it, rather than using the relationship as a launching pad toward their evolution. This fear remains a disruptive force in their life, and often causes the breakdown of their relationships, becoming a self-fulfilling prophecy and creating even more anxiety around love.

When vitality is established

The bridge between security and vitality is made of trust. When a person has confidence that a loved one will not harm or take advantage of them, the bond can strengthen over time, and all parties can grow through the creative process of reciprocity and mirroring. The outcome of such consistency in a relationship is called *object constancy*.

Put simply, object constancy is a stable, internalised image we hold of a person. We develop object constancy in a relationship when our loved one is consistently loving and accepting of us. Through repeated positive interactions, we eventually come to believe that we are worthy of love, and become confident that the relationship will remain into the future. When our loved one goes away for a period of time, we keep the internalised image of them inside our mind and heart, knowing that they will return.

Object constancy is strengthened above all during conflict. If we can have disagreements or arguments with our loved one without the threat of them cutting us off or walking away, we come to trust our bond with them even more. The relationship transcends differences. Whether they want to be in our life never comes into question, even if we are disagreeable or behaving badly. This is not to say, however, that object constancy equates to unconditional love. We do not get a free pass to mistreat others. A loved one can set boundaries with us, and they can get distressed when we hurt them. Disagreements and betrayals must be resolved, yet the integrity of the relationship is never threatened.

The easiest way to spot a lack of object constancy is in a baby, who grows distressed when mummy is gone, fearing she has abandoned them, but then relaxes when she returns. We can also see a lack of object constancy in ourselves as adults, where we become anxious and jealous when our loved one engages with someone other than us, causing us to fear that another person will steal them and destroy our relationship. If we have strong object constancy, outsiders do not shake our foundation, because the relationship has withstood the test of time and remained firm through many challenges.

Object constancy is not a given, and not everyone successfully develops it. Those who lack it can only know through the negative emotions that arise when they lose the time, goodwill or attention of their loved one. Those who have object constancy barely notice, since it is like the air they breathe.

As a result of object constancy, a child grows confident enough to challenge those in their environment. Secure in the knowledge that their loved ones will remain through thick and thin, they become more assertive about their need to actualise and individuate, and tenacity emerges.

3. Tenacity

The gigantic tension before the shooting of an arrow, and the total relaxation seconds later, is my way of connecting to the universe.

- Paulo Coelho

Vitality cannot flow forever unhindered. Firstly, your expression of life energy will cause friction with others who become threatened by your rising power. Secondly, when in a state of openness and love, a person is vulnerable to being manipulated and hurt. If enough abuse takes place, then that person will stop trusting others and close off. Thirdly, at some point, vitality will not be enough. You will need to be firm and penetrate with assertiveness if you want to achieve your goals. Whether defending yourself from harm or looking to impact the world around you, you will need to have something made of tougher stuff.

Put simply, tenacity is the capacity to tolerate the tension created by a build-up of vitality. Holding your own during a disagreement involves being in a state of stress, as does communicating your desires in a clear and impactful way. Expressing your sexuality requires you to sit with tension for a time. Interacting with others requires shifting between ease and pressure as the conversation evolves and loaded topics come up. Feeling emotions without dissociating from them involves tension, as does engaging in physical activity.

Tenacity shows that you mean business, that you 'have a backbone.' People notice when it is there. It requires laser-sharp focus and a strong will, and is a muscle which you develop by embracing challenge and healthy conflict. The tenacious not only accept tension, but gladly lean into it, knowing it is the only way to grow.

If vitality corresponds to what Carl Jung called the Anima, i.e. the feminine, tenacity would relate to the 'Animus;' its masculine counterpart. The Anima is abundant and ever-changing, while the Animus is laser-focussed and structured. It brings order to the world. Like taming a wild horse, tenacity helps you channel vitality in constructive ways and at progressively higher levels. The Animus and Anima must therefore work together to achieve wholeness. Without the ferocious power of the Anima, the Animus has nothing to direct toward a goal. Without the structure of the Animus, the Anima remains directionless and ineffective. Therefore, the stronger the flow of vitality within us, the more tension is required to create a container around it and channel it in useful ways.

Tenacity is also directly correlated to security, with its sturdiness and durability creating a feeling of safety and trust as a parent would in a child. Amid chaos, only the tenacious can restore order. When hell threatens to break loose, tenacity brings a welcome authority. Like the pangs of childbirth, nothing manifests without a constant rhythm of tension and release, a shifting from vitality to tenacity and back again.

Hate: The governing emotion of tenacity

When we give others the wheel, they can steer us in the wrong direction. Some people negatively impact our lives without our permission. Hate therefore helps us set boundaries, reclaim agency and rebel against a perceived abuse of power, aiming to halt its momentum and regain control. Hate also seeks to restore self-esteem as well as fairness to a relationship.

Hate only grows destructive if it merges with the death instinct. When someone interrupts or resists our expression of power, they blunt our life instinct, which leaves us prey to the magnetic and downward pull of death. Rage is a desperate attempt at regaining control so that we may resume our upwards trajectory toward a higher state. For those who are abused, bullied and oppressed for long enough, the death instinct comes to dominate their experience. Eventually, it becomes too much, and they turn it outwards, aiming to annihilate whoever enters their scope of vision. Others turn the death instinct toward themselves as self-hatred — growing reckless, self-destructive and even suicidal.

Tenacity is concerned with far more than this violent, split-off form of hate. Resistance, spite, stubbornness, coldness and contempt as well as rage can be useful tools. To resist, insist, and occasionally erupt with just cause, these are impulses which allow us to pursue an empowered way of life. Progress often calls for this kind of healthy conflict. When paired with the life instinct, hate becomes a useful way of demonstrating your strength and dependability, which is usually well-received and respected by others.

When tenacity is disrupted

We initially grow tenacity through family. When guardians are tolerant of assertiveness and tension in the home, then a child can develop comfort with hardening to get their needs met while relaxing back into vitality when satisfied. In rigid environments, those in power will not tolerate resistance, and will punish it with utmost prejudice.

For children who have their tenacity thwarted, their only choice is to drift back down to the level of vitality. They instead use appeasement and submission to influence their guardians into granting them their needs. The resulting personality is chronically nice and fears conflict. The most potent expression you can expect from such a person is passive-aggression. The 'nice person' has lost touch with their tenacity, dwelling within an invisible boundary that they are terrified to cross.

Without tenacity, a person must resort to wishful thinking to feel any sense of achievement and progress, since they are effectively unable to penetrate the world around them. The nice person's energy remains defanged, where neediness is the only tool they have to get what they want. Furthermore, without tenacity to create a container, the nice person remains unable to hold tension. Whether it is at work or in their personal life, they are always in *someone else's* container, and as a result, at the whim of other people's desires. A narcissist thrives above all when their target lacks tenacity. Without the capacity to hold tension, the target cannot set boundaries, and the narcissist can assert their influence with far more ease.

Becoming stuck in tenacity

On the other side of the coin is the chronically angry person. Rather than seeing tenacity as a tool to make progress, they turn it into a hammer to use whenever something frustrates them or causes them to feel shame. Anger for them is a way of life, where they remain on the edge of aggression at all times. This takes the joy and spontaneity out of their heart. Tension dominates their experience, sometimes being constructive, but mostly hindering their relationships and causing untold psychological damage to those who love them. Spending time with such people is always uncomfortable, due to the unresolved tension created by their anger boiling beneath the surface.

When tenacity is established

The person who successfully develops tenacity has learnt to create a container around their life energy, and can hold tension long enough to achieve their goals. For a person in a state of scattered vitality, the possibilities are endless yet unrealised. In a state of focussed tenacity, a dream can become a reality. Filled with willpower and secure in their boundaries, a person's life energy begins to concentrate, bringing into focus a mysterious opening within the Self. This doorway into the divine allows them to live out the inherent potential of the Self and to flow with the world around them while shaping it to their will. As a result, the tenacious person can move to the next stage of development, which is establishing a fortified and sacred inner 'realm,' where the spiritual ground is fertile and full of potential.

4. Divinity

The divine is not something high above us. It is in heaven, it is in earth, it is inside us.

- Morihei Ueshiba

Have you ever found yourself in a situation of such joy, amazement and flow that nothing else in the world mattered to you? Have you been the centre of attention, and as a result, felt empowered and full of life? Or have you found yourself on the opposite end of the spectrum, feeling completely isolated, staring in on a group of people having a great time? Did you find yourself saying *"I don't belong here,"* or asking *"What am I doing here?"* Between these two extremes, you can be sure you have ventured in and out of the heart of divinity.

Divinity is a magnetic core which draws life energy toward its seemingly transcendental reality. Entering into it *feels* different. There is something sacred about it, almost uncanny. It gives those who embody it an alluring presence. Everyone wants to be around them, and they feel at home within themselves, happy to be *exactly where they are*. A person in such a state becomes whole, and feels like they are at the centre of the world.

Divinity goes far beyond self-esteem. It legitimises your right to exist, and gives you the unshakeable sense that you embody the truth — and that nobody can tell you otherwise. For a king or queen, this quality is reinforced by the people and the state. Others claim it was bestowed upon them by God. They are not far from the truth. Just as kings and queens possess it, so do their royal subjects. The only missing ingredients for the average person are *awareness* of its existence within them, and *faith* in their capacity to channel it. Like breathing or walking, a person who embodies divinity does so without effort. They merely remove the obstacles and allow this energy to act through them. While narcissists try to conjure the illusion of divinity in the minds of others, the divine person experiences it by simply being themselves. There is no ego involved.

A child is born embodying this state, believing themselves to be at the centre of the universe. Before the ego emerges, the child knows themselves only through bodily sensations and sees themselves only through the eyes of their mother. When the ego comes on the scene, the child begins to identify with a mind-created 'I.' This 'I' is shaped by the child's environment, which when abusive and dysfunctional enough, can leave them believing that they are illegitimate and flawed. Much like a cloud-covered sky, the child loses faith in themselves, and forgets that the sun exists. In this way, the ego acts as a filter which can either maximise the potential of the True Self, or lock it up in a psychological cage. If divinity is seen and encouraged by the child's loved ones, then the emotion of pride swells. Knowing that they have both the legitimacy and capacity to expand, the child feels empowered and confident enough to make their mark on the world.

Pride: The governing emotion of divinity

As children, our self-esteem is entirely dependent on how our guardians and family perceive us. Their approval inflated us with pride, giving us the go-ahead to keep being who we were and keep doing what we were doing. Whether grounded in reality or not, pride can have a profound impact on our personality. Narcissism is, of course, the perfect example of pride that is not grounded in truth. Because they lack true security, a narcissist cannot channel vitality from within. They have invested their pride wholly into a grandiose, false construct, and their target, lacking a sense of divinity, buys into this lie.

Self-sustaining divinity bases itself on a foundation of security, vitality and tenacity. It is reinforced by the knowledge that no matter what happens outside, your True Self will always be there, waiting for you to claim it. A person typically draws pride from their status, deeds and successes. For example, someone born into an affluent family or who excels at their craft finds a reason to have pride. They inflate physically and psychologically, feeling themselves brush up against the divine within. Unfortunately, such a way of experiencing divinity is always fleeting, dependent on external factors to maintain it. A family can lose its wealth, and skill and good fortune can only take you so far. Divinity is an energetic state drawn from the knowledge that no matter what happens outside, your core remains intact. Holding you back is your conditioning, belief system and emotional investment in how others perceive you, as well as a lack of faith in your True Self. The modern world can be a cunning place, providing ample 'reasons' for a person to lose touch with their spiritual centre.

When divinity is disrupted

Returning to the example of a child, as long as the parent engages, protects and validates them, the child maintains legitimacy. If the parent ignores, abandons or attacks the child, then the 'bubble' bursts, and the child falls from grace. Their centre is overwhelmed by the death instinct.

Divinity requires momentum. With a secure emotional baseline and trust in the world, vitality flows. With the capacity to hold that energy under tension, a person can experience the boundaries of their inner 'realm,' and divinity establishes itself. The loss of this fragile balance for long periods causes enormous damage to the psyche, and regaining a sense of the divine grows progressively more difficult as the years pass, and as negative emotional patterns take over. Yet those who lack connection to divinity never stop longing for it. As a result, they become more susceptible to the charms of narcissists, who are skilled at conjuring the illusion of grandeur.

Becoming stuck in divinity

Some families value reputation above all else. Achievements which bring pride to the group are showered with approval — anything else is dismissed at best, and attacked and ridiculed at worst. Moreover, success is high up on the list of valued traits in our society, which can further wound a person's sense of pride if they fail to measure up. Add to this being born into an underprivileged life, and the pain grows unbearable. Rejection, bullying, ridicule, falling short — all of it can add up. The result is a deep yearning to be valued by others, no matter the cost. When we pursue pride as the antidote for deep-seated pain, it becomes a despairing journey. Approval by others is fleeting, and is dependent on numerous factors which can be soul-wrenching to maintain. Narcissism is a classic example of this form of Sisyphean venture for validation which is never enough.

When divinity is established

Certain families value love, security, humility and community, which are all strengthened by connecting to one's divine nature. To give the best of yourself to others and be of service, you need to feel you have the capacity and the legitimacy to act outwardly. That is divinity at its best. It is the sacred essence of a container filled with vitality and trust. When your inner 'kingdom' is in harmony, everyone benefits.

However, there is still one missing element. Divinity unchecked quickly leads to an inflation of power, which in time corrupts. It needs a counter-force; something to keep it in check lest it develop into hubris. The civilised world is a petri dish of expanding forces which must coexist. Living in harmony with yourself is not enough; knowledge of the world and those in it is also required. You need to know when to shine and when to hold back. Just because you can, does not mean you must. Rather than always taking the limelight, there will be times when you need to support someone else in expressing their fullness. That is what being a leader is about. This skill requires not only intelligence, but also a connection to one's emotions and intuition via their gut-brain. Millenia of evolution have led us here, and establishing harmony within our 'realm' reveals the treasure-trove which we have inherited from our ancestors.

5. Wisdom

Wisdom comes by disillusionment.

- George Santayana

How do you *know* the truth? Is it because someone told you so, or did you confirm for yourself through research and analysis? How do you measure truth? Is it continually evolving, or something static and pure you discover like a rare mineral?

Divinity gives a person absolute certainty that their existence is ordained and self-evident. The uncanny nature of someone's energy and the purity of their conviction can be enough to convince the world that they embody the truth. This pride bubble can grow to dizzying heights, leading to the eventual psychological collapse of everyone who partakes in it. When power corrupts, what everyone assumed was the 'truth' collides with reality, and another truth asserts itself. This is nothing new, it is only the natural order of the universe reinstating itself by enforcing the cycle of life, death and rebirth.

We have all been there. Caught in a state of hubris, our conviction grows ever stronger, before something dramatic rudely awakens us from our hypnosis. Somebody gets hurt, or we lose the support of those around us. Eventually, our perspective shifts just enough to realise that we were living in a pseudo-reality of our own making — or someone else's. In response, our mind is forced to slow down and absorb the truth that had been staring us in the face the whole time. We finally 'get it.'

When considering the wise figures in mythology and popular culture, one notices that they never get carried away. What they seem to possess is a strong sense of humility and deliberateness in thinking. It is as though they are anchored to something which gives them uncanny insights into the state of the world. They seem to be 'weighed down' by the truth, compared to those inflated by pride who appear ignorant yet light on their feet.

A good leader keeps such a wise advisor in close company. The leader embodies the divine and aims to bring order and prosperity to their world. Yet even they, the one person deemed most legitimate, are prone to making mistakes. And as leader, the consequences can be grave. Because of this, they seek counsel with someone who, while not as 'divine' as them, is capable of channelling a quality which they sometimes lose touch with. This trait is the antithesis of pride, while also being something pride cannot survive without.

Shame: The governing emotion of wisdom

Shame is many things. In its mundane form, it is the glue which holds hierarchies together, dampening each person's ambition enough to ensure cooperation. At its worst, it is capable of crushing and even ending lives. For anyone who has experienced toxic shame, the last thing they would want is a closer look at it. Yet shame is the key to unlocking one's potential. Like taking the reins of a horse, shame can either bring you to a halt, or it can safely guide you forward as you gain more and more speed.

The dull ache of *healthy* shame is an indicator of where you stand. You feel it when you compare yourself to others, or when you lack the solution to a problem, or when you mispronounce a word in the language you are trying to learn. A person comes to believe they are inferior when they are continuously shamed over a long period. However, we do not feel shame because we are inferior, but rather because we have hit up against our limits, subjective or otherwise. The question remains: What piece of knowledge is required, what skill do you need or what adjustment must you make before you can evolve to where you hope to be? Shame helps you find out.

Shame, when channelled well, can immerse us in instinctual knowledge which we then adapt to our life. Its heaviness slows us down so we do not get ahead of ourselves. It has the capacity to help expand our knowledge, improve our skills, and deepen our relationships. Like gravity, too much of it immobilises us, not enough of it sends us hurtling out into space, and just enough allows us to productively navigate the world.

When wisdom is disrupted

The wise seem to be in constant touch with the True Self. While shame weighs them down, their slowness of being allows them to carefully tune into the universal truth contained within life energy, also known as 'the word of God.' This is only possible when one is centred and has their emotions in a manageable state.

The capacity to tune into inherent wisdom is lost when someone is forced out of their centre. Guilt, fear and toxic shame make it difficult to be in one's body, which cuts off the capacity for intuition. A person's centre is their compass, and losing it throws them into psychological vertigo. The result is perpetual confusion and doubt, and rather than trusting their instinct, a person is forced to delegate to others. They believe they are not fit to know the truth, and instead need to obtain it from outside. Their mind can only parrot supposed facts. Wisdom, on the other hand, draws truth from the Self, which contains an unlimited pool of universal knowledge. Above all, the Self holds a person's true nature, and therefore is the only authority for knowing what is best for that person. The uncentered are quick to forget this.

Becoming stuck in wisdom

Those who are consistently frustrated in their attempts to grow and be accepted will have their pride wounded, and toxic shame will take over as their primary state. Their life energy is dampened, and rather than engage the world through spontaneous action, they revert to deep analytical thinking and contemplation to 'work out' their predicament.

Rejection, manipulation and abuse all harm a person's pride. Without a connection to the divine, a person carries around a sense of illegitimacy and inferiority into every situation. When toxic shame becomes a state of being, a person cannot align within their Self, and therefore is unable to channel vitality, tenacity and divinity. Spontaneity is lost, and that person lives a life of perpetual despair and conformity. Evolution is a slow process for the person filled with toxic shame. With no vitality to help them evolve, no tenacity to defend and assert themselves, and no legitimacy to carve out a realm of power, all a person has when shamed is their mind. They are like a blunt spear, unable to penetrate the world. They can imagine the possibilities, yet their potential remains a tiny fraction of what it could be. They see the world through a psychological window, growing observant and knowledgeable but having no capacity to do anything with this acquired wisdom. Rather than living life, they intellectualise it and seek to transcend it through the realm of knowledge.

For those trapped in toxic shame, the way out will be partially through knowledge of their obstacles. Yet this will amount to nothing if they do not also act in the flow. If they choose to remain in the realm of wisdom, they may be able to assist others in growing, but they themselves will remain stuck.

When wisdom is established

Wisdom helps us manage the rising complexity which vitality brings into our life. As we evolve, wisdom transfers from the unconscious to the conscious mind, where our knowledge is limited. Therefore, the wise person is aware that while they may have the whole truth within, they will never consciously know it all. Nonetheless, they rest easy, since whatever knowledge they do need can be made available.

At its best, wisdom is applied in the flow of life. A person feels energised and legitimised, and only deviates course when they intuit that it is expedient. The person of healthy wisdom uses idle time to contemplate before returning to the flow to apply what they have learnt. Most importantly, the person of wisdom understands that they do not know everything, and nor will they ever. They remain curious while trusting their intuition, knowing that wisdom will always have limits if not combined with experience and right action. Above all, a person of wisdom is aware that true knowledge goes beyond the mind, and that the analytical brain may not make sense of an experience until long after all is said and done. Such is the depth of wisdom.

The nature of power

Power without love is reckless and abusive, and love without power is sentimental and anaemic.

- Martin Luther King Jr.

The five developmental forces, along with their corresponding emotions, give potency to life. Fear thrusts you forward, and taming it gives you the confidence to face the unknown and seize opportunities. Love creates transcendental experiences and unlocks your creativity while evolving your relationships. Hate gives shape to your boundaries and assertiveness to your actions and lets others trust that you have a backbone. Pride lights up your potential and gives you legitimacy in the world so you can shape it in your vision. Shame slows you down enough to absorb the necessary knowledge for self-reflection and practical living. When all five are skilfully combined, you have the core elements of power.

Like the ingredients for a cake, it is difficult to differentiate between each one when you only have a final product. While we live within the realm of power at all times, we generally have little awareness of how it comes together, let alone how we can influence it. As long as we remain wrapped up in the ego and the stories it tells us, we will eat whatever cake the world gives us. When power structures solidify in our minds, we forget that they can be changed. Yet change them we can, starting with understanding how power is formed and organised.

The archetypes of power

Due to our helpless nature early in life, actualisation relies on an outside figure. As already discussed, this higher power is structured into the following fundamental archetypes:

1. **The great mother:** A loving figure who provides acceptance, mirroring, nurture and warmth.
2. **The great father:** A benevolent figure who provides guidance, wisdom, protection and support.
3. **The family:** A home base or tribe which provides identity, belonging, meaning and security.

Even when we leave home, we join clubs, friendship groups, workplaces, sports teams, political organisations, and so on. All of these stem from the family archetype, which remains integral throughout our lives.

In childhood, we experienced the five forces *through* these archetypes. At the time we were relating not to the human beings who were our parents, but to the divine figure we expected them to embody. We never considered that we could express these energies for ourselves.

The most powerful gain hegemony by successfully projecting the great parent archetype in the context of the current zeitgeist. Demagogues do this in times of crisis. Narcissists do it to gain narcissistic supply.

In relation to the great parent, power comes in two forms; personal and social. *Personal power* arises when we stop channelling the great mother and father archetypes through our parents and undertake the path to individuation, which entails embodying those figures in ourselves. *Social power* comes when we channel the great father or mother archetype for others; in parenthood, leadership or otherwise. Personal power is having influence over your own feelings, thoughts, decisions and actions, whereas social power is influencing how others feel, think, decide and act. In the case of personal power, a person breaks their dependence on an outside figure and consciously connects with the True Self. They free their vitality from the control of others, which gives them the capacity to act in their own interest.

When it comes to relationships and social structures, we often underestimate the part that love plays in enabling power. Although influence over others can be obtained through fear and money, in most cases it is voluntarily granted to those who can persuade others to forfeit it. That is, power is given to those transcendental people who can win the worship of others by promising them a higher state of being. These figures gain support not only by embodying the great parent archetype, but also through the myths they create which detail *why* we should submit to them in the first place.

The mythology of power

Power is a story, a thread which weaves the five forces together and tells the tale of how our desires will be fulfilled — or not. It is a story we tell ourselves, and if we lose trust in our personal power, becomes a fiction others feed us instead. This narrative is supposed to pave the way for us to get what we want. It is, in our mind, the ideal path toward actualisation.

Most of the time, we are held back from personal power by the stories of those who tell us we are incapable. Narcissists aim to crush our self-esteem by turning our shame against us. If that fails, they wall off our True Self within a house of fear and confusion. Imagine living within the confines of an isolated town and being convinced that there is nothing worthwhile outside those walls. Now take those walls and imagine them assembled in your mind.

Narcissists are master storytellers. They start by fishing for your desires, and then weave together a story of how the two of you will fulfil those wishes. Perhaps the purest and most fundamental yearning we have is for a special someone who will make our life better. This hope is rooted in our early experiences of the great mother and father. The narcissist awakens this core desire and convinces us that they are the only one who can make it come true. The reality is naturally different. The narcissist's empty words aim only to convince. Once the cracks appear, the storyline changes from desires fulfilled to tales of the incompetent, hopeless fool the narcissist is forced to tolerate. Shame, fear and doubt become the weapons of tyranny. A glare, a snide or ridiculing remark, a judgemental comment; these reinforce a story which aims to create an imbalance between you and the narcissist while hampering your personal power.

Self-development uses the five forces to restore personal power, and we achieve this by unravelling the forces from our internalised stories. Most importantly, we free the five forces when we disentangle them from the archetypes of the family, the great mother and the great father. We do so by becoming aware of the stories tied to those archetypes, and then observing how the underlying emotions keep the stories in place. From a young age, our life narrative becomes psychologically solidified, and we lose awareness of it. Our conscious reality remains stuck at this level, and we never look closer at the emotions and patterns which drive our beliefs. Worst of all, we lose awareness of the stories themselves and take them as gospel.

It takes courage, and a willingness to tolerate states of chaos before we can face the fiction which keeps us stuck in dysfunction. Creating a new reality is an alchemical process, forged by experience and emotion. In our relationships, it is easy to get caught up in the ideas of others, especially when we are attached to them.

Attachment: The highway of power

As vitality flows between two people, a bond gradually forms through which the relationship evolves. Much like a highway between two cities, *attachment* permits the sharing of energy and allows the people involved to influence and nurture each other. As the connection deepens, the other person becomes indispensable, and the idea of separation becomes progressively more painful. An example is the post-breakup pain we experience for weeks or even months on end. It is the consequence of a rupture in attachment.

Before they can develop, a child must establish a safe base within the mother. They cling to her at all times, and cry and scream when left alone. These protest behaviours are caused by threats to the attachment, and are fuelled by the terror of abandonment. The tiniest disruption causes immense pain for the child. Like an emotional umbilical cord, the attachment between mother and child sustains the True Self. Ideally, the mother is attuned and loving enough for the child to trust that she will always be there. This culminates in a *secure attachment style*, wherein the child can connect and separate from loved ones with minimal fuss or anxiety. A secure attachment involves a continuous, attuned connection between mother and baby through the use of touch, proximity, eye contact, sound making, facial expressions and the mirroring of emotional states. The child's alignment with their True Self relies entirely on this relationship, and any extended break in the connection can cripple their development.

Nobody can be flawless in their mothering. Breaks will occur when the mother is distracted, fatigued or stressed. Yet the attachment bond is durable, and can sustain temporary disruptions. As long as the mother is attuned and available most of the time, the child can maintain trust in the relationship. The child will then develop object constancy and a strong sense of Self, remaining in touch with their emotional world and having confidence in their ability to connect with and influence others. In short, a secure attachment with the mother acts as a blueprint for future relationships.

While we think of food and shelter as indispensable, we often forget how much emotional connection plays a part in our well-being. Without intimacy in our life, that is, without being truly seen and understood, we would quickly suffer at a core level. Therefore, developing and maintaining a secure attachment in our relationships becomes crucial, even though being attached to another person also makes us vulnerable to pain and abuse. This conundrum is solved by regulating the strength of the attachment using *activating* and *deactivating* strategies, wherein activating reinforces the bond, and deactivating weakens it.

Examples of activating strategies which aim to *strengthen* attachment are:

- Physical closeness and touch.
- Divulging your feelings and inner state.
- Thinking positively of the other person and focussing on their good qualities.
- Refusing to see the other person's flaws.

- Remaining in constant contact, including calling and texting often as well as spending lots of time together.
- Putting someone on a pedestal while seeing yourself as beneath them.
- Giving the person preferential treatment over others.

Examples of deactivating strategies which aim to *weaken* attachment are:

- Physically isolating yourself or withholding touch.
- Sharing less than the other person about your feelings and inner state.
- Cutting off your emotions and communicating superficially.
- Reducing contact by calling or texting less, or by going missing.
- Setting harsh boundaries.
- Blaming the other person when things go wrong.
- Judging the other person as inferior, flawed or unworthy in some way.
- Letting down or mistreating the other person to create emotional hurt in them.

Activating strategies are typically used to increase well-being and create a sense of security by helping a person feel closer to their loved one. However, fear and trauma can also arise in relationships when a person is abused, neglected or hurt by an attachment figure. To help combat feelings of vulnerability and fear, a person may utilise deactivating strategies, often acting manipulatively or hurtfully in the process.

Maintaining attachment while ensuring safety, integrity and space is where the power struggle in relationships is fought, where imbalances and dysfunctional patterns can emerge in endless ways. Who we attach to holds enormous sway over us. It is therefore crucial to understand how attachment can corrupt power in our relationships and derail our development.

The connection/actualisation continuum

We can think of power in relationships as a vehicle which runs on vitality. This ship is supposed to take the people who fuel it where they want to go. Power can also be a source of security, protecting those who surrender to it. Consider the child who snuggles into their parent, the person who looks to their partner for support, or the people who trust in their leader. Think of the times someone has believed in you, cooperated with you or paid you their undivided attention. That wind behind your sail, that exhilarating rush you felt, was power.

Relationships, above all, are about empowerment. Through mutuality and mirroring, people can enable and awaken each other's life instinct. It is like two artists co-writing a screenplay where they are both protagonists. This story can go anywhere if it is told in the context of the five forces. When security is established in a relationship, vitality flows between each person, and a democratic structure is tenaciously enforced through boundary setting. Both people have value and legitimacy in the relationship, and they explore and learn together as they grow in stature and wisdom.

For the narcissist, however, there is only one protagonist. Fear keeps everyone in check. Love is one-directional and only serves the narcissist's need for supply. Resistance and boundary setting are discouraged and attacked. Pride is reserved for the narcissist, and shame is used primarily as a tool to cut people down and remind them of their 'place.' This leads to a dysfunctional balance of power which stunts the development of a person's True Self. To challenge this hegemony, one needs to understand how the dysfunction first set in and what keeps it in place.

The scale for balancing power in a relationship can be illustrated on a continuum as follows:

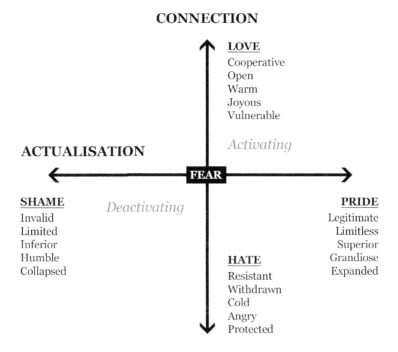

Figure 5: The connection/actualisation continuum.
Loving someone enables their pride, withholding love or ex-
pressing hatred aims to deflate their pride and bring them
back toward shame. Beneath it all is fear.

The connection/actualisation continuum dictates the following about relationships:

- Pride assumes high status, which by association calls for
  love via worship.
- Love is fuel for pride. Loving others empowers and legitimises them, and loving yourself empowers and legitimises
  you.

- Those inflated by pride can forfeit some of it by exhibiting healthy shame and making themselves vulnerable through love.
- Those who feel their needs are not being met or that others are taking advantage of them can use hate to make demands or push back.
- Subtly hardening through hate establishes boundaries.
- Love and hate temper how much power we hold over each other by regulating the strength of the attachment.
- If a person does not have enough power in the relationship, and cannot assert themselves through hate, they experience shame to compensate.

For the connection/actualisation continuum to apply, there must be *engagement*. When one person is indifferent to others, then power cannot be had. To experience power, we must first engage a person by *polarising* them and drawing them into the realm of emotion. We achieve this by creating the promise of transcendence through higher states of being. Without this, power falls flat, and a person must instead resort to fear, shame, drama and other forms of manipulation to engage the other person. In the case of the child, they are reliant on their guardian, and so their fear of abandonment keeps them engaged and attached at all times.

Losing balance

The consequences of drifting too far in any direction on the continuum are many, beginning with too much pride:

- **Pride:** The parent has undeniable control over the child, which can corrupt their power. If the child tries to resist by expressing their hate, and the parent digs in their heels and becomes even more full of rage, then the path to pride, or hate as a means to balance power, is blocked. The child is left with three options: loving through their split, self-hatred or shame.

- **Love:** When the child is left to choose between love, shame and self-hatred, they usually opt for love and repress the other two. Toxic shame and self-loathing are painful. If a genuine connection is not present, the child will project the split onto the parent and convince themselves that the parent is 'good.' They will overvalue the parent and ignore their bad qualities while becoming appeasing, hoping to obtain positive regard in return.

- **Shame:** Some domineering parents will entertain the child's love projections while remaining shut off themselves, knowing that it maintains their position. On the other hand, neglectful parents may be incapable of tolerating sentimentality. They disdain authenticity and set rigid boundaries, leaving the child no other option but to feel shame. The child drifts down the continuum and internalises powerlessness and inferiority as a way of being.

- **Hate:** Children who are constant targets of their parent's rage and have no healthy object of hate will internalise self-hatred as a state of mind. Repressed anger stays inside until they find themselves in a relationship with someone of lower power, e.g. a child or a spouse, where they end up using the relationship to unconsciously 'hand down' the hot potato of internalised self-loathing.

When the five emotional forces are considered this way, it becomes clear how relationships achieve balance in many dysfunctional ways. When a certain dynamic goes on long enough, a person internalises their emotional state and 'becomes' it. Those who cannot express hate and cannot experience pride become sentimental, submissive and passive-aggressive. Those who are robbed of their right to love and be loved become shameful, and those who are the recipients of rage attacks may internalise hate as a state of mind and become bitter. Finally, when a person drifts too far into pride or shame, they lose touch with reality and dissociate. Mental disturbance then arises to compensate.

Imbalances on the continuum also affect attachment. If someone of value is dismissive or emotionally distant (hate), a person tries to bridge the gap by using activating strategies to restore the bond. If a person perceives someone to be of higher status than them, they also may activate to move closer to them (pride). On the other hand, people may deactivate from those who they feel are too clingy (love), or who they perceive to be of lower status (shame). Empowerment is found when all five forces are balanced in a relationship, which is an outcome that requires a carefully-managed upbringing.

Permission to launch

The attitude of faith is to let go, and become open to truth; whatever it might turn out to be.

- Alan Watts

Balancing the five developmental forces is an art form, a juggling act which no parent gets one-hundred-percent right. Ideally, a family will provide safety and support for the child while respecting their individuality. After the child achieves a secure attachment with the mother, they internalise that feeling of security and use it to separate from and rejoin the family unit without guilt or anxiety. The healthy family affords the child this privilege because the guardians have their needs met by themselves, each other, close friends, and other adults in the extended family. With their needs sufficiently secured, the parent happily provides a warm, protective structure for the child until they leave the nest to live out their purpose.

While supplying the child's needs, the healthy parents place a minimal burden on the child to reciprocate. If there are multiple kids in the family, the parents will take responsibility for all of their needs, and gradually teach them to look after their own physical and emotional well-being, as well as where to search when they need help. In families with two parents or guardians, the spouses share power while channelling great parent energy. The aim is for the child to become autonomous, confident, capable and self-assured. Above all, the child's strengths and weaknesses are respected, so that they feel as valued as their siblings. Clearly the guardian will never achieve this perfectly, but they will do their best.

By allowing authenticity and encouraging rights, the healthy guardian enables each family member to contribute and provide value. As a result, the children thrive and become willing participants in the home. Their death instinct fades and gives way to a lust for life, as their perspective widens beyond fantasy and they embrace reality.

Resolving the split

Ideally, the guardian in a healthy home will mirror the child, cater to their needs, and offer them love and acceptance. When the guardian sets necessary boundaries, they remain calm as the child expresses their frustration at being blocked. In a fit of rage, the child splits from the divine being and directs their anger at the tyrant. The guardian will allow this, as it helps the child vent and hence maintain emotional health. If the guardian's split is triggered and they bite back at the 'bad child' with fury of their own, the child will experience immense terror and turn on themselves. The child splits themselves into good and bad, and directs their hatred at the bad child. This secondary coping mechanism is how the child deals with an untenable position. As a result, self-hate is born, and becomes increasingly destructive as the child grows.

On the other hand, if the guardian can be consistent enough and allow the child to project both the divine being *and* the tyrant, then the child can sufficiently internalise the great parent and use it to self-soothe during stressful situations. This maturation process requires patience and support. There are no shortcuts. By being present, loving and understanding, the guardian enables the child to integrate the subsequent positive emotions into their sense of Self. This leads to high self-esteem and a feeling of being 'ok' and 'good enough.'

The full expression of the split is one of the greatest gifts a parent can offer their child. The more balanced, accepting and consistent the guardian is, the more likely it is that the child will move to the next phase of their maturity. They transition from hyper-vigilance and fantasy to what Melanie Klein refers to as the *depressive position*. From this baseline state, the child comes back to Earth and sees reality for what it is. They begin to humanise their guardian, realising that the figure whom they love, the divine being, and the figure whom they hate, the tyrant, are one person. They develop shades of grey in their thinking and find that their parent is a human being capable of making them feel both good and bad.

In the absence of parental resistance, the child will feel safe enough to simultaneously hold both loving and negative feelings toward their guardian. The imaginary constructs of all-good and all-bad collapse, and the child instead sees a mortal person with strengths and flaws, and no longer an enigma in their mind. Their experience of the guardian varies often, and that is ok — there is no threat to their life. The relationship continues regardless.

After this crucial moment in the maturation process, the child can give up their worship and rely on their personal power. By dropping the all-good and all-bad positions, they can stop projecting onto others and instead see people as peers. The result of this is the collapse of the great parent, along with the emergence of terrible loneliness. Mummy and daddy may still be around, but they are no longer divine figures with limitless strength and wisdom. Their faults become progressively more visible to the child. Challenges arise for which the parent has no clear answer, and the child is forced to look within, where they come face to face with a mysterious yet resourceful Self.

The Orphan emerges

The picture that people get when considering the term 'Orphan' is that of a child whose parents suddenly died in an accident or abandoned them at birth. Yet the Orphan as an archetype is not the outcome of tragedy, but a rite of passage leading toward actualisation.

In a child's mind, the great mother and father are real phenomenons. As long as these projections exist, the child vicariously feels powerful and immortal. There is no room for death and suffering in a split state of mind. 'Mummy' and 'daddy' — with all of their strength and omnipotence — will handle everything. Once the split is resolved, however, these all-powerful figures collapse. The human mother and father may remain, but the divine beings who reassured the child are gone — at least for now. This is a time of grief but also opportunity. No longer bound by illusion, the child takes the open road toward individuation. Yes, they are exposed to the potential horrors of mortality, but they are also in a position to channel their energy in previously unimaginable ways.

The child who resolves the split and confronts the Orphan will meet with the sobering reality that they are alone in an unpredictable world, and responsible for where they end up. On the outside, nothing has changed, but on the inside nothing will be the same again. The person who reaches Orphanhood stops looking outside for answers and learns to trust their intuition. Where they relied on fantasy and external reassurance, they instead problem solve and deal with their life more practically. They educate themselves and act from a position of confidence and reason, rather than fear and wishful thinking. The depressive position which arises from a resolved split brings about a sobering acceptance of reality. Nobody knows what is best for you but you. The True Self becomes the primary source of wisdom and guidance as you launch into life.

Takeoff

Family is everything. It is also a launching pad. As we grow older and our Self-actualisation goals evolve, we outgrow our family and embrace a life of metaphorical Orphanhood. Purpose and belonging remain crucial needs, but they no longer just come from family. We are anchored within and supported by the five developmental forces. The world calls to us, and our successful exit is a sign of parenting done well. We leave as mature, autonomous adults ready to contribute to our society and able to maintain emotional balance. We develop healthy attachments to others and efficiently maintain them in ways that meet our needs and encourage mutual growth.

Yet life does not always go to plan. The development of the Self, like any process, can be disrupted. When thwarted, the psyche compensates in dysfunctional ways, many of which maintain our sanity but come at a gigantic price.

PART II:
THE AGE OF NARCISSISM

The True Self versus the world

Keep your face to the sunshine and you cannot see a shadow.

- Helen Keller

The True Self is divine in its mission. Like the sun, its goal is to shine brightly and empower the game of creation. Yet much like the sun, the light of the True Self casts a shadow.

If the True Self is an ever-shining, always-expanding star, the archetypes of the psyche can be seen as its solar system. The True Self lies at the centre of this universe, photosynthesising and giving life to everything. Driving it toward manifesting into the world is what Sigmund Freud called the *id*.

The id

The id is the True Self's pursuit of pleasure and avoidance of pain, being driven by urges, desires and needs. Our need to be loved and seen, our desire for sex, our urge to avoid abandonment, all of these drives and more lie at the heart of the id.

The id is powered by the life instinct, and operates on what Freud called the 'pleasure principle.' When you are hungry, you eat. When thirsty, you drink. When you want attention, you demand it. If you like something, you take it. If something is uncomfortable, you avoid it. When someone bothers you, you get angry. The id thrusts us away from the death instinct and wills us toward life. Much like a child, it is blind in its pursuit of gratification — until it faces the consequences of its actions, of course.

The ego

Our drives can clash with others, and our environment does not always accommodate us. To get what we want, we sometimes need to resist our urges. Instead, we might need to first analyse, predict and understand the world around us to know how to best fulfil our drives, which is a task for the mind. With each experience, we eventually form a map in our brain for how to best navigate our environment.

As we move through the world, we begin to notice differences between ourselves and others. Some people seem confident, others more withdrawn. Some are more powerful, others subservient. Furthermore, how people treat us shifts based on how we act or do not act. By withholding certain drives, we notice we get better treatment. Other instincts, on the other hand, are welcomed. In time, a concept forms in our mind of how accommodating the world is and *who we are* in it. This idea of who we are and, above all, who we *can be*, is our ego.

The ego is a construct the mind uses to negotiate and interact with the world on our behalf. It determines how we *can* behave in the world, not just how we *want* to. Over time, this concept of ourselves evolves based on the messages we receive from those around us. If we are constantly celebrated and loved, our ego believes us to be worthy of love. If we are neglected, ridiculed or abandoned, we see ourselves as inherently bad, and learn to repress our drives.

The descent of the shadow

Beginning with our parents, there will be a specific set of drives which the world deems unacceptable. In some families, crying is not allowed, nor is protesting or getting angry. Curiosity and excitement can be crushed by an intolerant parent. This creates enormous tension between a True Self that wants to energetically expand, and an ego which deems it 'wrong.' As our drives clash with the world, the tension gets too much. To cope, we reject these impulses outright and determine them to be bad. Yet they do not disappear. They remain within us, in an area of the Self which Carl Jung called *the shadow*.

The shadow contains the urges, desires, traits and needs we were unable to satisfy or express. Because they were rejected by those we loved, and because they were so painful, we dissociated and pushed these parts deep inside, and 'forgot' them. In the conflict between holding onto love and expressing our authenticity, we sacrificed core parts of ourselves to be accepted. As we grew, we developed amnesia to ensure we never had to face these 'flawed' parts, unaware that the past would eventually come back to haunt us.

The great escape

Between a rigid ego and a bloated shadow lies unbearable tension. The healthiest form of release is to satisfy those urges within one's environment. Yet when we have determined those drives to be bad, the tension remains permanently in place. We are then forced to vent through addictive behaviours and substances, acting-out, overworking, binge-eating or binge-watching, and other forms of escapism.

Another powerful way we release the tension of the shadow is through *fantasy*. In this way, we can numb our pain and create the illusion of satisfying our drives. We imagine a perfect person who will save us from our prison of agony. We daydream of our circumstances magically changing, or we visualise going to another place where life might improve.

Fantasy can also infect the concept of who we are, i.e. the ego. If we are constantly rejected, neglected and mistreated, the tension of the resulting pain leads us to compensate by imagining ourselves as desirable, valuable, or even superior. While this can provide relief, it inevitably clashes with reality. Much like a drug, when fantasy runs out, we need a higher dose to get back to where we were. Also, the stronger the shadow, the more powerful the fantasy must be. In extreme cases, when enough of the True Self is cast into the shadow, it becomes lost. Fantasy then becomes the only defence, where imagining oneself as superior crystallises in the ego and forms into a grandiose *false self*; a construct detached from reality.

Meanwhile, the shadow lurks, ready to burst out unexpectedly. A Cold War emerges between the 'all-bad' shadow and 'all-good' grandiose false self, ready to turn hot at any moment. The ground then becomes fertile for narcissism to grow.

The making of a narcissist

I trust no one, not even myself.

- Joseph Stalin

The connection/actualisation continuum, with its emotional forces of fear, love, hate, pride and shame, is a useful tool for illustrating how narcissism might arise due to a loss of balance. In the case of pride, a child can grow up in a cold, grandiose environment, incessantly pushed toward being more and achieving more by an overbearing parent. The parent is themselves usually driven by an unrelenting thirst for *more;* more status, more money, more attention and more recognition, and forces their child to partake in this doctrine. Growing up in such a shameless environment suffocates the child's authenticity and increases their chances of becoming narcissistic. But the question remains: Where did this thirst originate?

Original rupture

During infancy, a child needs a consistent, balanced attachment to the mother to establish harmony with their True Self. A lot can go wrong during this fragile process. Mothers can be overwhelmed by their environment. Their ancestors may have lived during a time plagued by conflict or war, where survival and stability were a higher priority than emotional well-being and actualisation. Intergenerational trauma can plague a family, passed on through behavioural patterns, belief systems, addiction and even DNA. This leads to systemic dysfunction becoming like the air a family breathes. Those who grow up in such an environment often adapt by becoming callous, ruthless, manipulative, emotionally dysregulated or emotionally detached. As a result, they behave in destructive and unpredictable ways.

Mothers with this kind of personality are incapable of sustaining the steady openness and warmth the child needs. Instead, they push away the child who frustrates or triggers them. Other insecure mothers, on the other hand, might have a difficult time allowing their child to separate and individuate. Such a mother clings tight to the child and does everything in her power to manipulate them into staying by her side. She may become intrusive, controlling, attacking or judgemental, too caught up in her inner turmoil to relate lovingly to her child. Consequently, the child's ability to safely connect and separate is compromised, resulting in an *insecure attachment style* which can be classified into the following types, depending on the nature of the rupture:

1. Avoidant attachment

There is a widespread belief that a child should not be 'spoiled' with attention, which is common in many societies that recommend leaving the child to 'cry it out.' The problem is that attachment is all that shields the child from the death instinct. The child is not faking their need for connection. In some cases, the mother is either unwilling or too over-whelmed to comfort the child. When a child's pleas and cries are consistently blocked or ignored, terror arises, and the child dissociates from the mother to cope. This protects the child from the harrowing, overwhelming terror of neglect, but also dampens their desire for attachment in the process. As a result, the child gives up and disengages from the richness of life. They develop a fear of closeness and come to prefer emotional distance over intimacy. This is illustrated by the child who stops noticing when the mother leaves the vicinity, and is indifferent when she returns.

People who lean avoidant experienced little warmth early in life. Their guardians were dominated by their mind, preferring to analyse and judge reality rather than experience it directly and vulnerably. Emotions were threatening in the family home, and so the child learnt to deaden their feelings to the point of mastery. An avoidant person seems calm and in control at all times, appearing unaffected by the chaos in the world. Yet this is an illusion, as they maintain a highly-anxious and shame-filled Self beneath the surface. They are also quick to disengage and dismiss the feelings of others, spending copious amounts of time alone to remain in control. Even a socially-inclined avoidant holds others at bay by keeping the relationship superficial and 'playful,' rarely exposing their emotions or being intimate. If intimacy does happen to grow in their relationships, the avoidant's fear takes over, and they sabotage in covert ways that catch the other person blind-sided. The avoidant has a push-pull way of relating, connecting for some time before disappearing for long periods. Such deactivating strategies aim to reduce anxiety in the relationship to a level that feels safe for the avoidant. This is intended to avoid vulnerability, which the avoidant grew up experiencing as a source of rejection and pain.

2. Anxious attachment

An insecure mother may impose herself on her child to get her needs met. This kind of behaviour is abusive because the mother is not considering the fragile inner world of the child — she is concerned only with herself. The child must experience attachment on their terms, and the mother must put her drives aside to have any chance of intuiting the child's needs. Smothering and controlling the child makes them anxious, since the child does not know when the mother will be responsive and in what way. Over-stimulation and under-stimulation are both frightening to the child, and having a mother incapable of skilfully managing the child's emotional baseline adds to this anxiety. When the child reaches out for comfort, the mother may feel overwhelmed and back away, terrifying and shaming the child in the process. Yet the child continues to reach out because they know that their mother sometimes engages them, albeit unpredictably. The child is unaware that the mother is attentive on her terms, coercing and manipulating them into behaving how she wants.

In other situations, one parent could be warm and loving, and the other cold and dismissive. The parents may be around sometimes, and then missing the rest of the time due to outside commitments. The common thread in all of these situations is inconsistency. In response, the child develops a neurosis around love much like a gambling addict, desperately seeking it out but not knowing when it will come. They are close to giving up hope, before the parent suddenly becomes available for a period of time. Such intermittent reinforcement creates anxiety around love, wherein obtaining it becomes the primary focus of the child's life. They put aside all curiosity, and focus on finding ways to secure their parent's love once and for all. This never happens, of course, since the parent is available on their own terms, and not the child's.

Anxious attachment is also known as 'preoccupied attachment,' since obtaining and keeping love for the anxious person is a primary focus. Feeding this anxiety is a crippling sense of low self-worth, brought on by the pain of abandonment. Furthermore, because they had no control over their access to love, they came to believe that love is a scarce commodity which they must earn through their actions. The anxiously-attached person has a strong need for affection, attention and reassurance in relationships, especially romantic ones. When in the presence of someone they admire, they will abandon all boundaries and use activating strategies almost neurotically. Their belief is that if they are nice enough and give enough of their love, resources and time, they will prove themselves worthy of being loved in return. This never works. The anxiously-attached only ever get taken for granted, denying their needs for the sake of pleasing others. They rely heavily on passive-aggression to communicate their distress, and when they over-give to the point of exhaustion, their rage at the unfairness of the relationship comes to a head and they erupt.

3. Fearful attachment

In addition to neglect and intermittent reinforcement, some children live in an abusive environment. Usually the guardian is emotionally unstable or badly traumatised. As a result, the child may be the target of rage attacks, or a sudden and violent invasion of their boundaries in the form of pinching, spanking, slapping and physical and sexual abuse. A parent may be loving and attuned one moment, then cold and spiteful the next. Any behaviour which displeases the parent could lead to punishment at any moment. There is no pattern to these reactions as far as the child can tell, and they grow terrified of their home environment. The intensity of the attacks is far beyond what the child can absorb, and they grow traumatised as a result, dissociating from their experience and retreating into their imagination for refuge.

In the face of such madness, the child splits off and holds their terror inside using a mixture of psychological repression and permanent body tensing. Later in life, any unlocking of the trauma comes with intense fear. The child cannot process assaults on their being. What makes such an environment so horrendous is that the child relies entirely on their abusive guardian for survival, so their urge for connection becomes fused with torment. The child is caught between the fear of abuse and the terror of abandonment, not knowing whether to reach out or pull away.

The fearfully-attached possess both avoidant and anxious attachment styles, quick to activate or deactivate depending on how threatened they feel. They flip flop between two modes, being warm and emotionally open one moment, then cold and distant the next. They desperately seek love like the anxious person, but are terrified of it like the avoidant, yet more so due to their trauma. The fearful person feels safe when boundaries are low and they are deeply connected to others. Their intensity makes them charming, so people feel drawn to them. Yet the fearful person can only handle so much intimacy, and can pull away with the same intensity they connected with, which can make others feel abruptly abandoned. Also, due to their trauma, they have many core wounds, which act as emotional 'landmines.' The fearful person is therefore easily triggered and offended, and tends to have a hard time trusting others. They overcome this by idolising people and placing them on a pedestal. Yet their trauma is never far away.

In all three insecure attachment styles, the child associates intimacy with pain. Their map for love is distorted, having been adapted to suit the whims of a rejecting, deadened, tyrannical or inconsistent parent. The insecure attachment styles are also not black and white. Usually, a person develops a mixture of all, with one more dominant than the others depending on the relationship and the situation. In any case, the insecurely-attached child ends up with a low tolerance for vulnerability and will struggle with closeness and intimacy. Yet the child's problems go much deeper than their disruptive and deformed way of relating. The damage done runs all the way into their core, infecting every element of their being.

Original wound

Children who grow up in dysfunctional homes experience unfathomable terror. The parent's anger, neglect and unpredictability are extremely destabilising, and can shock the vulnerable child's tiny body. Such an untenable situation leaves the child overwhelmed and devastated.

When a person feels threatened, their body pumps out adrenaline to compel them to either attack, or escape the situation as quickly as possible. This is known as the *fight/flight* response, which is a survival instinct common to most animals. In the case of a child, neither of these is an option. They do not have the power to fight nor the capacity to escape. Their tormentor is far bigger and stronger than them, and is also who they rely on for survival. Therefore, their *freeze* response activates, where they dissociate and become immobile. This serves to numb the terror, and to stop the child from doing or saying anything abrupt that might get them hurt. However, the child cannot remain like this permanently. They still have needs, and must be able to actively convince their guardians to support them. This gives rise to the fourth trauma coping mechanism; the *fawn* response.

Humans fawn so they can convince a stronger figure that not only are they not a threat, but also a cooperative and useful ally. In short, the fawner aims to soften the other person into a more loving stance. When the child fawns, they become appeasing and submissive toward the parent, focussing on determining what calms the parent and makes them happy. If successful, fawning alleviates the threat and makes the parent more likely to treat the child well.

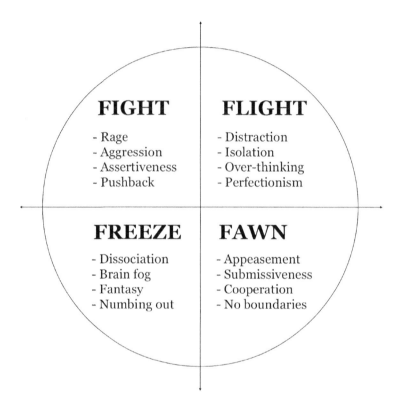

Figure 6: The four trauma responses.

Fawning is no magic pill, however, and can only go so far. Because the child in an abusive home has nowhere to turn, the fear also has nowhere to go. Worse still, the child has no way of processing what is happening to them. Mammals who escape threatening situations physically 'shake off' the incident in order to release the excess adrenaline. Humans have no such coping strategy. If a person cannot come to terms with the shock of an overwhelming situation, they become traumatised. This generally happens after major accidents or natural disasters, and is known as *post-traumatic stress disorder,* or PTSD for short. In such cases, the sheer magnitude of the event shocks the nervous system beyond what it can handle. Consequently, the fight/flight 'alarm bell' remains permanently on, and the body continues to produce adrenaline for a threat which no longer exists.

The abused child is traumatised in much the same way. Unless each frightening event is successfully processed and resolved, the energy remains trapped in the body and splits from consciousness, leading to a pressure cooker effect. The more fear there is, the bigger this 'ball of fire' becomes. The 'stress' component of PTSD is the exhausting burden of living with this excess energy. It is a constant, gnawing anxiety which never goes away. The longer the neglect and abuse continue, the more such experiences fuse, until the fight/flight state remains permanently active. This feeling of constant fear and impending doom is *complex post-traumatic stress disorder,* or C-PTSD for short.

What makes C-PTSD 'complex' is that it is not tied to a single, traumatic accident or event, but has instead developed over a long series of frightening and overwhelming experiences in a relationship. C-PTSD is also not isolated to fear and anxiety. An over-exposure to any negative emotion contributes to the trauma, including shame, guilt, grief, humiliation and helplessness. The horrifying spectre of abandonment, along with a series of painful emotional and physical experiences coalesces and becomes a permanent fixture in a child's psyche. This leads to an internal rupture which alienates the child from their True Self, irreparably altering their core.

Symptoms of C-PTSD might include:

- **Low self-esteem:** Children are grandiose by nature. They believe that everything which happens to them is their doing, both good or bad. Therefore, when the child is never celebrated or accepted for who they are, and when they never truly feel in control, their natural conclusion is that they are unworthy and incompetent.
- **Fear of abandonment:** Being neglected, emotionally cut-off or angrily attacked leaves the child believing that their parent might leave them forever. This results in a crippling fear of being alone, along with a paralysing terror of death by abandonment. This fear emanates from the child's core, so it is irrational while being irresistible in its immensity and strength.
- **Abandonment wound:** The abandonment wound is like a bottomless pit. It leaves you with a despairing sense that you will always be alone. With their low self-esteem, the traumatised child constantly believes that people will leave them, since they are, of course, utterly worthless and flawed.
- **Panic Attacks:** Repressed trauma has incredible power, and when it spontaneously breaks into consciousness, can take shape as a panic attack. Panic attacks are like volcanoes of fear, erupting and overwhelming you. They feel like

death, as though the terror will devour you until there is nothing left. It is a horrible, crippling experience.

- **Chronic emptiness:** Because the traumatised child is cut off from their True Self, its nourishment becomes inaccessible, leaving them with chronic emptiness as a permanent state. This makes the child vulnerable to neurotic behaviour, addiction, and neediness, all with the hope of filling the void.

- **Emotional flashbacks:** The traumatised child is submerged by a constant torrent of negative emotion. A flood of shame, guilt, fear, anger, sadness, despair, self-hatred and more always lurks beneath the surface, controlled by a hairline trigger. These emotional flashbacks are a core feature of C-PTSD. When activated, they take the traumatised person back in time. The person shrinks in stature, regressing to their childhood self. They become uncertain, highly-sensitive to stress, easily angered, or mute and unable to assert themselves. They might grow shameful and hide away from the world. They could become numb and have a hard time focussing or engaging others. Emotional flashbacks are so insidious that it can be incredibly difficult to know you are in one. You simply start to feel, think, look and react differently, and usually only become aware long after the fact.

- **Dissociation:** For the traumatised child, reality is often an incomprehensible nightmare. As the pressure builds, the child splits away from reality and drifts into their imagination. In this other-worldly realm, the child can escape their pain while fantasising of a 'better' life. Dissociation provides relief, and is a way to numb the chaos emanating from the child's core. The price the child pays for this coping strategy, however, is high. The child develops poor memory and even amnesia, being unable to recall aspects of their day or even their entire childhood. The dissociated child often cannot identify the nuances in their surroundings. They remain naive to the happenings in the world, and as a result experience immense disruption in their development.

- **Difficulty focussing:** Trauma and emotional dysregulation are incredibly distracting. This naturally results in an inability to focus, since the traumatised child is constantly plagued by the chaos and discomfort within. Trauma also impacts brain development, and is a major contributor to ADHD.

- **Impulsiveness:** Never truly in control of their emotions, the traumatised person may engage in risk-taking behaviour such as unsafe sex, illegal drug use, gambling, over-eating, reckless driving or overspending and materialism in order to regulate how they feel. The traumatised person is also prone to addiction.

- **Extreme splitting:** The traumatised child sees the world in black and white. People are either a threat, or a source of fantastic pleasure. The world is wonderful and abundant, or horrible and terrifying. There is no in-between, no nuance in the child's reality.

- **Suicidal ideation:** Trauma pulls you deep into the death instinct. This is a harrowing state, as you are literally swimming in death. Here dying becomes a natural, normal thing. You can feel it, even taste it. You think about it, imagine it, even welcome it. This is suicidal ideation. If trauma dampens the life instinct enough, physical death becomes a very real possibility.

- **Constant anxiety:** C-PTSD permanently activates the fight/flight response, and the resulting anxiety is crippling. The traumatised person has a need to always be doing something or working toward something in the future. They can engage in incessant thinking and compulsive talking to distract themselves from their feelings. They might have a hard time falling asleep, with anxiety corroding their capacity to relax. Those carrying trauma also carry a constant sense of impending doom. They catastrophise often in their minds, being bombarded by 'what if' thinking.

- **Unprocessed grief:** An abusive parent does not tolerate crying, since allowing their child to cry is to connect with their own wounded inner child. So they shame and attack the child to stop the sobbing in its tracks. A child is magical in their thinking, and lives in a beautiful Utopia of their own making. As they brush up against the limits and harshness of the world, their delusion cracks, and they lose another piece of their fantasy. A healthy response to loss is grief. That is what a child does. They are grieving the gradual death of their childhood. They cry regularly as their awareness expands and they realise the world is not as wonderful and friction-free as they imagined it to be. *Children are growing into adults when they cry.* The abusive parent halts this process, contributing to the child's arrested development.

- **Arrested development:** The traumatised child remains psychologically and physically frozen in time. Their muscles and organs tense to resist emotion, they appear younger than they are. Because of their extreme split, they are unable to integrate nuanced views, and hence continue to see the world in an infantile way. They spend so much energy trying to avoid pain that they miss the ship toward maturity and integration into society. They have a hard time in social groups, and are often dismissed as being slow, immature or uncooperative.

— **Identity diffusion:** The traumatised child's experience of who they are is so chaotic and confusing, they can never remain anchored within their True Self. They have a hard time finding mastery in life, since they have no consistent internal experience. They are chameleons, always changing to suit their environment, but never fully embracing or integrating any particular way of life. When you believe your core to be 'rotten,' no outer identity will ever be good enough, and therefore the traumatised child constantly switches out identities like costumes.

— **Ruptured sense of 'home':** The traumatised child's fragile sense of Self extends into belonging and community. They can never feel at home anywhere, since home is integrated within the Self, to which they have lost access. Home is a spiritual place as much as it is physical. Each relies on the other. Therefore, the traumatised child experiences no rest. They grow frustrated and might move geographical locations often to find this elusive sense of home. This is a trauma which quickly becomes intergenerational, impacting a family tree across multiple centuries as the family lineage grows nomadic, never truly becoming rooted and integrated in any community.

— **Paranoia:** With their fight/flight response on a hairline trigger, the traumatised person can never rest. They are always hyper-vigilant. This becomes most evident in intimate relationships and social situations. In relationships, the traumatised person becomes clingy, jealous and terrified of abandonment, often perceiving rejection when it is not there. They also have a hard time trusting, which makes staying in relationships far more difficult. This paranoid state also makes it hard to identify when real threats arise, which can destabilise the traumatised person's sense of reality.

- **Repressed rage:** Having your boundaries broken, being humiliated, constricted, terrorised or abused all take their toll on the child who cannot fight back. Yet the body never forgets. Anger is a reasonable reaction to such treatment, but the child can never vent or express it. So they push it into the body, where it remains. Some traumatised children appear perfectly calm, with the anger nowhere to be seen. But it is there. It eventually rises to the surface as passive-aggression, over-the-top rebelliousness and resistance to authority, unexpected angry outbursts, covert revenge and humiliation of others, and in the worst cases, as extreme violence that seemingly comes from nowhere. There is no limit to the traumatised person's rage.

Shame run rampant

One of the most painful yet insidious wounds the traumatised child carries is that of not being seen. A child craves the acknowledgement and validation of their guardian's loving gaze. The parent needs to be present, calm and accommodating of the child's chaotic emotions. Only through being seen does the child feel legitimised. Neglectful parents are often too dissociated, distracted, depressed or emotionally unstable to see the child. As a result, the child will come into the narcissistic phase with a wounded sense of Self. When they express rage to protest this painful state of affairs, the child is counterattacked and forced to repress their anger. As a result, they project the energy of their death instinct back toward the 'bad child' as self-hatred. Rage accumulates, remaining dormant and unprocessed. Having no power to get their need to be seen met, the child concludes that they are simply not worth it, and moves down the continuum toward shame. They become tortured by an agonising sense of inferiority and worthlessness.

A caring, respectful guardian will do their best to shield their child from experiencing too much shame. In contrast, an abusive guardian will behave in ways which trigger it torrentially. Shame burns in every part of the child's being, robs them of their willpower, and leaves them in a state of despair. By being able to set boundaries through hate and feel connected through love, the child can experience some sense of healthy pride. They can even experience a healthy amount of shame, especially when resistance comes with compromise. The emotional forces become balanced. If instead the child is denied their right to be seen, they reach a point where they can no longer tolerate the pain.

The loss of control

To the child who projects their split, the parent's reasons for abuse and neglect mean nothing. A happy and loving parent is good, and an emotionally deadened or tyrannical parent is bad. The child has no hope of understanding or transcending the dysfunction of their situation. When a guardian neglects the vulnerable child, the child is exposed to a sense of impending terror from the spectre of abandonment. When a guardian attacks the child or grossly abuses their boundaries, the child experiences shock, eventually being flooded with toxic shame. Both forms of abuse threaten the child with annihilation; one is death by abandonment, the other is death by attack. In both situations, the child's foundation violently collapses from the psychological earthquake, along with their sense of Self. Devastated and having lost all control, they clamber to regain it — whatever the cost.

Melanie Klein referred to the death instinct response as the 'paranoid-schizoid' position, which is another term for the fight/flight state and its subsequent coping mechanism. The 'paranoid' part is the fight/flight state, which manifests as panic and dread. This fear has two sides; the fear of engulfment, and the fear of abandonment. The 'schizoid' component is a freeze response, where the child dissociates from reality, numbing their emotions and retreating into fantasy. This coping mechanism is the first line of defence the child has to regain a feeling of control. By escaping into their mind and splitting their experiences into good or bad, the child can direct their love and hate accordingly, conjuring an imaginary sense of connection and control. In abusive families, the child's power to hate is forbidden. Anger is met with greater anger, frustration with greater frustration. The shame and terror become too much. The child is forced to dissociate from their external experience and goes within to find reprieve.

Wrestling back control

It is the nature of trauma that even when the original situation is gone, the fear generated by the threat remains in the body. Unless this original wound is quickly depressurised and released, it remains in place, and the ego builds around it. The fight/flight alarm bell stays permanently activated, functioning outside of the child's conscious awareness. Meanwhile, the child moves on to life's challenges, even as paranoia and low self-esteem infect their every experience. This leaves them far less likely to trust others, since they are always looking through the lens of trauma. Add to that a string of shame experiences, which bind together with the trauma, and you have the perfect cocktail for a dissociated personality.

With trauma and shame consuming the child's reality, it takes little for them to realise that powerlessness leads to terror, and regaining power in any form alleviates it. At first, splitting is the only tool the child has at their disposal, but as they grow, they scramble to develop ways to gain control over their environment. They get their chance during the narcissistic phase.

As the child's ego emerges, a new 'self' forms over the traumatised one, bringing with it the capacity for the child to influence their environment and manipulate their mood. The child finds that imagining this emerging self as powerful offsets feelings of shame and vulnerability. They split this imagined self in two, committing entirely to their 'good child' and discarding the shame-based 'bad child.' They then reinforce the grandiose, ideal self by experimenting with controlling the people around them to prove their superiority. You can see this in the child who constantly asks for approval, who bullies other children, who compulsively creates fictional stories, deflects questions from adults to avoid accountability, or tries to gradually push the limits by misbehaving in covert ways. In each case, the child is acting out their imagined 'all-powerful' self.

In the face of insecure attachment and C-PTSD, there is usually a limited integration of the True Self into the ego, since experiencing it is too painful. By living through their false self instead, the child loses touch with their guilt, empathy and shame. Their world becomes an abstraction, a projection of their imagination. The worse the trauma, the more compelling and absolute this false self must be. The child might practice being aloof around family members, hoping to remain under the radar. They might also find that their innocence disarms the adults, and so might exaggerate it by being charming and obedient. They integrate these behaviours into their personality and use them as tools to distract both themselves and others from their traumatised, shame-based Self.

The price they pay for this solution, however, is immense. To find sanity, they sell their soul. They give up their need for secure attachment and actualisation, and instead, direct all of their life energy into maintaining their grandiose false self. The True Self remains buried, and is replaced with a pale imitation; a set of behaviours which make up a personality, aimed at gaining cooperation through deception, manipulation and control. Instead of genuine connection, the child enters the world of power; a realm where *they* pull the strings. This pseudo-reality exists in its own bubble, requiring others to engage and feed it to keep it alive.

Disposable people

To resolve the split, a person must have object constancy. This requires a secure attachment and a tolerance for imperfection. When relationships undergo rocky periods, or our loved ones show their flaws, our steady image of them remains intact. Emotional hurt is one thing, the relationship itself is something else.

A lack of object constancy is an inability to maintain a positive, realistic picture of the other person. Without it, a person has no real estate inside another's heart, and therefore can be dismissed before they can cause any harm. A lack of object constancy is also usually to blame for people who have a high turnover of friends or relationships. They are simply unable to maintain an attachment through the uncertainty that comes with loving.

Because the wounded child lacks object constancy, they create it artificially via their split. They begin by withdrawing their vitality from their primary loved ones and creating an idealised version in their imagination. This allows the child to regulate their fear of abandonment by imagining the people in their life to be perfect, loving and, above all, *loyal*. By relating to an image of perfection and cooperation, the wounded child can avoid being hurt or abandoned. Their loved ones are, after all, perfect.

The traumatised child, through their split, holds a rigid, binary view of relationships. When people are cooperative and non-threatening, the child sees them as good, and treats them as such. When the child feels hurt or offended by others, they re-cast them as all-bad. From there, they can easily distance themselves from that person, allowing the child to 'avoid' being abandoned or humiliated. In a perpetually-vigilant state, the wounded child is relating based on how a person makes them feel in the moment. Also, by dealing with others in such a way, the child can avoid the potential hurt which comes when people become 'real.'

The unshakable false self

Although a child is magical in their thinking to begin with, they usually get a chance to test their fantasies against reality and tone down their delusions. For the traumatised child, reality is terrifying and painful. Grandiose fantasies are all they have to offset their trauma.

Eventually, a convincing, tightly-layered false self develops as the child moves into adulthood. With a dense, rigid ego, there is no space for the True Self to express itself, robbing the child of the experiences needed for growth and actualisation. Peeling off the layers of this false self subjects the child to a torrent of painful emotional flashbacks. Consequently, the child maintains a tense and armoured body, their breathing shallow and constricted, all to stop the repressed trauma from rising into consciousness. Meanwhile, the child clings to their paranoid delusions and grandiose images. This state may often be detached from reality, but it gives the child a sense of safety and sanity.

The more compelling someone's false self is, the harder it becomes to challenge it. People cannot see that beneath the traumatised child's facade they are forever vigilant, always on guard, unable to establish a foundation for mutually-beneficial, authentic relationships. What perpetuates this unshakable false self and keeps it functioning well into adulthood is that a) it exists beyond the child's realm of awareness, and b) it maintains the sanity of the child, along with their psychological health. It is an integral part of them, and no matter how intelligent and resourceful they become, the core remains untouched. To challenge this false self is to provoke the child's identity, which to them is what allowed them to survive the terror of childhood. Not even the most loving intentions can convince the wounded child to let go of their defences. Their paranoia is deeply entrenched and out of reach. To go beyond the ego and expose their True Self, the wounded child will need to have some level of trust, which by now they have long abandoned. The purpose of childhood is to offer a child plenty of time to build a secure attachment and to learn how to manage the five emotional forces in relationships. The wounded child gets minimal opportunity to achieve this. When they do grow old enough to escape their dysfunctional environment, the time for unconditional love and total dependence is over, and the chance to establish a mature emotional foundation is long lost.

When trust dies

A key ingredient for the True Self to thrive is intimacy via a secure attachment. To be intimate with someone is to be truly seen by them. Not only are they present with you, but open hearted. You feel safe expressing your thoughts, emotions and doubts to them. The intimate other looks upon you with love, and is delighted not only by who you are, but also by the fact that *you simply are*. This kind of emotional resonance breeds confidence and power in a child. The more intimacy you receive, the more your True Self feels safe to expand.

In short, intimacy is the absence of ego. Where the ego is a mind construct designed to filter a person's experience and guard their emotions, intimacy is the relinquishing of this protective layer. Such an act of faith allows humans to connect authentically, which creates a sense of well-being, safety and compassion. To allow intimacy, a person needs to feel the trust that only a secure attachment can provide. The less resistance and the more respect they receive during intimacy, the more confidence they can have in others. Their self-esteem grows, and they feel secure enough to express their emotions and desires. In a state of genuine connection, a person is also more likely to adhere to moral standards, because intimacy by design means functioning within the realm of our emotions, which includes shame and empathy. To maintain the connection, we are challenged to consider the feelings of the other person. This mutual space is beneficial for all parties, and it is in the best interest of everybody to handle each other's feelings with care.

Furthermore, it is the *promise* of intimacy which endears us to each other. Once our basic needs are met and we feel secure in our environment, we begin to crave deeper human connection. If the child has a dismissive or tyrannical parent, then this natural evolution is thwarted, as the path to intimacy is either blocked or compromised. To be seen, the wounded child must jump through the hoops of their guardian's expectations. The parent might provide some mirroring and care, although the condition of that love is the child's obedience. By being offered some path to love, the child remains endeared to their guardian and maintains the hope for true intimacy and unconditional love. Also, many children have older siblings who provide some mirroring and care.

In the worst cases, the child is perpetually abused or neglected without any offer of intimacy. They looked to their guardian to love them and were rejected, leaving them with a burning sense of inadequacy. Other times their behaviour brought on their guardian's wrath, and the resulting trauma became too much. It is precisely during these times of shame and terror that the child will look to their inner 'good child' to provide them comfort and escape. This good child is their grandiose false self, which creates the illusion that not only are they 'good,' but better, stronger, smarter and more capable of being seen than anyone else. They conclude that nobody can be trusted to cater to their needs, deciding never again to lower their guard. They may in some cases remain outwardly loyal to their guardian, but internally they split away from the great parent. In the meantime, the child's paranoia never wavers, and they must control their environment at all times. They remain hyper-vigilant, their bodies tense to block emotions, terrified of the death instinct and their toxic shame.

The child leaves their emotional world behind and connects with a construct of their imagination. In doing so, they effectively cease being human. That is, they refuse to be 'ordinary,' and no longer feel what an average person feels, hence allowing them to break free from the 'bondage' of humanity. Shame, morality, empathy and love cease playing a part in tempering their grandiosity. They give up the search for intimacy and stop trusting that it will come to them.

There is a price to pay for this Faustian bargain. While the traumatised child has gained a sense of power and pain relief, they have given up the sustenance of their True Self. Without the internal nurture of love, wisdom and humanity, the child becomes plagued by an eerie emptiness. To maintain their false self, they need to *feed it externally*. So the child rises above the realm of shame and intimacy and into the realm of power, unhinged and unhindered by their emotions. They observe their guardians and other adults, and take note of how those people obtain compliance. Grandiosity, aggression, trickery, charm and shamelessness become the child's ways of relating. Using these tools, they test their environment, fishing for weak spots in others and opportunities to manipulate and control. To survive and thrive, they need a constant supply of vitality for their false self. There is no resting in being for the wounded child. Attention, control and mind games are all they have.

If the wounded child manages to gain a monopoly over power, they use fear and emotional manipulation to enforce it. Where power is lacking, they turn the forces of love and hate against others to obtain it, withholding attention to gain the upper hand and feigning love to draw back those who pull away. This is the traumatised child's way of using attachment to their advantage. They are especially quick to target those who have an anxious or fearful style. They themselves will lean in any direction they see fit, using all manner of activating and deactivating strategies to manipulate and dominate others. They find that leaning avoidant makes the other person anxious to fill the gap, and charming the other person lowers their boundaries. A power imbalance then emerges in the relationship, and they even go as far as threatening the attachment to enforce compliance, knowing how painful abandonment would be for the insecurely-attached person. In all cases, the wounded child's aim is power and control. Above all, they want to avoid feeling helpless or vulnerable.

Beyond attachment, people also respond positively to the child's shamelessness, impressed by their apparent confidence, ambition and self-control. Without the negative emotions of their True Self, the wounded child takes on a clean, godly appearance. They find they can make intense eye contact, their posture improves, and they intimidate more easily. They use all of their craft and cunning, seeking out ways to manipulate their environment for the purpose of obtaining power. They relish the resulting feeling of control, fantasising about how far they can take it. In time, narcissistic supply becomes their drug of choice, and the narcissist is born — along with an accompanying entourage of hidden personalities to help enforce their doctrine.

The narcissist's kaleidoscope of faces

Three things cannot be long hidden: the sun, the moon, and the truth.

- Buddha

What makes narcissists so insidious is that they do not always fit the DSM-5 criteria of 'inflated self-esteem, lack of empathy, demanding of attention, and sense of entitlement.' A narcissist can come across as needy, desperate, appeasing or apologetic. They can seem warm and loving, with a deep desire to connect. They can forfeit the spotlight, and declare how wonderful *you* are. They can then act from the shadows, inflicting harm and punishment on you in horrible ways. They can be brazen, reckless and treat people like pawns, manipulating, cheating and lying at will. They can be one person in front of strangers, and someone else entirely at home. And even with you, they can be one person one second, and switch suddenly. This can be utterly crazy-making, as the tender, charming person who attracted you morphs into a cold, sinister, rage-filled monster. It is as though they are many people in one. The truth, sadly, is not far off.

It can be easy to forget that behind every polished narcissistic facade lies a fractured soul. Whether it was through abuse, neglect or having to live up to an inhuman ideal, the outcome remains the same — self-abandonment, avoidance of pain at any cost, and a burning sense of low self-worth.

Sometimes the grandiosity defence is not enough to compensate for this. The world is harsh and unpredictable, and reality often comes knocking on the narcissist's door. When their false self inevitably fails them, the narcissist needs to adapt. For that, they have an array of alternative 'selves' to get their needs met, defend against re-traumatisation, and punish those who hurt them.

The typical narcissist is not out for world domination. Narcissism has one purpose; garnering narcissistic supply. Supply props up a false self. This false self is the tip of the spear which penetrates the world while defending the narcissist's wounded core. But what about the rest of the spear? Those who carry Complex-PTSD are themselves also complex. They can be dissociated and paranoid, moving between conscious states like a dream to navigate their tangled web of wounds. Often they do not aim to hurt others, but rather act out of desperation. Other times, however, they *do* aim to hurt others, for which there is an insidious reason. More on that shortly.

To brush someone off as a narcissist without widening your lens is to miss the bigger picture. This can leave you uninformed at best, and exposed and vulnerable at worst, as some-one you perceive *not* to be a narcissist might be presenting one of their many alternate 'faces.' To educate and arm our-selves, we therefore need to delve into the world of *personality disorders* to get the entire picture.

The narcissist's hidden army

To maintain a continuous, harmonious sense of Self, a person must have their core emotional needs met. Like a smoothly-running engine, any breaks in those needs, and the entire sys-tem splutters and eventually collapses.

C-PTSD not only disrupts a person from getting their core needs met, but also irreversibly fractures the Self. This culmi-nates in a family of *core wounds* which reshape the child's be-liefs about themselves and the world, and cripple their capaci-ty to thrive. As a result, pain emanates from the child and per-meates every facet of their experience. They get a constant sense that 'something' is wrong with them. These unbearable pulses from within are the Self signifying that its core needs system is damaged and requires some kind of resolution to stabilise it. The core needs, their respective core wounds, and the accompanying resolutions are outlined as follows:

Core Need	Core Wound	Resolution
Love	I am unloved	I am loved
Connection	I am abandoned	I am connected
Resilience	I am weak	I am strong
Significance	I am not enough	I am enough
Acceptance	I will be rejected	I am wanted
Legitimacy	I am bad	I am good
Worthiness	I am unworthy	I am worthy
Safety	I am unsafe	I am safe
Visibility	I am unseen / unheard	I am seen / heard
Competence	I am stupid	I am smart
Growth	I am stuck	I am developing
Desirability	I am undesirable	I am desirable

Figure 7: The core needs/wounds table. The C-PTSD core consists of a series of unmet needs, the pain associated with them, and the resulting limiting beliefs.

Core wounds quickly become intolerable, and must be resolved by any means necessary. Robbed of a stable experience to call 'Self,' the child begins a frantic effort to 'patch up' these gaps, gradually stitching themselves together using various compensation mechanisms. For this crucial task, the human mind has a series of tools to help maintain psychological balance and ward off insanity. The traumatised child restores the integrity of their Self and gets their core needs met using measures such as amnesia, deceptiveness, seductiveness, aggression, paranoia, fantasy, fiction, provocation and more. These coping behaviours manifest in the form of various 'protector' personalities, which ease the pain of the child's core wounds and help them temporarily find the required resolutions, both real and imagined.

The protectors act as allies who get needs met and defend against psychological pain. These personalities exist in all of us, activating during times of stress, yet become especially pronounced and dysfunctional in response to C-PTSD. In their most extreme forms, they take over a person entirely and become personality disorders.

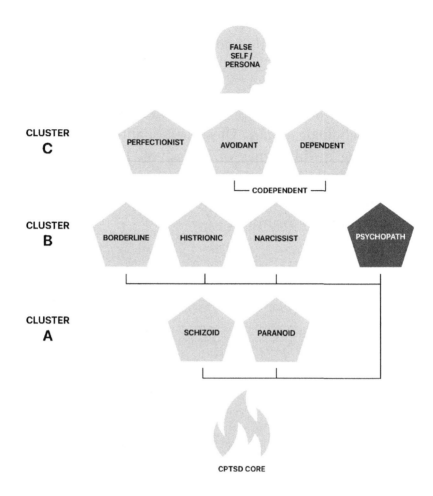

Figure 8: The protector personality map.

The protector personality map demonstrates how narcissism lies among numerous C-PTSD states. The primitive and passive 'cluster A' personalities are closest to the core and protect against threat. 'Cluster B' forms the active or 'dramatic' states which aim to garner narcissistic supply, seduce, achieve goals, defend against hurt, and of course, get core needs met. 'Cluster C' states aim to calibrate closeness and control in a relationship to ensure a sense of security and order.

The protector personalities are as follows, with each one moving progressively further away from the trauma core:

Schizoid

Seeks: To escape reality.
Fears: Exposure.

The first line of defence to the terror of neglect and abuse is to dissociate, or 'check out' of reality. The schizoid sees the world through a psychological window. They feel numb to their humanity, never able to absorb the entirety of their experience. They appear aloof or distracted. The schizoid has one foot in reality, another in imagination. They can spend vast periods of the day fantasising and imagining great successes, escaping their life and going somewhere else, doing something better or being someone new.

Schizoids can be creative, since they have a unique 'outsider's' perspective. They can think laterally, and their mind goes places the normal person's rarely would. The narcissist draws on this state for their grandiosity, leaning heavily on it to defy reality and imagine themselves as superior and great.

The schizoid has a flat emotional affect and an apparent indifference to people's opinions. A low-level enthusiasm might come to them, but it quickly fades. They prefer solitude over the company of others. The schizoid might take over after a relationship breakup. In such cases, the person might isolate themselves, become asexual, or avoid social engagements for an extended period.

When narcissists are exposed, humiliated or have their supply suddenly snatched away, the schizoid might activate to help them cope. Narcissists also grow more schizoid as they age, becoming progressively more reclusive. This is usually brought on by dwindling narcissistic supply and resentment, as their self-centredness and exploitation push people away. In response, the narcissist channels the schizoid into their grandiosity to avoid the shame of isolation, declaring that they much prefer their own company over wasting their precious time on others.

Paranoid

Seeks: Emotional and physical safety.
Fears: Threat to emotional and physical safety.

The paranoid is convinced that someone is out to get them. They believe the person walking behind is following them home. The people in their lives are manipulative and plotting to abandon them, humiliate them, use them, even to poison them. Although they have no proof, the paranoid is convinced that their partner is incessantly cheating on them. They perceive betrayal and threat at every turn while being convinced that it has already happened. If someone is not at their phone or is out for too long, they must be up to something. Trust is fickle in the paranoid's life. They have difficulty forgiving others, and have a tendency to hold grudges.

Trauma is enough to trigger anyone's paranoia and leave them on the constant lookout for threats, with their fight/flight system ringing at maximum level. Making matters worse is that many dysfunctional households harbour dark secrets and duplicity. Wounded and abusive parents often lie, withhold information and manipulate in the shadows to avoid accountability, causing the traumatised child to internalise mistrust as a permanent state of mind. The paranoid lingers beneath the surface as a constant suspicion, but takes over during times of stress. This can cause the traumatised person to lash out or even cut off relationships suddenly.

Paranoia often originates from *real threat and betrayal.* Hyper-vigilance is a useful energy for pre-empting abuse, testing reality, and ensuring we can trust others to mean what they say and do what they promise. Yet when it becomes a permanent state, paranoia can make deciphering reality and truth extremely difficult. A person with a paranoid protector will often attract someone with a personality disorder, who might act deceptively and dishonestly to avoid abandonment or the shame of accountability. It is a vicious cycle. Dysfunction breeds lies, which breed mistrust, which breeds fear of abandonment, which breeds further dysfunction, and the cycle repeats.

Borderline

Seeks: Love and emotional regulation.
Fears: Abandonment and emotional dysregulation.

The borderline is the first active protector personality, which is telling, since the name describes a person on the border of sanity and psychosis, between control and chaos, capable of falling head-first into panic, fury or depression at any time.

The borderline is prone to experiencing most of the core C-PTSD symptoms, and so suffers greatly. Their solution for this is to seek out the perfect love, aiming to regulate their inner turmoil through an 'ideal' partner. By establishing love with the perfect person, the borderline can calm their fear and alleviate their suffering through a bright future with a beloved who will never leave them.

Having failed to achieve the depressive position, the borderline is prone to seeing people as all-good or all-bad. When they polarise in the positive, they will attach to that person at warp speed. At first, the borderline idealises their partner. The relationship is the most amazing thing that has ever happened to them. Their partner is a dream come true. This love will manifest into a bright future filled with abundance and prosperity.

However, no fantasy can withstand the test of reality for long. Within the first few weeks or months, the partner's flaws come into focus, and cracks appear in the illusion. The trauma resurfaces and challenges the split. To help the borderline fend off the resulting discomfort, they externalise the feelings and blame their partner. 'All-good' flips into 'all-bad,' and the 'devalue' phase begins. The borderline criticises, judges, shames, punishes and 'points out' the partner's flaws. Nothing the partner does is ever good enough.

The main traits of the borderline are:

- **Abandonment anxiety:** The borderline clings to others, demanding their constant time and attention to feel secure in the relationship.
- **Fusion:** The borderline only feels secure when completely enmeshed, hoping to have the other person co-opt responsibility for their emotions, thoughts and decisions. It is only a matter of time, however, before they lose their sense of Self and feel engulfed and devoured by the other person.
- **Approach/avoidance:** The borderline seeks fusion with others *and* simultaneously has abandonment terror. Any perceived break in their fantasy of perfect love triggers their abandonment anxiety, and with it, threatens their mental stability. Therefore, if the other person disappoints the borderline, acts independently, or creates emotional distance, then the borderline pulls away abruptly as a defence. They go through phases of being deeply connected and in love, before suddenly growing cold and critical without warning. While this may produce a short-term feeling of control, the borderline's fear of being alone compels them to re-engage, and they cling to the other person again. Before long, they feel engulfed and again pull away. The resulting push/pull dynamic naturally results in constant blow-ups and fights with the confused loved one. The

relationship then becomes plagued by arguments that lead nowhere, emotional outbursts, bitterness, mood swings and chaos.

- **Fluctuating self-esteem:** The borderline alternates between supreme confidence and crippling self-doubt and self-loathing.

- **Identity diffusion:** The borderline has a weak sense of self and constant self-doubt. They have an unclear, shifting self-image, changing their values and behaviours as necessary to be accepted.

- **Chronic emptiness:** A hollow feeling of emptiness is a C-PTSD symptom against which the borderline has little internal defence.

- **Object inconstancy:** The borderline has difficulty keeping a consistent, internal image of the other person. When their loved one goes away, it feels as though they no longer exist. This makes it easier for the borderline to cheat, and also makes them desperate to keep that person around as their abandonment terror threatens to take them over.

- **Emotional lability:** The borderline often drowns in their emotions, unsure of their feelings. They experience extreme shifts in mood, and can bounce between intense euphoria and terrible depression. They are often unsure how they feel about others, and are prone to suddenly and abruptly ending relationships. They have weak impulse control and demonstrate risky, reckless behaviour. They tend to hold in their chaotic emotions, desperate to stay 'normal' and not hurt others, until they erupt suddenly in a violent rage, throwing temper tantrums and acting out in ways they later regret.

- **Self-harm:** Borderlines are known to self-harm through cutting, abusing drugs, binge-eating and promiscuous sex.
- **Suicidal ideation:** The borderline skirts the edge of the death instinct, sometimes playing with the idea of suicide as a way to end the torment.
- **Dissociation:** The borderline experiences gaps in their memory. They sometimes derealise and lose touch with reality, feeling like overwhelming events are happening to someone else, especially when they are shame or guilt-inducing, such as when they cheat or betray someone. They might create a fiction to compensate for their amnesia, hoping to keep a 'sane' storyline to avoid abandonment or going over the edge.

The borderline struggles with arrested development. Therefore, playing the helpless child or victim comes easily to them. The borderline makes themselves submissive in the presence of others, hoping that person will take up the saviour or parent role and magically rescue them or solve their problems. They struggle to form horizontal adult-to-adult relationships. Their innocence and playfulness are endearing to people the borderline comes into contact with. If someone has a latent saviour complex or harbours covert narcissism, they will gravitate to the borderline and pick up the slack. Such people are more than happy to play the role of the 'perfect' partner.

The borderline's splitting and magical thinking aim to shield them from their trauma. The borderline is constantly vigilant, perceiving abandonment and threat at every corner, and because of this, acts out in ways that ensure abandonment. They are forever testing their loved ones, pushing their sore points to check if that person will stick around. Together with their approach/avoidance cycles, the borderline puts others on constant edge. The other person has no idea when the borderline's mood will switch, or when and how the borderline will accuse them, judge them, criticise them or simply erupt and act out. The person usually has no idea they are being put through a washing machine of splitting, paranoia and repressed anger.

Histrionic

Seeks: Attention.
Fears: Rejection.

It is natural to want to be desired. However, when this need fuses with C-PTSD and narcissism, the results can be devastating.

The histrionic craves attention. They are often attractive, sexual, vain and overly concerned with their appearance. They objectify both themselves and others, believing that to be worthy of love, one must be desirable. The histrionic therefore seduces people into giving them what they want by having an irresistible appearance and energy. They may also act overly dramatic or provocatively to garner attention. They often say things that polarise or shock to get someone's attention, even reverting to wild accusations. For example, they might declare: "You don't love me. You don't care about me."

The histrionic needs constant reassurance and approval, and hates to be alone. They want to be complimented regularly and be the centre of attention. When it becomes your turn to speak, however, their attention often wavers. They panic when you do not respond to their communications immediately, and then try to provoke a response. If they do not get the attention they crave, they will act quickly, often flip-flopping their emotions, going from victim, to angry attacker, to passive-aggressive, all in the hope of forcing you to engage them.

The histrionic regulates their self-esteem with attention. They flirt naturally and effortlessly, and prefer the company of the opposite sex, often using them for gratification. They might turn the conversation to sex at unexpected moments. Their need to feel desirable can lead to triangulation, where the histrionic introduces a sexual threat into their relationship dynamic, hoping to provoke their partner's jealousy. When the partner is not showing enough affection and desire, the histrionic triangulates to 'remind' their partner of how desirable they are. They might even go as far as flirting with another person in their partner's presence while denying their true intention, claiming it was 'just being friendly.'

In extreme cases, the histrionic may damage their own property or fake a crisis to get their partner to come to their rescue, or hide something to force their partner to solve the 'mystery.' In relationships, they usually want to move in together quickly. They have a high moral code, but rarely live up to that standard. They are quick to call out others on social and racial justice issues, but only do this to appear self-righteous and draw attention to themselves.

Psychopath

Seeks: Justice and dominance.
Fears: Humiliation or failing to get their way.

What would you do if you had no emotions, no empathy and no conscience to hold you back? Would you steal, cheat, and manipulate? Would you lie to your loved one's face if you thought it would benefit you? Have you ever found yourself on the verge of doing something 'immoral' toward someone, imagined the rush of power it would give you, before suddenly holding yourself back?

The term 'psychopath' comes with enormous stigma. People typically associate it with violence, murder and inhumanity. However, we need to overcome this stigma if we are to understand it, and above all, spot it in those who are lower on the spectrum. Inside all of us is the seed of the psychopathic self, waiting to flower under the right circumstances.

The psychopath is the fixer and equaliser. The one who cleans up the mess and gets things done. The one who could not care less, who gets a rush of power when having their way with someone. They lurk in the shadows, paying close attention to the world around them. Meanwhile, they keep a black book of 'misdeeds,' waiting for the perfect time to strike and deliver their revenge. The psychopath adheres only to the law of the jungle, where the strongest survive, and the weak and naive get what they deserve. For the psychopath, any means justifies the end. They take pleasure in dishing out revenge for perceived slights, and have a tendency toward humiliating others and exploitative, sadistic sex. The malignant narcissist acts mostly from their psychopath, often with no remorse or empathy.

Vindictiveness comes easily to the psychopath. The psychopath deflects and blocks out the inconvenient truth, and lies compulsively. They do everything in their power to achieve their ends, which includes avoiding abandonment or exposure. The only thing keeping us from activating the psychopath in its horrific power is our conscience, which we channel via our True Self. Without our inner compass and outer environment to keep us accountable, there is no telling what we might do. There is a reason why many of the highest positions in our social hierarchy are occupied by fully-fledged psychopaths. Unhindered by their conscience, the psychopath forces their way to the top, and while at the top, becomes even more psychopathic due to a lack of accountability.

The psychopath is the strongest card the narcissist has to defend against the spectre of psychosis. The psychopath is a judge and executioner. Faced with disrespect, humiliation or insult, they punish others to restore balance and ensure justice, waiting for the perfect moment to strike, which might be months or even years in the future. The narcissist carries immense shame and feelings of low self-worth, and so the psychopath supports them in offloading those feelings to others in a way that avoids accountability. The psychopath will covertly attack others on behalf of the traumatised individual. In extreme cases, the psychopath will become violent.

If a person's conscience does arise to counter the psychopath's malignant behaviour, the psychopath blanks out their memory and denies everything. The psychopath creates fictions to cover up their behaviour and avoid accountability. They have no morality or plan, often acting on the whims of the moment. It is this personality which can cause the most damage, both to those the narcissist comes into contact with and to the narcissist themselves, whose reckless behaviour loses them not only supply, but the trust and love of others.

The psychopath is always lurking. If the target finds themselves suddenly reeling and shocked, caught utterly off guard, it is often the psychopath who has plotted and executed their plan with utmost prejudice. When someone becomes wholly detached from their True Self, they embrace the psychopath as a default state. The further up the spectrum they move, the less their conscience is there to stop them. Many narcissists, histrionics and borderlines can drift in and out of the psychopathic state during times of stress or threat, although this does not last long. In the borderline's case, they often experience guilt and shame for their actions after the influence of the psychopath wanes.

The psychopath is hyper-competitive. They take the narcissist's need for attention and status and pursue it to the fullest. The psychopath will torture their loved one on behalf of the borderline to ensure the loved one remains small enough to control, hence losing the confidence to leave. The psychopath, through the histrionic, will flirt, seduce and pursue a desired person without shame, even in the presence of their partner, often for mere revenge. This often causes immense destruction to the relationship, but the psychopath does not care. These actions are carried out in the heat of the moment. The person is simply not present when the psychopath takes over.

All for one, one for all

Trauma is like the Earth's core, and the cluster B protector personalities form the outer shell. The C-PTSD core remains tightly packed as the pressure of the real world threatens to break through and expose it. Abandonment, betrayal, engulfment and abuse, perceived or otherwise, all pose threats, forcing the relevant protector to emerge. There is no guarantee, however, that a narcissist will demonstrate all of these states. Some will be more dominant, and others may not show up at all. It depends on the narcissist's personality and the nature of their injuries. The more extreme the original wound, the more likely it is that all of them will emerge, especially the psychopath. When they are in their charm mode, the narcissist can be hiding any of these protectors behind their false self. It is only when your attachment to them grows and your defences lower that the cracks in their polished armour appear. Yet when push comes to shove, it is the psychopath who emerges to take charge, doing *whatever* it takes to protect the narcissist.

As you may have noticed, the cluster B personalities often overlap with narcissism. The borderline can be hot and cold, just like the narcissist. The histrionic is self-absorbed, and wants to look good and draw all the attention. The psychopath is callous, lacks empathy and has no issue exploiting others for their own gain. This is not by coincidence — the many sides of the kaleidoscope are connected to the same source. The protectors all have the same core trauma, and need each other to achieve their objectives. For example, the borderline needs love, and if making themselves seem desirable or superior gets it, then they will do it. The protector personalities also come in all configurations. While one protector might dominate, human beings are unique, and so are their adaptations to trauma. You can have a grandiose borderline, an emotionally-labile narcissist, a histrionic narcissist, a psychopathic borderline, and so forth.

When protectors fuse, they override symptoms of the others, making it difficult to diagnose. For example, a narcissistic borderline will experience a more stable sense of self-esteem through their narcissist protector, will not experience suicidal ideation, and will not self-harm. However, they may still experience emotional lability and maintain their fear of abandonment. Using this model, we can pull back from our narrow view and learn to see through a *cluster B lens* instead. Toxic is toxic, regardless of how it shows up. Rather than grow confused by a person's haphazard behaviour, we come to expect any of the behaviours, from any of the personalities, at any time.

The histrionic and borderline tend to be attributed to women, and the narcissist and psychopath to men. Yet all protectors can exist in both sexes, and will merely express themselves with the flavour of the person's gender and personality. Love bombing applies across all of the cluster B types, with the narcissist, histrionic, borderline and psychopath all looking for immediate and intense attachment in order to gain supply, attention, love or control, respectively.

Emotional instability also overlaps. The histrionic will be upset at not getting the attention or reaction they want. The borderline reacts negatively to perceived abandonment or because their idealised image of the other person is threatened, and they need to take out their uncomfortable emotions on someone. The narcissist, of course, reacts with rage when narcissistically injured, made to feel inferior or when their false self is attacked or discredited.

Environment determines fate. A person might alternate between protector personalities daily, depending on the needs of the moment. A protector might be stable and dominant most of the time, such as in the case of a grandiose narcissist. A protector might arise unexpectedly during conflict, before the default personality reasserts itself. If the power dynamic in a relationship shifts in the target's favour, the narcissist might revert to a borderline state, as their grandiosity shatters and fragments of their True Self rise to the surface. During a crisis or breakdown, a protector personality might collapse and give way to another, more primitive defence. A default protector might also fall apart as a person ages and their power in the world fades.

Codependency: The avoidant/dependent dance

Unable to find inner balance and confidence alone, the traumatised person develops an over-reliance on relationships to regulate themselves and define who they are. This is a recipe for disaster, as paranoia, splitting, dissociation and other C-PTSD symptoms make maintaining a harmonious relationship nearly impossible. The traumatised person is constantly overwhelmed by negative emotions, and projects them onto others to help them cope. The battlefield in such dysfunctional relationships is attachment, where a struggle ensues for that elusive sense of safety, security and love.

All of the insecure attachment styles struggle with boundaries. Anxious people, having experienced precarious connection, require consistency above all. By completely dissolving boundaries, the anxious person hopes to fuse with their loved one, gaining constant and predictable access. Avoidant people feel unsafe with intimacy, and put up strong boundaries to feel safe. Fearful people flip-flop between both modes on a dime, dropping all boundaries and connecting deeply before brutally raising their shields without warning. An insecurely-attached person forgets where they begin and the other person ends. The other person's needs either become theirs or become a threat. This painful, dysfunctional way of relating is *codependency.*

Since intimacy creates vulnerability, the potential of being hurt is too much for the insecurely-attached, which leads to a constant see-saw of a relationship. The *dependent* leans anxiously into the relationship, while the *avoidant* pulls away. The dependent directs their love *outwards* toward the other person, while the avoidant directs their love *inwards* toward themselves as grandiosity. The fawning dependent is often wide-eyed and clingy, the avoidant is aloof and appears arrogant. The dependent tends to devalue themselves, while the avoidant over-values themselves to maintain separation. Both personalities are shame-bound, compensation strategies for trauma.

The dependent is overly reliant on the relationship to regulate their self-esteem and sense of safety. Because they feel like they need others more than others need them, they tend to become overly giving and sacrificial, hoping it convinces others to meet their needs. The dependent usually puts up with the abusive and destructive behaviour of others, too terrified to lose them and face being alone. The relationship is all that is keeping the dependent from falling into their chaotic borderline state, where paranoia, panic and emotional dysregulation await them.

Although it seems on the surface like the dependent is simply being nice and giving, there is a darker side to this protector. Behind their submissiveness, the dependent is passive-aggressively demanding. By sacrificing everything for the relationship, the dependent creates a hidden contract with their partner; *I will give to you unconditionally, and you will love me unconditionally.* The dependent leans on their loved one no matter how badly they are treated. They grit their teeth and bottle up their pain at not being seen or 'respected' for what they do, smiling through thick and thin to maintain their 'perfect' appeasing front. In doing so, the dependent ensures that their loved one both takes them for granted, and is never accountable for their actions. Even from their submissive position, the dependent's behaviour gives them a feeling of control. As the dependent fulfils the other's every need, the loved one feels progressively more guilty and obligated to remain with the dependent. Leaving someone who sacrifices every-thing for you makes you a horrible person, after all. The loved one has little awareness that these feelings exist, due to the hidden contract being enforced upon them by the dependent. Also, by casting themselves as the 'saviour' who always comes to the rescue, the dependent hopes to gain the high ground in the relationship.

Such a boundaryless relationship is not sustainable, however. The need for safety comes hand in hand with a need for au-tonomy. A person requires firm boundaries to know who they are, and must defend the integrity of those boundaries if they are to grow and actualise. Yet the insecurely-attached person is not equipped with healthy boundary setting. Something has to give. The result is a push/pull dynamic, as one person steps into the avoidant role, and the other into the anxious depen-dent role.

To feel safe, one person leans toward the other for love. The other person, feeling engulfed, then pulls away to restore their sense of autonomy. The person who leans in then feels reject-ed and unsafe, and doubles down on their neediness, causing the other person to pull away even further. This causes im-mense hurt, and the dependent person finally gives up. The avoidant person, now feeling the pain of a void in love, grows anxious and leans in, and the cycle continues. This exhausting game is never resolved, since one person only feels safe with closeness, and the other person only ever truly feels safe with autonomy. Injecting chaos into this dynamic is the fearfully-attached person, who not only exhibits the predictable push-pull dynamic, but also an unpredictable response when their trauma is triggered.

In this codependent dance, the partners can flip-flop between the anxious and avoidant roles, other times the roles stay firmly fixed. Narcissists generally remain on the avoidant side, while their partners tend to be dependent. Behind this dance is a fear of abandonment and fear of engulfment. The codependent relationship is therefore a classic breeding ground for narcissistic abuse, where the narcissist attracts a target with a dependent personality. Both are playing roles which betray their authentic selves. The narcissist's false self is grandiose, and the dependent's submissive false self worships the narcissist's false self.

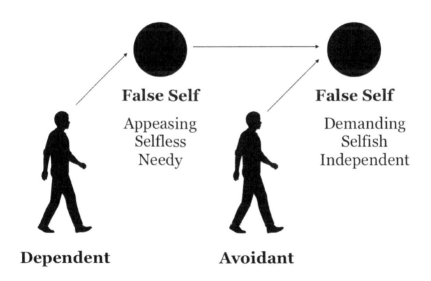

False Self

Appeasing
Selfless
Needy

False Self

Demanding
Selfish
Independent

Dependent   **Avoidant**

Figure 9: The narcissistic, codependent relationship dynamic. As the power balance shifts, the avoidant be-

comes progressively more narcissistic, drunk on their power over the dependent.

Due to their neediness, a dependent person is instantly at a disadvantage in the relationship power balance. Their partner is 'high value,' and they are the 'inferior' one. The dependent generally enters a relationship with low-self esteem, which creates the need to prove themselves to their 'superior' partner. This shifts the power balance in the narcissist's favour, which allows them to take advantage of the desperate and needy partner. As these two people progress in an enmeshed state, a natural hierarchy ensues. One has the high ground, the other the low ground. Narcissists naturally thrive in such an environment, where the power imbalance gains them easy access to narcissistic supply. Yet the dependent partner is not innocent in all this. The narcissist exerts overt, *hard power*, while the dependent exerts covert, *soft power*.

Soft power includes people-pleasing, being submissive, charming or appeasing the other person, all of which obligate them to stick around. Hard power includes ordering the other person around, yelling, threatening, ridiculing, shaming, dominating and directly controlling the other person. Typically, a narcissist will use soft power at the beginning of their relationship with a dependent partner, then revert to hard power when they feel threatened or sense the other person has sufficiently lowered their boundaries.

At some point, the dependent will feel scorned and upset with the narcissist's constant use of hard power and selfishness, and will apply hard power of their own while threatening to leave the relationship. The narcissist senses the end and reverts immediately to soft power. Once the relationship is restored and the dependent is appeased, the narcissist will switch back to being selfish and harsh. This is what lies at the core of the narcissist/dependent relationship dance.

In the case of long-term relationships, a codependent style will typically dominate, especially after a drawn-out power struggle, where the 'house-broken' person loses their willpower and comes to accept their role.

The perfectionist

Due to their sense of Self being shattered into countless fragments, the traumatised person grows hungry for structure and order. The perfectionist personality is an antidote for this, where a person:

— Becomes overly preoccupied with setting and maintaining rules.
— Becomes obsessive-compulsive about how and where things should be.
— Sets impossible standards for themselves and others.
— Develops a rigid morality, and a heavy-handed set of ethics and values, based on the needs of their wounded self.

By becoming dictatorial in their rule-setting, as well as self-righteous and rigid in their morality, the perfectionist can feel an imagined sense of power, order and safety in their life. They avoid failure at all costs, and never take risks. Much like codependency, this protector can overlap with the others. Paired with the avoidant, the perfectionist morphs into a tyrannical parent-like figure who can overpower and dominate their anxious partner. The perfectionist ensures not only order, but also the moral high ground, as being perfect makes them divine, and being the 'rule-setter' makes them the de facto 'ruler.' Through constantly telling others what to do, how to behave and what is right, the perfectionist firmly plants themselves in a position of power and control.

The chaos behind the face

To successfully hide the narcissist's dysfunction, the false self must create an air of flawlessness, superiority and power. Lurking behind this perfectly polished persona, however, is an entire cluster of protective personalities and coping mechanisms. Life is full of stress, unpredictability and suffering. As the narcissist faces the harshness of life, they alternate continuously between these protector personalities, hoping to maintain their false self while avoiding exposure.

The false self is the front guard, which interacts with people while the protectors remain on alert. The paranoid stands by while determining the level of external threat. The schizoid numbs pain, filters out reality, and creates desirable fantasies. The histrionic seduces, while the borderline works to cultivate a perfect love with a replacement parent who will regulate their emotions and never leave. The avoidant maintains a safe emotional distance when threatened. The dependent charms and cultivates closeness. The perfectionist ensures order and moral superiority. These protectors safeguard the integrity of the false self, as the core trauma continues to bubble beneath the surface. Meanwhile, the psychopath maintains a watchful eye, always ready to pounce, manipulate, control, lie or punish to ensure justice and integrity.

Yet while the narcissist has many allies to call on, they cannot control the world. They only have so much power. Often a narcissist grows up in an environment which offers little reinforcement for their imagined superior self. Sometimes catastrophe strikes, and the narcissist is either abandoned, exposed or betrayed to the point of collapse. In such cases, a re-organising of the entire personality is required to ensure survival.

Hiding in plain sight

Like the smooth, glimmering surface of the ocean on a calm, sunny day, the false self hides various lurking predators. These personalities can rise to the surface, then disappear just as quickly. They can remain active for long periods, or dormant 'underwater.'

For example, when the histrionic actively tries to seduce or gain attention, they are in their *overt* state. If they are abandoned by their object of desire, then the overt personality falls apart due to histrionic injury. The histrionic may double down and lash out, or withdraw completely, especially if they are broken up with. Over time, the histrionic goes 'underground' into their *covert*, schizoid state and avoids sex and people in general. They remain this way for a time, waiting to restore their confidence and find an opening to reassert themselves as desirable.

The overt and covert states are well-known for narcissists. 'Classic' narcissists are easy to spot. 'Covert' narcissists are notoriously difficult to identify by those not intimately close to them. Yet *all* of the protector personalities have both a covert and overt state.

If the narcissist can gain steady supply without opposition, then they will remain in their overt state. Celebrities, politicians, narcissistic parents, company managers, cult leaders and dominant friends all flex their narcissism as far as they can. If a narcissist finds themselves low in a hierarchy, where their need for superiority and grandiosity is constantly challenged or ignored, then they may enter into their covert state to avoid repeated injury. The environment shapes the narcissist, and their life situation determines how long they remain in their overt or covert state. A narcissist can be abrasive and dominant with their children, yet switch to becoming appeasing and cooperative in the workplace when faced with a powerful, narcissistic boss. That is, they are overt in one environment, and covert in the other.

The covert narcissist can also be difficult to spot at the beginning of the relationship. It is easy to dismiss someone who is acting too abrasive or stuck up. Yet a covert narcissist is typically polite, friendly and deeply interested in you when you first meet. They remain in their covert state until they sense your attachment growing, wherein they gradually switch to their overt state as the balance of power shifts in their favour.

Covert narcissists also behave altruistically, since those who are seen as 'immoral' are typically shunned. It is for this reason that narcissists, through their histrionic, often gravitate toward social justice causes, as it forces people to view the narcissist as being on the 'good' side while placing the narcissist at the centre of attention.

A house of cards

The false self, above all, aims to protect from pain. This solution becomes a problem in itself, however, as the more narcissistic a person becomes, the more they must deny reality. The more reality challenges the narcissist, the more they must double down on their grandiosity. They recruit more people for narcissistic supply, manipulate further, and work harder on their image. Eventually, the house collapses, and the narcissist switches to their covert state. The narcissist withdraws from reality to soothe the pain of their disillusionment, while dreaming of a future where they can assert their grandiosity and rebuild their house of cards.

Sometimes the narcissist's false self is challenged or exposed in a way their ego is ill-equipped to cope with. The calm, confident, seductive exterior collapses, and the narcissist comes face-to-face with their trauma. In such an instance, they revert to the borderline state and become inundated by shame, terror and rage. They act out, attack and lash out in unpredictable ways. They sob, beg, and guilt the other person, using all of the tools at the borderline's disposal. If damage control is needed, the psychopath may activate, and the narcissist will lie, manipulate or even become violent to punish the other person and restore their dignity and dominance.

This cycle plays out repeatedly, as the narcissist's house of cards withers to the point of permanent collapse. There is no perfect love to save them, and their desirability reduces as they age and lose status. At this point in life, a narcissist typically withdraws from society and regresses to the cluster A level. Moving from narcissist, to histrionic, to borderline, through to schizoid and paranoid, they approach their core wound. There is no more pretending. The narcissist becomes cynical, passive-aggressive and bitter, embracing conspiracy as worldview and reality.

The young narcissist looks down the barrel of this downward spiral and senses that they are running on borrowed time. They know that they must avoid this fate at all costs. They have no other choice — they must obtain narcissistic supply, or 'die.' What they fear is ego death, but this may as well be the real thing. While at the height of their 'power,' the narcissist therefore employs an instinctive strategy to obtain and hold onto narcissistic supply as long as they possibly can.

The narcissist's playbook

I play into the perception of me, but it's not really me.

- Kim Kardashian

The narcissist needs others to maintain their power. Where people usually nurture bonds through empathy and cooperation, the narcissist must convince people to enter their fantastical sphere of influence using alternative means. For this, the narcissist relies on the art of persuasion to sell their false self while manipulating others into meeting their narcissistic needs.

The art of persuasion

At the heart of every narcissist, behind their elaborate false self which can fool almost anyone, lies a timeless methodology. Coined by Aristotle over two thousand years ago, the 'three pillars of persuasion' have remained a universal blueprint for influence, and are outlined as follows:

Ethos (Appeal to credibility)

To have ethos is to project competence, divinity and authority. How a person dresses, their body language, their expression, and their ability to demonstrate success and status all come together as ethos. Think Adolf Hitler. He tailored his appearance and body language to create the impression of authority, showing abnormal discipline in honing his image. He rarely faltered in public, maintaining perfect posture and controlled body movements. The illusion of greatness had to be seamless and absolute. Hitler also touted his war record as proof of his bravery and loyalty to his country. Kim Kardashian is another example. She has dedicated herself absolutely to her image, surgically sculpting her body and perfecting her movements, posture and behaviour to create the illusion of divinity and perfection.

Ethos is potent. It persuades without making demands. In the uninitiated mind, the presence of a person of apparent strength, beauty or competence demands submission. While the average narcissist may not be as devoted as Hitler or Kim Kardashian, they will still develop a strategy of some kind. They adapt their body language, facial expression and attire to appear to have more status than they do. Narcissists will also flaunt and exaggerate their achievements, hoping to convince an audience of their high value.

Pathos (Appeal to emotion)

Appearance and reputation are how the narcissist makes their target receptive to influence. However, to cause a real shift, the narcissist must engage others by appealing to their emotions. The narcissist will make sometimes subtle and sometimes outrageous claims and accusations in the hopes of throwing people off-balance. They will also make sweeping, passionate generalisations to polarise people.

A narcissist explicitly targets the emotions of the five developmental forces. Their words can strike fear in the target, or cause them to feel shame using ridicule. The narcissist can appeal to a person's sense of pride by questioning their worth and forcing them to redeem themselves. The narcissist can win the target's love with charm, or anger them to force an outraged reaction. In every case, the purpose is to throw the target off-centre and force them to comply with the narcissist's agenda. Our tendency to act from our emotions makes us all vulnerable to the pathos of the narcissist.

Logos (Appeal to logic)

The narcissist's end game is to gain access to their target's mind. While disarming a person and destabilising their emotional balance are powerful tools, the narcissist must strike at the person's core beliefs to ensure effective control. By consistently questioning and challenging a person's reality, the narcissist can change how others see the world and themselves. For example, a narcissist might say: 'Your friends don't care about you,' or 'That's not what a good friend does.' Depending on the situation, the bare minimum such a statement achieves is to have you questioning your friendships, which eventually might culminate in you distancing yourself from them. In this way, the narcissist goes a way to isolating you from those you care about. The narcissist is relentless in their assault on their target's mind, using a barrage of subjective statements and questions aimed at reprogramming their target's core beliefs.

For maximum effect, the narcissist will use all three pillars simultaneously. They cultivate their image while discrediting and mocking those who threaten them (ethos), while questioning and attacking the reality of their target using emotion-triggering statements (pathos), and convincing yet subjective arguments and statements (logos). Using ethos, pathos and logos, the narcissist can neutralise those who threaten their power, disarm their target, pull the target into their reality and then manipulate the target into submission. Used on the uninitiated, this psychological assault is incredibly effective.

Shapeshifting

To endear themselves to the target, the narcissist needs to behave in an appealing way. The narcissist is an opportunist, and their role is spontaneous, coming about as required.

Examples of the narcissist's guises are:

- **The loyal friend:** The narcissist will listen attentively and agree wholeheartedly with what the target is saying. Regardless of what the target shares, the narcissist will be unconditional in their support and hearty in their praise. If the target complains about another person, the narcissist will be fierce in their mutual condemnation.
- **The fun friend:** The narcissist will joke and laugh with their target, generally at someone else's expense. Because it is all in the name of fun, the target will usually not object.

This dynamic creates a feeling of being 'buddies' who have a great friendship.

- **The wise orator:** The narcissist will speak passionately and confidently, exhibiting their alleged strength and knowledge, which gives them an air of authority and compels their target to pay attention, hoping to be enlightened by this captivating figure.

- **The victim:** When in their borderline or histrionic state, the narcissist will express how difficult things are for them or how life has dealt them terrible misfortune. The target then feels compelled to empathise and invest in the narcissist's 'problem.' Many people like to problem solve because it activates their saviour complex, or because problem solving helps distract them from the difficulties of their own life. When the narcissist plays the victim, the target will not only empathise, but also propose solutions for the problem. The narcissist has no intention of correcting their problem, however, usually brushing off these suggestions and instead keeping the focus on their alleged misfortune.

- **The actor/charmer:** The most charismatic characters are usually narcissists in their histrionic or psychopathic state, their seamless persona impressing and disarming the people with whom they come into contact. Their eye contact is magnetic, and their zeal and lack of hesitation make for intriguing interactions.

The narcissist will mix and match these roles, shifting shape depending on the person. All of these guises are intended to disarm the target by giving them an ego boost.

The greatest guise of all

The most potent shape the narcissist can take is that of the great mother or father. This archetype usually activates when a person resonates with our parent's face, voice tone, body movement and/or personality. Furthermore, a narcissist can seem arrogant and unreachable, which is a posture that many parents take with their children to project an air of control. Being exposed to this activates our parental complex, wherein we regress to our childhood self, and begin acting in ways that seem foreign to our adult self. When we are in our child, we become submissive, impulsive, and lose our boundaries. This gives the narcissist unparalleled power over their target, much like a parent has over their child.

Subliminally aware of this, the narcissist will emulate the body language and emotional coldness of a critical parent, which immediately activates their target's split. The target then feels an irrational and desperate desire to pull their head in and avoid disappointing or upsetting the narcissist. Because the parent-child relationship was so lopsided and absolute, the target regresses to such a state naturally, much like riding a bicycle. The great parent's gravitational pull is almost irresistible. The target has no idea that they are now interacting with an archetype rather than a person.

Before the narcissist can switch to condemnation, however, they need to charm their target into lowering their boundaries. They do this by playing the role of attuned parent, listening attentively while allowing a one-sided relationship to evolve. The narcissist will pay careful attention to what their target needs, and will fulfil the target's wishes as perfectly as possible.

The better the narcissist is at channelling the great parent, the more their target projects their unresolved split and psychologically regresses. Their body softens, their ego loosens its grip, and they become agreeable as they slip into a submissive state. With enough time, the narcissist will endear themselves to their target, allowing them to drop the guise and switch to tyranny, shaming and terrifying their target while extracting narcissistic supply.

Scapegoating

The best way to explore your shadow is to consider the qualities you loathe in others, since these are likely disowned aspects of yourself which lurk inside you. In the narcissist's case, they avoid their shadow like the plague and focus on their false self instead. By creating a grandiose 'light,' they can avoid their darkness. However, when reality challenges this delusion, the repressed emotions of the shadow come howling out. The narcissist's first defence against this is to attribute those emotions to someone else.

Scapegoating frees the narcissist from their shadow and bolsters their grandiosity. It is also a duality-based tool they use to boost their ethos. By putting others down in the presence of a third party, the narcissist creates the illusion of being 'good,' since they are the one pointing out the 'bad' person. This can be as subtle as poking fun at somebody they perceive to be weaker than them, pointing out somebody's alleged incompetence, gossiping about someone they secretly despise or can be as overt as lashing out at a minority group.

Scapegoating is compelling for many reasons. It allows the narcissist to discharge their shadow onto another person, effectively relieving them of the burden of feeling negative emotions and pent-up rage. Scapegoating also helps the narcissist recruit allies by using a method of divide and conquer. The narcissist relies on scapegoating to create an 'us versus them' narrative, using ethos, pathos and logos to convince others to join the 'us' team. For the uninitiated, taking the narcissist's side when they scapegoat can be an addictive ego boost. Owning your shadow is confronting and painful for anybody, narcissist or not. Life is simpler when you can disown your negative emotions and direct them at someone else. The narcissist knows this and uses it to powerful effect.

Propaganda

Propaganda is usually attributed to fascist and authoritarian regimes, but narcissists also use it. The purpose of propaganda is to hijack a person's mind by filling it with a series of carefully-cultivated and lopsided messages. It is a tool for misdirection, distracting the target from seeing the narcissist's true nature.

The narcissist will use pathos and logos to overwhelm their target. They tell far-fetched stories which have a grain of truth while making outlandish fabrications. Often, their 'story' is so compelling that it becomes believable. They communicate with conviction, spurring vivid images and rousing their target's emotions. But behind it all, propaganda is about creating an alternate reality and maintaining a target's engagement. It is a smokescreen, and nothing more. Once it seeps in, however, it can be hard to see through.

Gaslighting

Because the narcissist is in a dissociated, split state of mind, their behaviour cannot be understood through the lens of logic or 'fairness.' A normal person who bumps up against harsh reality will feel a spike of shame, then shift their approach to harmonise their inner reality with the outer reality. They empathise with others, consider the greater good, and then try to cooperate in a way that honours their needs as well as those of others. They understand the golden rule, that one should treat others as they would like to be treated. A narcissist, however, does it the other way around; outer reality must be manipulated and altered by any means necessary to support *their inner reality*. As a result, gaslighting is born.

Gaslighting is nothing personal. A narcissist, along with many of their associated protector personalities, becomes lost in their paranoia. They dissociate often while plagued with multiple, conflicting emotions or states. Their inner world is pure chaos, and they struggle to make sense of this confusion. Meanwhile, they know that on the surface, they need to be perceived as 'normal,' and of course, superior. Due to dissociation, the narcissist also has gaps in their memory. This is a horrifying reality to face, and the only way to fill the gaps is to create a fiction of what happened.

There is no logic to the narcissist's mind-boggling storytelling. Their sense of self is completely fragmented, with no cohesive train of thought, emotion or narrative. Therefore, they stitch together a Frankenstein narrative using any trick or lie they can come up with. To avoid the horror of what they are doing, they believe this fiction as though it were true. In this way, the narcissist is not lying. They are simply creating an 'alternative' truth.

This manifests in such behaviours as:

- **Questioning:** The narcissist will challenge your memory and argue against your interpretation of events. They will counter with phrases such as "that's not true" or "are you sure I said that?"
- **Blame-shifting:** When you express your distress at being mistreated, the narcissist will point out *your* bad behaviour. They will tell you that if they had a dollar for every time you did the same thing, they would be a millionaire.
- **Trivialising:** The narcissist, after hurting you in some way, will tell you that they were only joking. They might call you "too sensitive" or tell you that life is too short to create drama out of nothing.
- **Diverting:** The narcissist might simply try to change the topic, or ask you if you can just forget it and move on. They might shame you by telling you that your relationship could be amazing if you just stopped sweating the small stuff. By offering you an easy way out of conflict, they make you look like the person who wants trouble.
- **Compassion:** In the middle of being called out, the narcissist will tell you they love you and how terrible it is for

the two of you to be in this situation. This causes you to soften, and consider dropping it altogether to get back to the love.

DARVO

The narcissist cannot bear to see themselves as an abuser, since it challenges their perception of themselves as all-good. As a result, they will do everything in their power to explain away their behaviour and cast you as the persecutor instead. Again, arguing with the narcissist using logic is pointless; they are not in the same reality as you. They will drag you into a washing machine cycle of nonsense by denying or playing down what they did, pointing out your supposed bad behaviour, and then drawing attention to themselves and the pain that *they* have to go through because of *you*. This is what Jennifer Freyd coined as 'DARVO,' which is an acronym for 'deny, attack, reverse roles, victim, offender.' It is an insidious way the narcissist avoids their shadow by reframing situations to cast themselves as the innocent person.

Projective Identification

To maintain their 'all-good' image, the narcissist can only feel emotions which belong to a 'superior' person. Shame, guilt, sadness, doubt, anger; none of it acceptable. Therefore, the narcissist must find a way to covertly syphon their negative emotions into others instead. This is yet another shadow-denial process which Melanie Klein labelled 'projective identification.'

Projective identification is done in disguise, usually beginning as a harmless 'chat' about something small you did wrong. As the conversation progresses, the narcissist will slip in their judgements and 'hint' toward other things you do wrong. The conversation then gradually and casually 'drifts' from a reasonable heart-to-heart into a hypnotic monologue. On the surface, you are locked into a normal conversation. However, using *subtext* and *conversational drift*, the narcissist will make sweeping statements which cast you in a negative light. This is done so cleverly that you unconsciously take on the 'all-bad' role and its associated feelings while still believing you are having a normal conversation.

Projective identification is what typically leads to 'reactive abuse,' where a target takes on and acts out the narcissist's shadow emotions without consciously grasping how it happened. They only wake up from the shock of being triggered, where before that, slowly but surely, they felt the temperature inside them rising like boiling water, before they snapped from being cornered into the 'bad' position. As soon as their trigger hits, the narcissist then springs up and points the finger, piling on the judgements to drive home their point that the target is bad. In this way, the narcissist a) relieves themselves of their negative traits and emotions, b) gains the moral high ground, and c) reinforces their false self as being 'all-good.' To top it all off, they even force the target to blame themselves for the argument. All the while, the target has no idea how it all happened, and is completely unaware that the narcissist had injected them with their poison without their awareness. It is absolutely crazy-making.

Many of the gaslighting behaviours can leak into the other protector personalities. The malignant narcissist's psychopath can gaslight in order to dominate, punish or torture you. The borderline can gaslight to regulate their overwhelming emotional state by offloading their pain onto another person via DARVO and projective identification. The narcissist also uses gaslighting to ensure the integrity of their grandiose false self. With each protector personality, the behaviours are the same on the surface, yet their underlying process is different.

Triangulation

Triangulation is the bread and butter of all cluster B personalities, wherein the abuser introduces a third person into the relationship dynamic with the aim of tipping the power balance in their favour.

Triangulation comes in two forms:

- **Physical:** The narcissist flirts with someone in front of you while neglecting you, invites someone to mutual events and parades them, or spends increasingly more time with someone while talking them up in front of you.
- **Verbal:** The narcissist talks about the other person favourably or compares you to them unfavourably. They often drop the person's name into conversations, and gradually build them up in your mind. In a narcissistic family, a parent will do this between you and your siblings, often comparing you to your 'superior' sibling or so-and-so's child. In a romantic relationship, this is usually done with an ex or a potential successor, where the narcissist reminds

you of what the other person did right when discussing what you do wrong.

Triangulation can make you feel the following:

– Jealous.
– Undesirable and unattractive.
– Threatened.
– Afraid of being abandoned.
– Insignificant.
– Inferior.

Some reasons a narcissist might triangulate are:

– **It makes them feel wanted and in demand:** Having multiple people show interest in them makes a person feel like a valuable commodity. Telling the people about each other then creates competition and amplifies insecurity, making the 'competitors' feel inferior and unworthy. It communicates: "You are not special, let alone the only one, so you must fight to please me."
– **They want to control you:** Triangulation can trigger a person's jealousy and fear of abandonment, making them grow needy and insecure. They then become desperate to feel close to the person at the centre of the triangle. These feelings of insecurity make you reactive and panicky, and therefore easier to control. You are always on edge, doing everything you can to prove your worth and avoid being abandoned. A mother or father can also triangulate to get

their way and direct their children how they want. In all such cases, it is about control.

- **It helps them win an argument:** If so-and-so also thinks the same way as the narcissist, then that's two against one. Often it can be dozens against one, since apparently "everyone" feels the same way as the narcissist.
- **Fear of commitment:** The narcissist might keep multiple people around to avoid being 'stuck' in one relationship with all their eggs in one basket.
- **Backup:** Having multiple people in their harem allows the narcissist to have their pick of narcissistic supply, as well as to have options when the relationship with their target gets rocky.
- **Grandiosity:** The narcissist can never make someone as special or more special than them. Triangulation keeps others feeling insignificant and tips the power distribution in the narcissist's favour.
- **Revenge:** When the narcissist grows vindictive or resentful, they may triangulate simply to inflict punishment on their loved one.

Ultimately, the motives for triangulation depend on the protector personality. The narcissist uses triangulation to reassert their superiority and put their target 'in their place,' which is on the bottom. The histrionic triangulates to prove that they are still desirable, to garner fresh attention, and to remind their partner that they have options. The borderline looks to pull their partner in and keep their love by provoking their partner's jealousy and fear of abandonment. The psychopath, of course, looks to punish their loved one by causing them maximum pain.

Devouring the target

Intimate relationships nurture the soul. When two people connect authentically, they separate feeling seen and satisfied. The ego, on the other hand, is insatiable. It has only ever been a survival tool, a layer which rests above the True Self. For all of its ingenuity, the ego can never give a person peace and fulfilment. Our resting mode was always supposed to be the True Self. By disowning it and dwelling in a mind-created state of paranoia, the narcissist creates an untenable situation. Once a grandiose false self has established itself, it must be fed at all times — without exception. The larger it grows, the more it takes to satisfy it, and the more painful it becomes when supply runs out. Like any addiction, a lull in narcissistic supply creates a crisis.

By gaining control over their target, the narcissist has secured their drug, and they begin a process of devouring their target one transaction at a time. They diminish their target's freedom and self-esteem and demand reassurance of their grandiosity at all times. Meanwhile, they project their negative emotions on their target via shaming and projective identification. The target's willpower and confidence quickly wane from the consistent assault on their being. There is no mercy from the devouring process; the narcissist's thirst for narcissistic supply is unquenchable. Who in their right mind would agree to such a fate? Within this question lies the key to understanding how the narcissist maintains control for so long; being the target *is not in their right mind.*

The narcissist's wonderland

All fantasy should have a solid base in reality.

- Max Beerbohm

Before a target can be lulled into a narcissist's world, they need a compelling reason to lower their boundaries. For this, a narcissist creates a fantastical, hypnotic realm which promises to fulfil all of their target's desires.

Above all, a narcissistic relationship is a world of illusory potential. The narcissist, who lives in a dissociated state, is adept at awakening the target's magical thinking. From the get-go, the narcissist communicates to their target that they will be going on a spectacular adventure. Maybe travel the world. Achieve the perfect love, or create the perfect family. Be protected or taken care of forever. Find riches and obtain immense status, or pursue a mission which will change the world. The narcissist and their target will transcend reality, and create something the world has never seen.

The narcissist's realm is abundant. It promises infinite money, sex, power, status, fame, wonder, belonging or love. It is divorced from the 'limits' of reality, able to accommodate any vision. The narcissist's realm is also *dreamlike* and *mobile*, capable of being transported to another place at any time.

Washing away reality and fuelling this realm is *limerence*, where someone becomes infatuated and obsessed with another person, feeling their heart bursting with joy and amazement at the mere thought of them.

Limerence is characterised by the following:

- **Intrusive thoughts:** The person is on your mind when you wake, and as you fall asleep. You think about them constantly throughout the day, whether you like it or not, and feel an irresistible need to be with them when they are not around.
- **Dramatic change in priorities:** You put aside your hobbies, your friends, even your long-term plans in order to align your life with this person.
- **Emotional dependence:** You do everything you can to keep that person's approval, feeling incredibly anxious about 'doing something wrong' which might upset them. You read into every communication, decision, boundary or facial expression, terrified that this 'perfect' relationship might suddenly fall apart.

In a romantic relationship, limerence is often mistaken for love, as we believe we have finally found 'the one.' What we fail to realise, however, is that limerence is a powerful holdover from childhood; an immature form of love based on splitting. When fused with trauma, limerence carries into adulthood, where we split people into the divine being and ignore their flaws. The core difference between love and limerence is that love comes from *abundance*, whereas limerence comes from *lack*. That is, when we meet someone who seems to possess traits that we ourselves lack, limerence emerges to compel us to merge with them. This can be in romance, friendship, business or in our personal development. In all such cases, we feel limerence because we believe that person will somehow make us whole, and we do everything in our power to maintain this feeling.

When a narcissist sees their target in this state, they grow bolder, knowing that they have the target exactly where they want them. The narcissist then goes about fuelling the target's limerence, carefully playing into the role of perfect lover, guru, saviour or whatever role the target casts them into. Swept up by fantasy, the target enters a trance-like state where boundaries and scepticism are washed away. There are no rules to bother with in this realm, and above all, no outsiders to deal with. The narcissist's fantasy is safe, contained and exciting. It is timeless and without worry, and will remain that way forever — or so the target thinks.

The idealise, devalue and discard cycle

To bolster their grandiose realm, the narcissist must recruit people. Yet not anyone can qualify. This club is exclusive, and has two entry requirements:

1. A willingness to provide narcissistic supply.
2. Proof of perfection.

For this reason, anyone the narcissist associates with must be *useful* and/or *high value*.

The narcissist's bread and butter is to have a harem of subjects and admirers in their psychological pantheon of targets. If a target is willing to offer attention, sex, resources or services, then the narcissist will idealise them as worthwhile subjects — so long as they remain loyal. Eventually, the narcissist may grow bored of the target, or the target fails to live up to their initial promise. The target might resist too much, make demands, or worse, offend the narcissist. In other cases, the target's flaws weigh down the narcissist. In all such cases, the narcissist recoils and quickly discards the target.

Then there are the exceptional ones. Those who possess the beauty, strength, knowledge, status or skill to be *truly* idealised. The narcissist is immediately struck by such a 'high value' person, and looks to merge with them completely. This makes sense when you see it through a narcissistic lens. If the person who enters into a relationship with you is high value, then you too are high value by association.

By devouring the attention, resources, services or status of others, the narcissist can elevate their sense of godhood. The narcissistic realm is a one-person cult consisting of countless subjects and deities. The narcissist is either being worshipped, or worships others as a way to prop up their grandiosity. The narcissist also idealises people in order to feel safe enough to connect. By imagining a person to be unconditionally loyal or perfect, they can bond with someone who will never leave or disappoint them.

Yet this corrupted religion is just a fantasy in the narcissist's mind. The narcissist's entire life is dedicated to feeding their grandiosity. They use real people, exploit real resources, hurt real feelings, and cause real damage — all while buffering themselves from the reality within, which is the self-hatred, shame and rage they internalised in childhood.

This truth is never far away, however, no matter how the narcissist deludes themselves and others. Behind their facade, the narcissist carries the paranoid protector, who is always on the lookout for betrayal. If the target deviates from their role in the narcissist's fantasy, the narcissist will take names. Targets might act recklessly or carelessly and upset the narcissist. They might offend the narcissist, sometimes on purpose, as their patience with the narcissist's rigidity, perfectionism and controlling nature grows thin. The target might cheat, or they too might carry wounding which compels them to hurt the narcissist in terrible ways. In such cases, the narcissist receives an electrical jolt which causes their fantasy projection to flicker, allowing reality to seep through.

In extreme cases, such as cheating and other forms of betrayal, the narcissist's grandiosity becomes irreparably injured. They respond by deciding that the target is no longer useful or perfect, but rather bad, or even disgusting. Beneath the narcissist's fantasy realm lies immense paranoia, shame and anger. When you sufficiently betray or disappoint the narcissist, their deeply-repressed toxic dump of trauma oozes out and takes them over. Rather than see this for what it is, the narcissist *externalises* their pain and discomfort, and directs it toward the target, i.e. the horrible or worthless person. The narcissist decides then and there to *discard* the target, which heralds in the *devalue* phase. From this point on, the narcissist lays the groundwork to rid themselves of the other person.

If the narcissist's life is deeply entwined with you, then they need to slowly push you away. So they turn cold and contemptuous, judging, criticising, stonewalling, attacking or ridiculing you at will. Because you are still caught up in the fantasy, this will come as an enormous shock. You will grow flabbergasted, humiliated and sick to the stomach. In some cases, the narcissist may simply ghost you or walk away without another word.

The target, now used to the warmth of the narcissist's unconditional positive regard, panics and begins questioning themselves during the devalue phase. To get back into the narcissist's good graces and return to the idealisation phase, they turn up their attempts at appeasement. Their hope is to restore themselves in the narcissist's eyes, hence re-injecting the relationship with the original 'idealisation' drug.

For the target, bonding with your dream person at first feels amazing. However, the traumatised core of the narcissist remains beneath the surface. The target forgets that, in time, all drugs wear off, and the bad feelings re-emerge as the cruel, blistering cold reality asserts itself, and the narcissist's true nature comes through.

A cruel, vicious machine

Within an endless loop of idealisation, devaluation and discard, the narcissist leaves behind a trail of destruction. Their wonderland of fantasy drugs up their target, their cruel devaluation crushes the target's self-esteem, and finally, their brutal discard leaves that person traumatised. The narcissist does not learn from this process, usually convinced that it was *they* who were hurt and betrayed. This is partially true. The only missing element is the timeline. The narcissist *was* hurt and betrayed: *as a child.* Their rage is, above all, toward their neglectful and abusive parent, and their trauma is what keeps this horrible wheel spinning.

The narcissist's realm is fickle, recruiting and spitting people out at a rapid pace. Yet they have no other choice. The show must go on. The greatest challenge for the narcissist, therefore, is to maintain supply at all times. With ethos, pathos and logos, and through shapeshifting, scapegoating, propaganda, gaslighting and triangulation, the narcissist has many potent tools. They look out into their world, observing and studying their environment for the best sources of supply. They find that society is a collection of hierarchical structures with seats of power. The company has management and CEO positions, political organisations have ministerial positions. The narcissist also looks closer to home and finds opportunity in a structure which is not officially a power hierarchy, but can be converted with some adjustment: the family. This offers legitimacy for the narcissist's lust, providing the best chance for the narcissist to capture what they most desperately need: *permanent supply.*

The narcissistic family

Wherever I look, I see signs of the commandment to honour one's parents and nowhere of a commandment that calls for the respect of a child.

- Alice Miller

To sustain a grandiose false self, the narcissist needs narcissistic supply. As they go through life, they reign over younger siblings and relatives, or find weaker classmates in school to 'befriend.' They shame others while acting shameless, using people as building blocks to prop up their ego. They scapegoat to build up their reputation and avoid their shadow. Instead of building relationships on empathy, mutuality and support, they make others extensions of themselves. They draw in their target with charm and weaken their target's self-esteem with ridicule, all under the guise of connection. The narcissist can only have a positive sense of Self when in the presence of someone they can control. If there is nobody present to mirror their grandiose self back to them, their unresolved childhood trauma comes to the surface, and they become filled with uncertainty and dread.

The narcissist then grows older, and has probably gone through dozens of friendships. Most people eventually sense the emptiness and exploitation of the relationship, and consequently distance themselves. The narcissist's false self sustains cracks, but they reinforce it with replacement targets. They might also charm a potential lover, hijacking their partner's split, morphing their own behaviour to match what their partner perceives as ideal. Such a ruse works for a while, but often ends in disillusionment and breakup, or the narcissist grows bored and leaves.

It takes great effort to seduce and keep people around. The narcissist might look to elevate their career if they are capable, eyeing off high status positions such as a managerial role. In their personal life, however, there is no steady stream of narcissistic supply. It is only a matter of time before the idea of marriage and family comes up.

The core of the narcissistic family

All cultures see family as one of the pillars of success. At first, understanding is given to any person below the age of thirty. But as they near that daunting milestone, the urgency grows. The expectation of finding somebody and beginning a family looms over all single people. Friends and relatives remind the unmarried person as they grow into their twenties that the clock is ticking. Finally, if the person manages to cross through this rite of passage, their family and friends rejoice.

The celebrations vary between cultures, but the overwhelming message is clear: *You have made it.*

For the narcissist, this rite of passage carries little weight compared to their grandiose self. They remain locked in what feels like a life and death struggle to maintain and reinforce the illusion of power and control. It is inevitable then that family would become an extension of this world. Although it harms the people they come into contact with, in the narcissist's mind, the end justifies the means. When the narcissist seeks a partner, they look for someone who will not only over-look their grandiosity, but enable it. As children arrive, they too become an extension of the narcissist; objects which serve and uphold the narcissist's grandiose false self.

Hijacking the child's worship

Due to their vulnerability and subsequent split, children have a strong need to look up to and adore their parent. Therefore, whatever the parent says or does is taken as gospel. In a healthy family, the parent reflects reality back to the child, en-couraging them to channel their personal power and gently challenging their fantastical thinking. As the child's True Self develops and their split resolves, worship fades, and with that, they reach a sobering reality; their parent is not invincible, and will not magically solve all of their problems. Over time, their guardian gradually cedes power, and they learn that they must take responsibility for their own life. The child experi-ences an ambivalence toward the world and themselves, aware that between 'good' and 'bad' are many grey areas of uncomfortable truth. Without their black and white projection, the child reverts to reason and intuition to establish truth instead of reacting from their split. The warm blanket which protected them during childhood is gradually removed, leaving them feeling exposed and vulnerable to a complex world, but also free to grow and actualise as they see fit.

The narcissistic parent, on the other hand, thrives on their child's infantile nature. Being the subject of a human being's worship gives the narcissist a feeling of power and control while reinforcing their grandiose false self. When the child tries to assert themselves, the narcissist becomes threatened and cuts the child down with rage and contempt. If the child tries to assert their grandiosity, the narcissist responds by shaming and ridiculing them. The child can never be allowed to go rogue; they must remain within the narcissistic parent's sphere of influence at all times. Only the narcissist can sanction the child's power. In extreme situations, the narcissist uses the death instinct against the child, threatening them with abandonment or violence. In time, the child's will breaks, and they become locked in a psychological prison of fear. They live under a constant shadow, never able to experience the full spectrum of what life can offer. Toxic shame runs riot, and their sense of trust shatters. Healthy object constancy and actualisation become pipe dreams. The child is forced to dissociate and dwell in fantasy in order to cope.

A dysfunctional balance

Even before overt abuse takes place, a core problem in a dysfunctional family is the parent's lack of presence and inability to serve the children's needs. The parent's focus is wrapped up in a particular addiction, while their spouse struggles to fill the void and put out fires caused by a lack of structure and nurture. With the parental system occupied by the elephant in the room, the roles become reversed. Instead of the parents catering to the children's needs, the children adapt to the parents' whims.

While addiction can impact the narcissistic family, it is the parent's grandiose self which creates the void and forces the children's focus toward the parental system. What should be a nurturing and loving structure intended to raise children instead becomes a mini-autocracy geared toward the parent's grandiose agenda. The narcissist projects their paranoid split onto their family, using it to decide what is 'good' and what is 'bad' — i.e. what is acceptable and unacceptable. They also project their split onto their children, deciding who fits the role of 'good child' or 'bad child.' The children are not aware of what is going on, they only feel the distress of disapproval and rejection. Eventually, they learn that they are not the focus. The children realise they must instead work to satisfy the narcissistic parent's expectations, hoping to earn the parent's favour and attention. This dynamic creates a power scramble among the children, and the more kids in the family, the more likely it is that somebody gets left out. By suppressing their needs and turning their attention toward the narcissistic parent, the children and spouse achieve a balance, albeit a dysfunctional one intended to prop up a grandiose false self.

The narcissistic family doctrine

The one unquestionable myth about a narcissistic family is that it is a happy family, and on the surface, it appears so; after all, nobody seems to be complaining. A closer look, however, will reveal deep-seated frustration and stunted development held in place by a domineering parent. Rigidity and fear reign, and spontaneity and vibrancy are only allowed if they do not challenge the narcissistic parent's grandiosity. For the spouse and children, the rage of the narcissist is terrifying, so they will play along with the happy family image while suppressing their resentment at being controlled. To help them cope with a cold and loveless environment, they project their split onto their family and identify with it as being perfect. To accept reality is too painful and unsettling. Meanwhile, the narcissist, with their grandiose and controlling nature, projects their shadow onto their family. The narcissist is never to blame for any problems; it is either someone else's fault in the family, or a figure outside of the house is scapegoated. The narcissist's false self is impenetrable, making healthy shame and communion impossible. Anyone brave enough to speak up is met with deflection or fury, leaving them no choice but fall into line.

Acceptance and approval do exist in the narcissistic family, but it depends wholly on a person's ability to serve the family image. In a narcissistic family, you will be valued based on:

- **What you can offer:** For example, the narcissist may value the firstborn boy, so being born male and first will instantly win you acceptance. In matriarchal families, it is typically the firstborn girl. A family could value education, so receiving high grades becomes a source of approval. The narcissist may prize success, so they will usually champion the most talented child. Being well-behaved and cooperative can also win points, since it helps bolster the narcissist's image of being a good parent. Being attractive can enhance the family image, and such children will be showcased in front of others.

- **How well you uphold the family image:** You are expected to represent your family enthusiastically in public. Acting happy in front of outsiders reinforces the family's reputation and validates the narcissistic parent.

- **Your capacity to conform:** The narcissist is rigid and demanding. To maintain balance in their grandiose mind, they need a specific, unchallenged reality. Because the children are dependent on the narcissist, they have no choice but to submit to this pseudo-reality. The children must go where the narcissist wants, agree with what the narcissist says, and behave as the narcissist expects. The children and the spouse effectively orbit the narcissist and submit to their whims, creating a 'togetherness' which unwittingly passes off as a happy family.

Being valued for some things but rejected and attacked for others creates ambivalence in the child, who only wants to feel safe and loved. They remain unaware of the narcissistic agenda of their parent. For the child, everything is a matter of the heart. For the narcissist, everything is a question of their false self. The more dismissive and authoritarian the narcissist becomes, the more the child splits to maintain their sanity. They create delusions about the goodness of the parent, and internalise the shame of being objectified and controlled. The child blames their 'bad' child for being unable to obtain love or satisfy their parent. The result is toxic shame and an exaggerated 'love' for a 'perfect parent' who only exists in the child's mind as a projection.

Roles in a narcissistic family

As the children and spouse fight for the narcissist's favour, a pattern emerges. They find that what they are curious or passionate about is overlooked, while certain behaviours seem to win approval. They follow the path of least resistance and start to get a sense of control and normality. They desire above all a stable family environment, and playing along helps them achieve it. Differentiating and asserting themselves results in ridicule, rage or neglect, while being a good sport wins them acceptance. The children and spouse do not realise that they are being groomed and led through a narrow maze which grows less apparent over time. By being continuously conditioned, the children and spouse fall into specific roles and become them, while the vibrant and spontaneous True Self is pushed underground.

The typical roles of a narcissistic family are:

Enabler

This is usually the spouse but can also include one of the children. The enabler is the narcissist's sidekick and most loyal ally, carrying out the narcissist's menial tasks and tending to their basic needs, as well as helping put on a happy front. The enabler also reassures the narcissist of their grandiosity by always remaining at their side, or more accurately, orbiting them. As long as the narcissist knows that the enabler is available to react and respond to them, they feel reassured. In return, this role gives the enabler an identity and wins them the narcissist's approval.

Golden Child

The narcissist will seek out a child to mould in their image and will champion them as *the* good child. The golden child is usually the oldest, but not always. If another child is more attractive or excels at a quicker rate than the eldest, then the role of golden child can go to them instead. The narcissist will give the golden child preferential treatment — as long as the child behaves as expected, achieves on behalf of the narcissist, and enhances the family reputation. The rest of the children are expected to cooperate with the golden child and give them the 'respect they deserve.' This child grows up believing they are unique when in fact, they have been groomed in the narcissist's image.

Scapegoat

The narcissist's spite never goes away; they only repress it. They need someone to dump their disowned rage on — a 'bad' child of the family. The narcissist will usually see the second oldest or the most vulnerable as the problem child, and will target them with disapproval and abuse. Where the golden child can do no wrong, the scapegoat can do no right. Other children in the family may unwittingly follow suit, taking the narcissist's lead by using the scapegoat as an opportunity to unload their own unacknowledged resentment and shame. The scapegoat is usually the first to act out or show symptoms of mental illness, due to the unbearable burden of being the dumping ground for their family's collective toxic emotions.

Surrogate Parent

The narcissist is emotionally absent and too preoccupied with their false self to cater to the basic and emotional needs of the children, while their enabling spouse is often overwhelmed with responsibility. When there are multiple children in the family, the narcissist will designate at least one child to play surrogate parent, telling them to "look after your brother/sister". This child-parent is expected to cater to their younger sibling's needs, and will be held accountable for their sibling's well-being and behaviour. However, the surrogate parent is not an adult; they are a child. To succeed in their role, they must put aside their core needs and desires. They become rigid and responsible to a fault. Their service as a surrogate parent allows their younger siblings space to thrive somewhat, but they themselves pay a hefty price. The surrogate parent is a martyr; they forfeit their childhood for the sake of their younger siblings. Raising children is difficult enough for an adult. When a child is expected to do it, their apparent 'failure' leaves the surrogate parent with an enormous sense of guilt which haunts them for a lifetime. Furthermore, because their worth is wholly tied to having a duty to fulfil, they usually grow up to become workaholics, or move straight into tending to children of their own to maintain their identity.

Lost Child

Any children who the narcissist has not designated a role will be neglected and encouraged not to rock the boat. The lost child is usually somewhere in the middle or can be the youngest. They grow up with a sense of not knowing who they are or how they fit into the world, going through depressive phases and feeling unwanted and unloved. The lost child retreats into their mind and dwells in their imagination. They may spend countless hours reading, binge-watching films or playing video games. This dissociated fantasy state gives the lost child a sense of calm and control. Meanwhile, they live with a burning sense of unworthiness. They feel as though nobody sees them, hears them or cares about them.

Divine Child

The narcissistic family also needs a torchbearer; a child unscathed by the world. This divine child is typically the youngest, and is often spoken highly of with no apparent justification. They differ from the golden child in that they are not the narcissistic parent's protégé with the pressure to perform. Rather, they maintain their status through staying unchanged and 'pure.' They are mummy or daddy's little boy or girl, and are expected to remain under the narcissistic parent's wing. They are also usually the joker of the home, providing levity and comic relief, which masks the tension in the family and distracts from potential conflicts. With the older siblings absorbing the pressure of living up to the narcissist's expectations, the divine child remains infantilised and absolved of responsibility, never allowed to separate and mature. The rules are simple; stay close and be the family's mascot, and you will have all your needs met and be held in high regard.

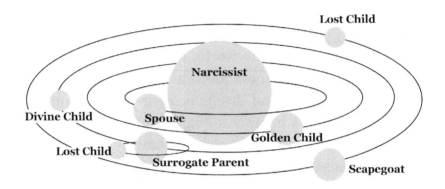

Figure 10: The narcissistic family system. *The narcissist exudes a psychological pull in the home which traps the spontaneity of the True Self inside a role while holding each family member in an endless orbit around the narcissist.*

The consequences of playing a role

Even though ultimate power is with the narcissist, the roles of a narcissistic family still give each person the *illusion* of control. The enabler's care-taking gives them purpose, the golden child's high-status gives them a sense of pride, the lost child's imagination drowns out the panic and creates calm, and the divine child's jokes allow them to dictate the mood of the family home. Only with the scapegoat is the absence of control a defining trait, as their outbursts create new opportunities for other family members to attack them.

The roles can also shift and vary. For example, if the golden child moves out or resists their responsibility, then a sibling may be promoted to golden child. Also, a child may play multiple roles. The golden child can play surrogate parent, and the lost child can also play the divine child. An only child is especially prone to numerous roles since they have no siblings to share the load. They will typically be designated the golden child, but also play scapegoat when the narcissist needs it and be expected to play the divine child to distract the parents and provide comic relief.

One can fool themselves into believing that the golden child has it best. Yet even though the roles are all different, they still betray the True Self of the child and are all shame-based. Also, by being coerced into a role, a family member is covertly told what is and is not acceptable in relationships. Their idea of what love is and what it takes to get it becomes distorted, creating deep-seated psychological damage.

The repercussions of being groomed into a role are enormous. The children and spouse of a narcissistic family usually experience the following:

– **Anxiety and depression:** Unable to grasp the narcissist's agenda, the child feels like they are being randomly rewarded and dismissed. The narcissist is like a slot machine which hands out approval and acceptance. For the child, this approval is what gives them a sense of identity and safety, and they remain addicted to the game, alternating between a cycle of hope and anxiety followed by despair and depression.

- **Emotional repression:** The family member must hold back their emotions so as not to disturb the fragile family balance. Negative feelings especially challenge the happy family image and are ignored, discouraged or attacked. The children learn to repress emotions such as anger and resentment, which leads to shame and depression. Also, by suppressing some emotions, the child is forced to suffocate all of them, which kills their ability to feel joy, stunts their growth and alienates them from their True Self.

- **Unhealthy beliefs about relationships:** Each member grows up with the idea that relationships are about which role you can play, being in constant competition, and about love being a limited resource which you must earn through your actions. The reality that love is a means and *not* an end, is about sharing and *not* about performing, is entirely lost on the child.

- **Inability to experience intimacy:** The child, who keeps opening their heart but is treated coldly without knowing why, eventually grows incapable of intimacy. The path to love becomes too frustrating. The child's subsequent insecure attachment style flows into all of their relationships. They become conditioned to expect rejection and controlling behaviour from others, and their erratic use of activating and deactivating strategies confuses the other person and destabilises the relationship.

- **Stunted maturity:** Due to an unresolved split, the child continues to see the world in black and white, all-good and all-bad. This immature way of living stops the child from seeing reality and integrating new viewpoints into their understanding of life, leading them to dysfunctional and harmful outcomes.

- **Toxic shame:** Being trapped in a rigid environment without having a say is shaming. For this reason, in order to exist within a narcissistic family, one must surrender all agency and feel constant shame. Add to that neglect and abuse, and these shame 'experiences' bind together, collectively amplifying as the child grows, culminating in toxic shame. When a child internalises toxic shame, any situation which even remotely reminds them of a past shame event can cause a flood of painful feelings to arise. This torrent functions autonomously and can render the child helpless, pulling them into a deep depression which can last for days at a time.

The only chance a person has to cope with the torment of living in a narcissistic family is to keep playing the game. As long as they maintain their role and remain in the hunt for approval, they can keep pace with their life instinct and stop from falling into despair. It is like running exhausted on a treadmill which never stops, or, as already illustrated, like being a planet or moon in perpetual orbit, always 'falling' but never able to change course.

The despair of orbit

When a satellite, moon or planet orbits another body, you have one object speeding past a larger object at the same rate as the larger object's gravitational pull, so that it is always in a state of free-fall. Narcissistic relationships follow this same law, but on a psychological plane.

First, if the orbiting object's velocity is too slow, it will suc-
cumb to the gravitational pull and crash into the larger object.
Therefore, the narcissist must ensure that emotional closeness
is regulated, so it is never too strong or too weak. By shaming,
questioning, ridiculing and attacking their target, the narcissist can psychologically slow them down and pull them in. If
the target gets too close, the narcissist pushes them away by
closing off emotionally. If the target threatens to 'shoot away'
from orbit and escape, then the narcissist increases their gravitational pull by charming the target and temporarily 'opening
up' to them.

This same dynamic plays out in the narcissistic family. Each
member's psychological velocity is being monitored and manipulated to ensure they never get too close emotionally yet
never gain the independence and agency to escape. Because
the child is always in motion, that is, 'on the way' toward approval, they feel like they may eventually get to their desired
goal: the love of the narcissistic parent. Instead, they remain
in an endless, despairing orbit.

The tragedy of the spouse

The spouse is in a particularly difficult position, caught between wanting the best for the children and keeping their narcissistic partner satisfied. Behind it all, the spouse is terrified
of abandonment and terribly low on self-esteem. The tragic
part of being the narcissist's partner is that the spouse receives minimal support while being expected to fulfil the
needs of numerous children. The narcissist is usually careful
to isolate their spouse physically and psychologically in order

to maintain control. As a result, the spouse's emotional needs remain unmet. Struggling to keep their head above water, the spouse leans on the children, growing demanding of them for attention or affection. This leaves the children feeling trapped and manipulated, causing further erosion of trust in intimacy.

Reality in a narcissistic family

The narcissistic family is publicly defined by the perfect family image while being privately held together by fear and shame. Each child is desperate for morsels of love while scrambling to measure up to the rigid expectations of the narcissistic parent.

In a healthy family, shame is balanced through equality, empathy and compromise. In a narcissistic family, shame is resolved through hierarchy and power. The problem with the narcissistic model is that the lower you are in the hierarchy, the more shame you will experience. Such a family model effectively creates a scramble to reach a higher position. The children subconsciously know that if they do not fight for what they need, they will be neglected and forgotten. In a narcissistic family, domination and strength stand above all else.

The narcissistic parent thrives on fear. The fight/flight state creates tunnel vision and arouses the death instinct while encouraging urgent action over rational thought. When the child becomes fearful, they lose the ability to think laterally, and are much easier to manipulate and control. Only the smallest prod is needed to make them cooperate. Love and support calm the fight/flight response and induce feelings of safety. Armed with this knowledge, the narcissist will threaten the children with abandonment to ensure cooperation and then give them morsels of acceptance to reinforce good behaviour.

The children of a narcissistic family are effectively being held hostage, unconsciously fighting for survival. Their situation *feels* like life and death. The child lives in an alternate reality, governed by the delusional, tyrannical, grandiose false self of their narcissistic parent. The child has no other option. Their fawn trauma response activates, and they cling to the narcissistic parent while denying the abuse taking place. This process of splitting and projecting as a result of fear is a milder form of Stockholm Syndrome, where the hostage bonds with their captor. Being caught in a terrifying situation with no power to escape or change it, the captive becomes overwhelmed by the death instinct. They split and identify with the captor as good, hoping to assuage their terror, reassuring themselves that the 'good' captor would not harm them.

The toxic nature of such a family becomes even more apparent when its dynamics are put under the microscope:

- **Worship:** Dependence is permanent in a narcissistic family. The shamelessness of the parent ensures that the only way to coexist with them is to submit to their will.
- **Personal power:** The narcissistic parent, by not being active in the child's actualisation and emotional development, communicates to the child that they are not capable of personal power. The narcissist continues to hold control in the family, and the children unwittingly continue to infantilise themselves to their parent.

- **Equality:** The children are left to fend for themselves and compete for the narcissistic parent's affection. The parent plays favourite while making little attempt to adapt to the children or encourage their strengths. This creates a dictatorial hierarchy focussed on the narcissistic parent.

- **Emotional openness:** Emotions are forbidden, instead being covered up with humour, pretend-happiness, ridicule and perfectionism. By not acknowledging feelings, the narcissistic parent does not have to be influenced by them. This frees them from being responsible for their child's emotional well-being. They dismiss the genuine expression of feelings as pointless and weak.

- **Communication:** Triangulation is the preferred method of communication in a narcissistic family. The narcissist typically compares the siblings to each other, using shame to dictate their behaviour by forcing them to try to 'measure up' to their sibling. Furthermore, to avoid being put in a compromising position, the narcissistic parent will express their feelings and displeasure indirectly, either through their spouse, through one of the children or by dropping hints. This covert way of communicating allows the narcissist to deliver their message while remaining unaccountable. If the narcissistic parent did permit direct communication, their agenda could be challenged, and their children emboldened. Due to this disconnect between the parental system and the children, resentment and concerns go underground, expressed only in secret between siblings or remaining unspoken.

- **Boundaries:** Boundaries are non-existent in a narcissistic family. The children are expected to comply at all times and are not consulted about their feelings or needs. Their mail is opened, and their diaries read. This enmeshed state allows the narcissist direct access to the children without having to navigate their boundaries. It is sold to the children by telling them that, in a happy family, "what's yours is mine, and what's mine is yours". Such a way of operating means the children experience overwhelming guilt and shame for wanting to act separately from their family. They learn to play along, even when it goes against their true desires. Worst of all, it crushes their self-esteem by reducing them to a cog in a machine without independent thoughts and feelings.

– **Accountability:** One thing is sure in a narcissistic family; the narcissist is never accountable for their actions or the family's problems. The blame always lies with the scapegoat, another of the children or an external source.

These dynamics are put in place by the narcissistic parent to ensure complete control of the family, and with that, total grip over their environment. Meanwhile, the parent remains practically untouched and uninfluenced. Although it is highly detrimental to the well-being of the rest of the family, the narcissist remains unwilling to loosen their hold for fear of losing control. Under no circumstance do they want to relive their repressed childhood experience of being powerless. Yet as long as they hold onto control, the emotional flow of their family unit remains stagnant. The family members repress their emotions, and their maturity is compromised. The principles of narcissism become internalised by the children, and each member develops a false self based on roles, power and manipulation.

A narcissistic mentality

The narcissistic family dynamic is unconscious, weaving into the hearts and minds of all members and shaping how they see the world. Without awareness, it is a pattern which can be passed down from generation to generation, mutating and adapting into different forms but remaining narcissistic and dysfunctional throughout.

Who develops strong narcissistic tendencies, and who remains within a healthy range depends on numerous factors which include birth order of the child, birth order of the parents, attachment style and personality type. It also depends on what role the parent played in *their* family of origin. For example, if the parent was a golden child, then their children will inherit a sense of entitlement. If the parent was a lost child, their children will usually inherit an introverted mindset and a general lack of self-esteem. If the parent was a scapegoat, then their children may be more prone to angry outbursts or having a victim mentality. There are, however, no absolutes. Narcissism trickles down a family tree over multiple generations in complex and unpredictable ways. Nonetheless, regardless of the role, every member of a narcissistic family takes on the dysfunction. That is, to live in a narcissistic family is to have a *narcissistic mentality*.

The narcissistic mentality, unconsciously absorbed, is the belief that relationships are defined by power hierarchies, and that you are either in charge, infantilised, or worst case; scapegoated or forgotten. Those are the only options: you are either high status or low status, strong or weak, useful or useless, worthy or worthless, either special or a nobody. There is no in-between; you are committed to the narcissistic family doctrine and agree to play your role, or you are out. And as long as you remain inside the narcissistic family, you must continuously fight to fend off the overwhelming sense of shame which is forced upon you. For some members, especially the scapegoats, it is only a matter of time before the pressure gets too much.

Stay and fight, or leave

The narcissistic family hijacks the child's need for a higher power. Rather than encouraging the child to resolve their split and fulfil their purpose, it infantilises and brainwashes them into reinforcing its grandiose image. It enslaves and exploits the child, keeping them in a state of perpetual infantilisation, doing everything it can to stop them from separating, finding their personal power and actualising. Because the narcissistic parent is shameless, the child can never reach a point of humanising them and consequently resolving the split. The narcissistic parent takes no blame, admits no fault, and allows their child no concession. If the child rebels, the narcissistic parent's rage comes out. They lash out at the child, blame them, ridicule them and shame them. These methods get results, especially when the child is young and has nobody else to intervene. As long as the narcissistic parent holds power and maintains their grandiose false self, the child has no external object of rage. They turn back on themselves and internalise their parent's anger and shame.

When the child becomes an adult, they are eventually faced with a choice; continue to submit or leave. Many children, especially those high in the hierarchy, remain close to their narcissistic family, unwilling to part with their deluded identity and source of narcissistic supply. Others, riddled by trauma, shame and crippling low self-esteem, having had their willpower sufficiently broken, are left psychologically crippled with no means to break away. They remain trapped in the dynamic for their entire lives. Some children, filled with an overwhelming sense of shame or anger, decide to leave and seek salvation elsewhere. Without consciousness of the root cause, however, they barely get far. Even in adulthood, they still cannot grasp the problem; they only feel a sense of unease brewing under the surface. The ability to become aware of and analyse one's beliefs happens later in life as the conscious mind develops, but this usually only happens for new experiences, not old ones. The conditioned role and narcissistic mentality remain deeply entrenched in the child's psyche.

For the anxiously and fearfully attached children who leave their family of origin, the split remains inside them in the form of an unidentifiable longing. Their anxious attachment style means they maintain the desperate hope of finding love from a higher power. They continue to unconsciously pursue the great parent in each person they meet, yearning for the acceptance and love which their narcissistic parent or older sibling did not give them. Due to their partially infantile nature, they easily surrender their personal power to people who they perceive as higher status. They judge each person they meet with a black and white criteria, quick to love and, in the case of fearful attachment, quick to dismiss. As they go through life, they continue to unwittingly seek out a resolution for their split in oppressive yet familiar relationships.

In their split state of mind which sees only all-good and all-bad, the child becomes much more susceptible to charm and manipulation. They drift through life while narcissists swarm, ready to play the perfect friend, lover or leader. The child's great parent archetype activates in response to charm, and they infantilise themselves to the narcissist. The more the child commits to the relationship, the easier it is for the narcissist to flip the script and assert their authority. Once the narcissist has fooled the child into projecting their great parent split, the narcissist can dominate and manipulate the child while relying on the split to keep the child trapped. The split carries immense power.

For the child who develops potent narcissism, they may outgrow and become disillusioned by their family system, which no longer serves their narcissistic needs or becomes too abusive. Their avoidant attachment style means they have abandoned the hope for intimacy. They may also leave, but rather than seek out love and acceptance, they go after power and control. The narcissistic child will search for prey, and seek out structures which allow them to reinforce their grandiose self.

In any case, the children who leave narcissistic families are doomed to repeat their family dynamic elsewhere. Their narcissistic parent has devoured their identity and merged it with the family collective. Without a separate sense of Self, the child does not know themselves as an individual, and will become vulnerable to being either influenced or devoured by other narcissists who promise them security or power. As the child enters adulthood and goes out into the world, they get a sense of déjà vu. They are ripe for recruitment into the narcissist regime.

The narcissist regime

History does not repeat itself, but it often rhymes

- Mark Twain

Members of a narcissistic family are victims of soul murder. Regardless of their role or place in the hierarchy, their actualisation was hijacked by a false self. In a narcissistic family, nobody wins. The concept of winners and losers goes out the window when you become aware of the exhausting struggle taking place, and the price each person pays to stay afloat. When nobody is permitted to actualise and express their True Self, everyone loses; the narcissist included.

A person raised in a narcissistic family often falls into systems which allow them to repeat their role. The eldest or golden children seek out relationships and social structures where they can be admired or in control, the lost children find positions where they can stay out of the limelight and avoid being put under pressure, and the enablers seek out relationships and places where they can reprise the role of helper.

Requirements for entry

Narcissistic realms exist in all facets of society. What makes such a space narcissistic depends on various factors. The key point to consider is what a structure *overtly* promises, and how it *covertly* functions. This hidden agenda is where we discover the narcissist regime.

A narcissist regime overtly promises security, belonging and growth, while covertly functioning as a source of narcissistic supply for the person or people in power. When you break it down, a narcissist regime is just like a narcissistic family; it is a group of people unwittingly trapped in a power grab while trying to outrun the dark cloud of shame. One person holds the influence, while everyone else is left to snap up the remaining positions of power.

Behind the scenes, the narcissist regime has a rotten core. It is a structure which nets aspiring narcissists, wounded or unwitting people, or people unconsciously looking to play out the same role they had in their family of origin. It offers security in the form of connection, purpose and structure while reducing a person to a source of narcissistic supply. The narcissist regime has no regard for the member's need to actualise. On the contrary, it counts on each person remaining precisely as they are. It never wants you to transcend or outgrow it.

A narcissist regime has most or all of the following traits:

- **Pseudo-transcendence:** The narcissist regime always *seems* like it is going places, or achieving or offering something. It promises power, love, adventure, unconditional positive regard, and more.

- **Isolation:** The narcissist inherently knows that the influence of anyone outside of their control threatens their fragile false self. Those not under the narcissist's spell can challenge them, shame them or undermine them. Worst of all, 'outsiders' can expose the narcissist's lack of superiority in front of those who *are* under the narcissist's spell, hence endangering narcissistic supply. To ensure the integrity of their false self, the narcissist will need to control all variables within their realm. The more the narcissist regime can isolate its members from outside influence, both physically and psychologically, the more reliant it can make them on it, and the harder it is to break free. This kind of tribalism runs on the idea that 'others' are inferior, stupid or reckless, and therefore cannot be trusted.

- **Lack of accountability:** The narcissist regime is always led by a narcissist, who shields themselves through triangulation, deflection and shamelessness, so as not to be impacted by their actions. If questioned about something, they either deny it, blame someone else, hand off responsibility, create a drama to distract from the core problem, or claim to have a magical solution.

- **Enabling:** The narcissist usually has one or more sycophants to validate them or communicate their message to members of the regime. This allows the narcissist to avoid menial tasks which they see as beneath them, as well as keep a buffer between themselves and others. Often the narcissist uses their enabler as a lightning rod for any blowback that their decisions create.

- **Propaganda:** The narcissist regime relentlessly pushes its doctrine, reinforcing the image of it being an amazing 'family' or a tight ship sailing proudly forward. The result is that members become indoctrinated into a pseudo-reality, feeling traitorous when questioning the status quo. The narcissist responds to any scepticism of their worldview with dismissal or rage.
- **Rigidity:** The structure can never be challenged, and thrives only on compliance. Grievances are sometimes heard but never addressed. Members often feel a sense of despair, wanting more say and influence but never getting anywhere. They may eventually learn that they are only valued for their loyalty. They fantasise about leaving but are unable to act due to having long given up their personal power.
- **Enmeshment:** There is a covert expectation for each member to serve the narcissist's needs and agenda. Boundaries are not respected, and members feel a suffocating pressure to conform and live up to expectations.

The above traits apply in various ways depending on the nature and size of the narcissist regime. Examples of the most common narcissistic structures are:

The narcissistic romantic relationship

The romantic relationship, when narcissistic, can be a unique form of the narcissist regime. Because it only consists of two people, the roles become obvious; the narcissist holds power, and their partner plays the role of golden child during the idealisation phase, and enabler and scapegoat during the devalue stage.

The fantasy in a romantic relationship is that of a 'Bonnie & Clyde' union. It is us against the world. The narcissistic romantic relationship promises the perfect, unconditional love. Shared goals, amazing adventures, a bright future, a happy family, even the potential to travel the world together.

The narcissist, at first, will charm their partner and shower them with attention, occupying their mind with a barrage of stimulation and excitement. The narcissist is attentive and attuned, withholding judgement and disapproval, creating the illusion of unconditional love. If the partner has not resolved their split, their repressed yearning for their neglectful parent awakens through the narcissist. The partner's defences break down, and limerence emerges. The narcissist takes on a divine form, and the partner comes to see the narcissist as the person who will save them from their misfortune.

From there, the relationship becomes rigid, enmeshed, and oppressive. The narcissist creates a smokescreen of drama and gaslighting, taking their partner on an endless roller coaster controlled by the narcissist's grandiose desires. The narcissist discredits the partner's family and friends in order to isolate them. The partner becomes trapped in a despairing orbit where they must fulfil the narcissist's needs, as the narcissist slowly wears down their self-esteem and sucks their life force dry.

The narcissistic friendship

When a narcissist befriends someone or is part of a wider friendship group, their grandiosity always dominates. The narcissist's group typically casts itself as the 'cool' ones, or as the 'outcasts' who refuse to conform to society. The narcissist is always chasing the next high, and always has a plan. They might lead their friend or friends on an endless series of pursuits in the form of an amazing event or 'hidden' party. They might cause trouble or damage public property to assert their status. Boredom is never tolerated. Alcohol or drugs are often involved in helping boost the grandiosity of the group and keep it from falling into 'normality.'

The narcissistic friendship group takes on the form of a narcissistic family, the difference being that it consists of peers rather than parents and children. A dominant group leader controls the group's movements, while the other members assume their roles. One member is usually the narcissist's protégé and enabler, emulating and supporting the narcissist while holding a position of importance in the group by association. The rest of the members who are not part of the inner circle tend to tag along and hover around the leader as lost children. The narcissistic group must also have a scapegoat who the narcissist can ridicule, while the rest join in. Shame trickles down the hierarchy and collects with the scapegoat.

The narcissist will talk a big game, keeping the group members hypnotised and engaged at all times. Shaming and ridicule are the tools of choice for keeping group members in line, the only people immune being the narcissist and their protégé — as long as the protégé behaves, of course. Outsiders are generally frowned upon and judged from a distance. This aims to keep the group isolated, so that the narcissist has uninterrupted supply and never feels threatened.

The narcissistic company

The narcissistic company is an elaborate, business-focussed version of a narcissistic family. It promises infinite potential for career growth, or sells the target a company vision for 'changing the world.' The CEO is a narcissist, the human resources person plays the enabling spouse, the department managers are the golden children, and the employees are responsible for the menial tasks. In each department, the manager handpicks certain employees based on their loyalty and tells them to manage their peers. These 'surrogates' are triangulated to create a buffer between the employees and the narcissistic department manager, allowing the manager to avoid accountability and to control their subordinates without being exposed to criticism. Some members are designated as divine children and encouraged to represent the company at public events as mascots.

The CEO sees the company and the employees as extensions of themselves. The lower in the hierarchy a person is, the more apparent it is that they are mere role players. Low-level employees in a narcissistic company are often lost children from narcissistic families who carry a sense of despair in their jobs, unconsciously knowing that they are only valued for their output. Not only are they the forgotten ones, they too have forgotten their potential.

The emptiness of working in a narcissistic company is offset by cultivating a company 'spirit,' similar to those in cults. This potent company mythology dominates the workplace and distracts from its dysfunction. Employees and surrogates, if their boundaries are weak, will be expected to work overtime hours, to offer their personal assets, and to comply without question. Their narcissistic manager will gradually push their boundaries, pressuring the employee further and further until they have a breakdown, or abruptly decide to leave from either too much stress, or when they grow disillusioned by it all.

Most people who work in a narcissistic company have no idea of its true nature until they decide to move on to another job. Their exit becomes a bitter experience, where they are either met with cold indifference or spiteful anger from their manager or CEO, who only saw them as a means to an end. The employee, who cared for the company and sacrificed themselves to it, leaves with a burning feeling of shame and anger.

The narcissistic movement

The narcissistic company offers financial stability and a job title. In doing so, it exploits its members in furthering the narcissistic goals of its leader, who only seeks money and status.

The company structure does have a drawback for the narcissist, however. Since the company inherently states that there is a boundary between work and personal life, this tends to overshadow the relationship between the narcissist and their targets, offering the target a layer of protection.

The narcissistic movement, which includes self-development and spiritual groups, has no such limitation. It has no need to pay its members. On the contrary, it allows the narcissistic leader to draw money from members by promising solutions for their woes, transcendence from their reality, and salvation from their pain.

Like the narcissistic family, the narcissistic movement lacks fixed boundaries, which ensures that members can more easily become enmeshed with the narcissist. Also, what makes the narcissistic movement especially potent is its focus on spirituality and growth. The movement targets people who are on a path toward self-discovery, offering them guidance and wisdom. It draws in those who are in a life transition, people whose identities have fallen apart due to relationship breakups or who are fleeing abusive families, making them perfect prey for a narcissistic 'spiritual' leader or guru.

The spiritual realm is personal and sacred. It is a place beyond the ego, beyond the realm of reason. In the absence of personal boundaries, a group must have a governing body to protect the rights of its members. Such a structure exists in a democratic society, and to some extent in a company. In a movement, there are no regulations besides the rule of law in that country. The group members surrender their identity and become vulnerable to the whims of the narcissistic leader.

The spiritual realm is also 'mysterious' and 'unexplainable.' The narcissistic leader plays this to their advantage, using the spiritual realm to explain away their behaviour. The narcissist goes beyond shamelessness, cultivating an image of benevolence and divinity. The members of a movement split into familiar projections and gradually surrender to the 'guru,' entrusting the narcissist to guide them, heal them or save them, depending on what the doctrine promises.

With the advent of social media, narcissistic 'gurus' have gained a powerful platform to grow their movement, offering get-rich-quick solutions to anyone willing to join. This comes in the form of already available, common-sense knowledge which they rebrand as 'one-of-a-kind.' Such schemes only act to syphon money from people by preying on their desires and weaknesses.

Coming to terms with a narcissistic world

A bad system will beat a good person every time.

- W. Edwards Deming

The leader of a narcissist regime seizes control of a target's mind and merges it into a system which serves their grandiosity. Regardless of whether it is a relationship, a family, a group of friends, a company or a movement, the idea is the same — the members' individuality is systematically erased while their vitality and resources are devoured as narcissistic supply. The members of a narcissist regime are cogs in a machine which pushes power up the hierarchy for the narcissist to claim, and pushes down shame for the lower-ranked members to collect.

A narcissist regime is a place where souls wither. It preys on the vulnerable, capitalising on the unresolved splits and weak boundaries of its members. It is a never-ending nightmare which keeps repeating in different forms; until you become aware and make a conscious effort to break free.

The first question we should be asking is: *How did I get mixed up in all this?*

Can you identify with the narcissistic family? Are you a highly-sensitive person who was caught off guard by a narcissistic friend, boss, lover or guru? Was there something about you which lured you into the narcissist's dystopian web? It takes great courage to explore such a confronting question. Nonetheless, it is a crucial step in exposing the source of narcissistic abuse and paving a path toward lasting freedom.

The same cloth

In a typical hero story, the antagonist often claims to be 'just like' the hero. The Joker, just like Batman, disguises his face and functions outside the bounds of the law. Luke Skywalker and Dark Vader both channel 'The Force.' The hero then argues that they stand opposite to the villain in their morality. The Joker worships crime and chaos, Batman stands for justice and order. Luke Skywalker is a rebel who channels the light side of The Force, whereas Darth Vader is part of The Empire, and believes strength comes from the dark side of The Force.

This hero story trope is not there by coincidence. Just like the villain 'happens' to appear in the hero's path, so too did the narcissist come into your life for a reason. The purpose of this trope is to direct the hero's attention to their *shadow*. Batman acts outside of the law, while his supposed goodness stems from his trauma as an orphan. He feels justified in fighting criminality on his terms, since it was a criminal who killed his parents without being brought to justice. Luke Skywalker champions the light side of The Force, all while struggling with his temptation to use the dark side to achieve his goals.

These storylines translate to reality in fascinating ways. The narcissist, like Batman, feels justified in inflicting pain on their target because they themselves were abused and betrayed. Anyone can relate to feeling resentment when they play fair while others get ahead by acting selfishly and manipulatively. The lure of the dark side is always there, no matter who you are. Narcissists chose to go over to the darkness. It is not uncommon for those who get crossed up with narcissists to be lured over as well, as the narcissist leaves them bitter and angry after their ordeal.

In defiance, we point a finger at the 'villain' and declare that we are nothing like the narcissist. The narcissist is selfish, manipulative and *evil*. We, on the other hand, are selfless, honest and good. How could it be that we were cut from the same cloth?

And yet here we are — on the tail end of a relationship with the narcissist.

If you look closely at any person partaking in a narcissistic relationship, what you always find is *trauma* and *fantasy*. You have people in pain using pseudo-reality to cope; two sides of a coin composed of the same material. Narcissists chose their poison, and we chose ours. This is the pill which hurts yet heals the most.

A hero can never transform meaningfully until they have tussled with their shadow. This is arguably the most difficult aspect of our hero's journey. To find the light, we must first explore the darkness within us which led us to the narcissist. Uncomfortable as it may be, we need to ask: Could the narcissist have dangled something we wanted, or were lacking? Or does the truth go even deeper?

Shutting down the show

The protector personalities exist for a reason. If someone wishes to enter into a long-term relationship and have children, they need to seduce a potential partner and gain their attention via the histrionic. The narcissist, when channelled in its healthy form, allows us to feel worthy of being seen and getting what we want. When push comes to shove, especially during crisis, we need to do away with our emotions and act, no matter the cost. That is, we need to be psychopathically driven. Sometimes intimacy leads to manipulation and pain, and we need to be avoidant, contemptuous even — above all with a narcissist. Sometimes we need to depend on others and lean in more to create intimacy.

Only when exposed to C-PTSD do our protector personalities become dysfunctional. The histrionic, having been exposed to childhood humiliation and rejection, will walk around with an agonising sense of being undesirable. This core wound might then overtake them, and cause them to try to recklessly seduce their best friend's husband, just to feel wanted for a moment. The anxiously-attached person or borderline will cling to a partner to the point of suffocating them and being abandoned.

The narcissist will alienate everyone in their life and end up bitter and alone, just to hold onto their grandiose sense of self. No sane person chooses such a fate. The suffering driving these behaviours must be monumental. Trauma is the emotional and psychological form of drowning in rough seas. There comes a point when reason checks out, and we act out in erratic, dissociated, even destructive ways. This is why no-contact and hard boundaries are recommended for toxic relationships. The person 'drowning' is not themselves, and will desperately pull us under if we do not remove ourselves from the situation.

The narcissist suffers from the same predicament. They can be open, romantic, almost clingy, living through their borderline self. Then they could switch and grow jealous as the paranoid activates. They could be distant and avoidant, stonewalling you for hours or days. They could then grow judgmental and controlling, enforcing their tyrannical order on you via their perfectionist. In their malignant form, the narcissist can strike from the shadows, wounding you in the most unexpected ways via their psychopath. If you pay close attention, you can spot the shifting states in their energy, their words, what they focus on, how they open to and close from you. It is all there. Covering it up was a dissociated dream state — a fantasy world. And we were duped into believing it was real.

Fantasy allows us to compensate for perceived lack. A healthy person aspires toward their dreams, yet manifests them in reality, taking one tangible step after another. They accept failure, deal with the pain and disappointment along the way, and are willing to alter their approach as reality changes. C-PTSD corrupts this entire process. Trauma makes accessing our emotions and gut instinct impossible. For some of us, it gets to a point where fantasy takes over our lives. We lose our grip on reality and on who we truly are, choosing limerence over healthy love, make-believe over true connection and reality.

At first, we saw the narcissist as magnanimous, loving and nurturing. They were *perfect*. Yet it was their false self the whole time. The truth shone through the cracks, yet we remained willingly ignorant. Why? Were we channelling our grandiosity vicariously through the narcissist? Maybe their desirability made us desirable. Their perfect exterior made them appear majestic, powerful and in control. In the face of this, our wounded inner child leapt into their arms. Their grandiose vision of the perfect love inspired us. *Their overt behaviours resonated with our covert desires.* They offered us a path toward transcendence — and we took it, swept away by their beautiful, 'perfect' world.

Grieving the fantasy

The narcissist sold us a fantasy, and we lapped it up because somewhere deep down we wanted it. We *craved* it. The perfect, sexy partner, and by extension, the perfect, happy home. We especially pined for this reality if we were deprived of goodness in our lives. Coming from a dysfunctional home makes a person want a perfect, happy home as compensation. Having an emotionally-absent parent makes the idea of an attuned, loving partner seem irresistible. We forget that in reality, all people are wounded and imperfect, and forming and maintaining relationships is hard work. Each person has unique desires, beliefs and values which will clash with ours. All relationships have phases of tension and pain, followed by routine and boredom. It is not all rainbows. How quick we were to forget this while pulled away by the fantasy.

When the narcissist arrived, we saw the beginning of a perfect union, which we hoped would lead to a happy future. The narcissist sold us this because we too would tolerate only perfection. The narcissist sees themselves as perfect, and because they are so self-centred, sees their relationships as an extension of this perfection. They never accept that they are limited or flawed, so as reality eventually bites and imperfections in the relationship arise, they lash out. *You did this wrong. You did that wrong.* The target feels like they are always striving for a higher bar, which keeps rising as they become increasingly more exhausted. And yet we put up with this.

For the traumatised soul, fantasy is the ultimate medicine. By striving for the perfect relationship, we deny the pain of our past. Most importantly, we reject the potential flaws in our present. Normal people who show imperfection are unsettling to us, because their imperfections show that they could let us down or leave us. They connect us with our shame, and our shame has proven to be painful and irredeemable. What remains when the fantasy dies? Life can feel bleak when it is realistic and 'normal.' By denying this, we were harbouring hidden grandiosity. Normal would never fly for us.

Reality is pain. To accept this is to see that the world is not what we had hoped. Coming into reality reveals our trauma. Our pain. Our tragedy. It exposes our shortcomings and broken dreams, our hurt and our longing. Our broken past. What could have been, yet never eventuated. We needed an escape. Enter the narcissist.

The system made me

We are all products of systems. A good system brings various people under its fold and empowers them. A corrupted system, on the other hand, perpetuates abuse and wounding based on the original wound of the person or people in power. This creates further wounding, which spreads into different systems. Entering or being born into a narcissistic system causes untold damage.

Ask yourself: What systems were you a part of? What systems were the people who abused you a part of? What systems might their abusers have been exposed to? Were you involved in abusive relationships, with a narcissist or otherwise? Were you caught up in a narcissistic friendship group, where you were humiliated and bullied? Did you work in a narcissistic environment, or were you taken advantage of in a spiritual or self-development movement?

Go further back. Does your family carry an original wound? If so, could that have affected your Self-development? Where might your family's original wound have come from? How far can you trace the truth of what got you here?

Where you stand in all of this will reveal itself when you are ready. Maybe you are sure that you grew up in a narcissistic family, and need time to come to terms with this reality. You may have slipped into a narcissistic relationship or narcissist regime and are now only just beginning to count the cost. You might have been subjected to tragedy in your childhood home in the form of death or divorce. Maybe your parents did not have the capacity to love you as you needed. Emotional neglect can be deeply painful and damaging.

Through asking such questions, you realise it goes beyond you. You come to see that *it is not your fault*. You had no control. To overcome the tragedy of the narcissist regime, you must see its corruption for what it is, and you must see yourself for who you truly are. With this level of awareness, change is inevitable. Regardless of how and when you fell into a narcissist regime, your concern now should be transformation. By coming to terms with the past, you can focus on the future. The recovery process then enters a crucial phase: *You must undertake your hero's journey.* At this point, you are no longer powerless; you are grounded in reality. With awareness and a wider perspective, infinite options are open to you. It is time to embrace a new way of being.

PART III:
THE HERO'S JOURNEY

Crossing the threshold

Our grandfathers had to run, run, run. My generation's out of breath. We ain't running no more.

- Stokely Carmichael

Somewhere along the line, our need for a higher power was hijacked without our awareness. It happens to all of us. Celebrities, sports stars, influencers, politicians, even the 'cool kid' stole our attention in school. What they all have in common is the promise of taking us to a higher state, of lifting us toward the divine realm and allowing us to rub shoulders with the gods. This undeniable drive of ours is the narcissist's bread and butter. They recognise and exploit our deepest desires to gain narcissistic supply.

Power is not necessarily evil. The world is built on it. It is the tip of the spear which penetrates life. Attempting to shoot down those who rise above us is futile; more will shoot up to replace them. We all need to expand, to actualise and fulfil our potential. Higher powers are blueprints for this. Having influential leaders initiate us into the world is crucial. Rather than blindly fighting power, we instead need to question who we surrender our love to and what those people do with that love. Are we blindly repeating our childhood patterns of worship? Who or *what* exactly are we relating to in our relationships? Are we trading our love for scraps; for the promise of salvation? Do we sense that we lack something and unwittingly seek it in someone else?

Our rational mind is incapable of finding the answers. Beyond the mind, however, things are different. By embarking on a conscious dive through the Self, we witness reality 'behind the scenes,' and intuit the truth. Anyone who undertakes a spiritual journey inevitably learns that there is knowing, and there is *knowing*. One is based on facts and concepts, the other is a doorway into the heart of truth.

To know from this deeper place, we need to get out of our heads and drop into the body. We typically avoid this descent because it makes us painfully aware of our shadow. It forces us to feel the chaos and turbulence of our repressed emotions. The ego craves predictability and stability, and the Self is anything but predictable and stable. Yet the hero's journey begins only when we choose truth and evolution over illusion and comfort.

To help map this descent, the following diagram outlines how the five forces of the Self are experienced in the body:

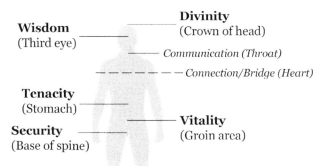

HEAVEN (Life Instinct)

Divinity
(Crown of head)

Wisdom
(Third eye)

Communication (Throat)

Connection/Bridge (Heart)

Tenacity
(Stomach)

Vitality
(Groin area)

Security
(Base of spine)

Grounding

EARTH (Death Instinct)

Figure 11: The five developmental forces of the Self in the body.

A deep breath into the belly helps illuminate our inner world. Life energy originates at the base of the spine in the form of fear, and changes in density and frequency as it lifts through the body. Vitality erupts from the groin, and tension builds in the stomach area. Bridging the five forces is the heart, which we need to keep open to ensure we can evolve. Binding this process are the life and death instincts, of which the life instinct circulates upward toward Heaven, while the death instinct moves downward toward Earth, being grounded through the spine, legs and feet.

In figure 11, you will notice the chest area is marked with *connection/bridge* and the throat is labelled *communication*. The throat is an outlet for life energy, while the heart is a conduit. When we are overwhelmed or hurt, we typically close our hearts and live in our head, blocking the flow of energy from below. This creates an ache in our chest, tightness in our shoulders and jaw, and a lump in our throat. We lose the ability to relate to and connect with others, and instead experience reality from the level of ego and fantasy, which can easily be hijacked and manipulated.

As we move deeper into the Self, we need to speak our truth. We also need to learn to open our hearts and welcome vulnerability. The saying that somebody 'has a big heart' relates precisely to this. The open-hearted do not close off and disengage when the going gets tough, they keep their chest open and their head held high, allowing the intensity and truth of the moment into consciousness. Energy then flows to their third eye and beyond the crown of the head, where they can react from a position of wisdom and power.

Returning to the analogy of the tree at the beginning of this book, we can imagine the Self to be an energetic cycle rooted low in the body while flowing upwards to the crown of the head. 'Grounding' yourself involves relaxing your jaw, shoulders, chest, stomach, pelvis and legs while directing your consciousness toward the base of the spine, down through the feet, and all the way into the core of the planet. When you sufficiently relax into this reality, the Self awakens and is ready to receive new experiences without the ego obstructing it. For many of us, this can be a jarring experience, and we quickly return to the safety of the mind.

As we will explore in the coming chapters, there can be no evolution without chaos. Upon looking deeper, we come to find that within the restlessness of the Self lies enormous intelligence. At some point during Self-development, you will achieve a certain level of enlightenment and begin to experience yourself and the world through an elevated state of mind, body and spirit. You begin to sense the latent possibilities within. As you come to *know* the power of the Self, you may look with curiosity upon those you worshipped in the past and ask:

Why not me?

That is, if they can channel the divine toward a higher state of being, then what is stopping you from doing the same? Could it merely have been self-defeating beliefs and conditioning holding you back? This becomes a seismic discovery, akin to striking oil.

Eight stages for Self-development

When someone believes they lack the ability to actualise, then splitting, worship and fantasy become their only options. By undertaking the process of Self-development, your natural resources will reveal themselves, and the impulse to forfeit your personal power to another person fades. When you finish reading the upcoming stages, you will know the path. After undergoing and experiencing the process, however, you will *know* where it leads. By crossing the threshold of consciousness, your world expands, ushering in a time of dramatic upheaval yet great opportunity.

The eight stages of Self-development are as follows:

1. **Awakening:** Explore how duality leaves you vulnerable to manipulation and put an end to it by embracing and loving your authenticity.
2. **Orphanhood:** Face and release your abandonment wound. Channel the strength of the Orphan archetype to carry you through the wilderness of reality.
3. **Metamorphosis:** Use the art of centering to mindfully carve through confusion and pave the way to your True Self, setting you up for transformation.
4. **Reclaiming security:** Ground yourself firmly within and learn to thrive in the face of uncertainty and fear.
5. **Reclaiming vitality:** Unleash spontaneity and evolution by merging with the flow of life and learning to truly see and connect with others.
6. **Reclaiming tenacity:** Welcome tension as an agent for growth, and use it to increase your assertiveness and capacity to set boundaries.
7. **Reclaiming divinity:** Learn to validate yourself from within while allowing the fullness of your energy to penetrate all facets of life.

8. **Reclaiming wisdom:** Tap into the vast intelligence inside you by embracing shame as an ally, using it for maturity, understanding and insight.

Which stages resonate and which you find challenging will depend on numerous factors, such as what role you previously played in the narcissist regime, your personality, your core wounds, and how far you have come in the recovery process. If you want to start with something practical, take a look at 'Stage Three: Metamorphosis.' If you struggle with low self-esteem, try 'Stage Eight: Reclaiming wisdom'. If anxiety is crippling you, 'Stage Four: Reclaiming security' will help. If you feel lonely and disconnected, 'Stage Two: Orphanhood' can give you perspective. Your intuition will tell you where to focus. If you are unsure, do the stages in numerical order and prioritise a particular stage once you get a feel for them all.

Transformation can be treacherous. While you work through the stages, it helps to understand the lay of the land. By knowing what to expect when you delve inside, you can label the uncomfortable emotions and sensations you encounter, which helps you avoid losing yourself in them. You will eventually come to see these remnants of narcissistic abuse as separate from you. They are layers of wounding which keep you from accessing the Self, and which need to be released through paradigm shifts, mindfulness and bodywork.

The layers of narcissistic abuse

The layers of narcissistic abuse are a combination of beliefs, thought patterns, behaviours and repressed emotions which constellate in the form of six recurring negative experiences.

Each is tied up with one or more of the developmental forces and tends to disrupt the natural flow of the Self. These six layers of narcissistic abuse and their accompanying traits are as follows:

1. **Conditioned role:** You have a sense of despair and hopelessness, along with the belief that nothing will ever change. The conditioned role also reveals itself as the crippling guilt you feel whenever you act independently of the people in your life.

2. **Complex trauma:** The traumatised person is plagued by paralysing emotional flashbacks and in some cases, panic attacks. They often dissociate into fantasy and experience crippling anxiety.

3. **Love hunger:** This manifests as a longing for affection from a 'special' person, as well as dropping all boundaries to be accepted by others.

4. **Pent-up rage:** This can manifest as passive-aggression, an inability to feel anger, or immense tension in the body, especially the jaw and shoulders.

5. **Abandonment wound:** The Orphan complex shows up as a deep, unfulfilled desire to belong. One also believes that they are 'strange' or different, and is plagued by chronic loneliness.

6. **Toxic shame:** Last but not least, toxic shame shows up in countless ways, including as an inferiority complex or low self-esteem, a crushing sense of heaviness, or the mind going blank when you find yourself in the spotlight.

These layers hold us back from Self-actualisation. Whenever we encounter them, we either act them out, dissociate and distract ourselves, or unconsciously attribute them to others. The way forward is to acknowledge them and begin the work of releasing. Like cleaning an Olympic-sized swimming pool one bucket at a time, transformation is a long and gradual process. With patience, persistence and grace, results will come. During this gruelling yet far-reaching process, each day provides a new opportunity to purify a bucket of repressed emotions and dysfunctional patterns.

During each of the eight stages, the layers of narcissistic abuse will be explored along with strategies for releasing — which needs to be handled with utmost care.

The pitfalls of transformation

Transformation is not a linear process. There will be good and bad days, as well as prolonged periods where you feel you have made no progress. Whenever you feel lost, it helps to remember the difference between *story* and *energy*. Repressed emotions feed the story, while the story reuses the emotional energy and keeps it from releasing.

You know you are engaging the story when you feel spikes of emotion in response to a particular thought. It requires a deft touch. You disengage from story by a) allowing the thought to pass by, and b) *witnessing* and *allowing* the underlying energy. Here you simply focus on and relax into your emotions and bodily sensations, even when they are overwhelming. Separating story and energy in this way is the foundation of the eight stages. You will often grow confused by waves of feelings and a barrage of thoughts. This is fine. Your challenge is merely to differentiate the energy from the story and to create space for the turmoil. There is nothing to 'do' during this time.

The five forces can overwhelm you. If you are unable to create a container around what you are experiencing, then pendulating in and out of that energy becomes crucial. This means establishing safe spaces where you can rest as you venture in and out of your overwhelming inner world. Examples can be your room or home, a therapist's office, a park, a cafe, or merely zoning out and watching a movie or reading a book. As soon as your emotional baseline has returned to a manageable level, you can resume the process.

Other times an emotional flashback may awaken, and before you know it, you have been taken over by one of the developmental forces. A classic example is a panic attack, where repressed trauma bubbles to the surface and floods you with inescapable terror. A toxic shame attack is another one, where a crushing feeling of inferiority can cripple your self-esteem for days, while you sink into a psychological swamp of darkness and heaviness. A rage attack is another, leaving you furious and unable to calm down. Another is the aforementioned limerence, where you fall in 'love' with an idealised person to the point of unhealthy obsession. It is during these episodes that we may question and criticise ourselves. There is only one response to such doubt, and that is direct confrontation. Here is where faith comes in. Transcendence is about alchemy, and alchemy is about allowing the natural process of the Self to play out. When faced with an energetic wave you cannot cope with, rather than seeking escape, try something new: *direct your focus into it*. Notice the thoughts that accompany it, but do not engage them with your mind. If you do lose yourself in them, do not beat yourself up. Be conscious and allow everything that is there, no matter how threatening it may feel. *Go deeper into the phenomenon and meet it head-on with the light of your awareness*. Have faith that your psyche will adapt and expand to cater for an excess of emotional energy. This approach to transformation will be explored in-depth in 'Stage Three: Metamorphosis.'

The initial period of transformation is the most confronting, especially if you have an abundance of repressed emotions to purge. Like flying through a storm, it can take time before you break out of the turbulence and into clear weather. Often a person approaches transformation in a somewhat balanced state, but upon activating their unconscious, is quickly met by a hornet's nest of crippling intensity and confusion. The human body is nonetheless adept at coping with states of being which it knows you are not prepared to handle. This is useful to remember, since a) you can rest assured knowing that you have a built-in protection mechanism, and b) you can maintain a 'live to fight another day' attitude. *Easy does it*. The longer you do this work, the more capable you become, and the more you can handle. What bewildered and overwhelmed you yesterday can become not only manageable today, but laughable. Such is the essence of alchemy. There is no need to put unnecessary pressure on yourself. Your only expectation should be to persevere, to be courageous, and to have faith while respecting your limits. The results will come when the time is right, and that time is different for everyone.

With that in mind, let us move on to Stage One.

Stage One: Awakening

Life isn't black and white. It's a million grey areas, don't you find?

- Ridley Scott

Picture the stare of a narcissist. This unflinching, all-seeing eye casts out a pulse of judgement that leaves you feeling naked and exposed. It is as though the narcissist sees something in you which nobody else does. The second they lock on, you sense yourself lured into their realm, compelled to act or speak without being sure why. There is just *something* about this stare which profoundly impacts you.

The piercing stare of a narcissist has three characteristics:

1. **Judgement:** It makes you feel small and defective, as though there were something you need to fix, compelling you to prove yourself worthy of the narcissist's presence.
2. **Tension:** It creates a cold, enclosed void and waits for you to fill it, putting you under pressure to reveal more vulnerable parts of yourself to 'please' the narcissist.

3. **Magnetism:** It weakens your resolve, making you feel you have no choice but to engage the narcissist.

There is something deeply unsettling about the all-seeing eye. It is forever directed outwards, scanning its 'territory,' determining if someone is a source of loyalty or threat, while using the resulting tension and magnetism to coerce that person into providing narcissistic supply. Under the watch of this all-seeing eye is where the devouring process takes place, wearing down the target and stripping away their identity, until all that remains is an unadulterated source of supply. The weapons used during narcissistic abuse take many forms, including shaming the target, ridiculing them, terrifying them, sowing doubt in their mind and bombarding them with charm or drawn-out monologues. But first the narcissist must lock their target in with their stare while gauging their target's weak points. Does the target look away? Do they squirm under the pressure? Do they blush, fidget or blabber nervously?

When a person with healthy shame makes eye contact, they take the edge off the tension by expressing warmth, looking away occasionally, as well as using head gestures to indicate that they acknowledge what you are offering. The narcissist's stare, on the other hand, is cold, static and unyielding. It offers nothing to its target except an eerie sense of being watched. The narcissist may smirk and say nice things to create the illusion of niceness, but their eyes reveal their true intention. Awareness of it is one thing, being able to confidently hold eye contact is something else. Your capacity to remain firm within the tension tells the narcissist that you have a spiritual boundary which they cannot cross. Above all, it informs them that your sense of Self is solid and that you see through their game, which is *duality*.

Exposing duality

As long as you avoid the malignant, all-seeing eye, you remain vulnerable to its effects. In Greek mythology, the hero Perseus used a shield to reflect Medusa's deathly stare and slay her. Your hero's journey also involves you having the courage to face the narcissist's menacing gaze and live to tell the tale. In your case, however, your shield will be *awareness*. This includes a consciousness so potent, you gain the ability to see through the all-seeing eye, deep into the recesses of the narcissist's being. The aim is to cultivate a character that is formidable, where the narcissist is the one forced to yield or look away. You do this by anchoring yourself within, allowing you to engage the world with abundant tenacity and self-esteem.

Your hero's journey begins in the land of duality, where narcissism thrives through a strategy of divide and conquer. Narcissists succeed here by creating an air of exclusivity, wherein they and their 'allies' are good and righteous, and everyone else is not. Meanwhile, control is enforced by the all-seeing eye, which has the potential to lift you to the heavens, or crush you beneath the weight of toxic shame.

When the all-seeing eye locks onto its target, the narcissist is determining how invested the target is on a particular axis of the connection/actualisation continuum. If the target is centred, then they are not over-invested in any way. Instead, they are comfortable with uncertainty and awake to reality, able to shift between love and hate as well as shame and pride. The centred person will be at ease with vulnerability while being confident in setting boundaries. They will expand and step into tension without getting lost in hubris, and can welcome the viewpoints of others without feeling threatened. Once the narcissist sees this, they will back away. The potential target is too aware, able to see through their game.

Then the narcissist lays eyes on another potential target, and their all-seeing eye lights up. The target leans in with their puppy eyes while fidgeting nervously, trying to make a positive impression on others. The target sets no boundaries. They want to prove themselves loveable by repressing all resistance and negativity, fearful of being seen as narrow-minded. Such a person is caught in the game of duality within the *connection* axis of the continuum. Their mindset is based on the scale of 'loveable' and 'unloveable,' and they invest tremendous energy trying to stay on the 'right' side. They are excellent fodder for the narcissist, and the strategy is simple: charm, hook and extract narcissistic supply.

On the *actualisation* axis of the continuum, the concept is the same, except the target is over-invested in pride. That is, their sole mission is to be seen as 'good enough.' They believe that gaining the favour of people they perceive as high status will elevate their worth and grant them access to what they desire. Such people are typically driven by hope, forever searching for the elusive realm of 'good enough.' The narcissist's strategy is again quite simple: act shamelessly to create the illusion of being higher status while shaming the target and attacking their pride. As a result, the target becomes trapped in an endless scramble to prove themselves and restore whatever ounce of self-esteem they felt they had.

We all fall victim to duality, regardless of whether it is connection or actualisation we seek, or both. The more invested we are in any direction, the more strongly we respond to charm, bravado, empty promises, ridicule and shaming. A centred person is proficient with all the emotional forces while never being over-invested. That is, they can let go because they know duality does not determine their worth.

Toxic people can only thrive when there is an over-investment in duality. Remaining on the 'good side' is an impossible challenge in a narcissistic relationship, since the playing field is constantly changing. If you are stuck in any of the developmental stages, then the narcissist will only need to find which one and push the appropriate button. The wind of change comes when you awaken to this. Shine the light of your awareness on the narcissist's exploitation of duality, dare to disengage and return to your centre, and the game collapses.

Moving beyond duality

Because enmeshment can make it hard to know when we are caught in someone's duality, time in solitude gives us a chance to re-centre ourselves and mindfully reflect on our interactions. However, we cannot grow in a vacuum. Our relationships mirror who we are while demonstrating where 'we' end and others begin. That is, boundaries are to relationships what a wall is to a house — without the former, the latter cannot exist.

The core challenge we face in relationships is knowing when we have given up our personal power. For many of us, it can happen so seamlessly and feel so familiar, that we believe we are still 'us,' even though we have become enmeshed with the other person. In many cases, the resulting power mismatch can keep us in a submissive, infantilised state, whether in a romantic relationship or otherwise. Without a 'power' police to watch over our relationships, it can be challenging to maintain a grounded sense of Self.

A way to connect authentically is to partake in an environment of sharing which goes beyond duality. This can involve joining an egalitarian group where everyone has an equal chance to participate. This can be a theatre group, poetry slam, dance class, survival group, spiritual circle or book club. It can even be a group of people who get together each week to share vulnerable stories and be heard. This kind of sharing community will support your growth if it a) can respect your boundaries while b) offering mirroring and support. When we see ourselves acknowledged in the eyes of people who have no agenda other than being in communion with us, we get a sense of how empowerment feels. If such a dynamic can be achieved without judgement and grandiose showboating, then duality collapses, and genuine connection is established. Nobody is 'bad,' and nobody is 'ideal.' Everyone is merely a human being with the courage to share their True Self with others.

Revisiting worship

You may need help when you first try to awaken to your authenticity and power. Another method besides the group-sharing approach is to consciously and purposefully lean into the split by re-creating the parent-child relationship via therapy.

A therapist can model the great parent by offering firm boundaries while helping you express yourself. Attempting this in an enmeshed romantic relationship or even with a friend is a recipe for disaster. It is best to engage somebody while clearly defining the terms of the relationship. By infantilising yourself, you make yourself completely vulnerable. It helps to have pre-established rules and boundaries which protect you.

The longing for the great parent does not disappear once you become aware of it. The split began with your parents and so must be resolved through creating and internalising experiences of the great parent. By consistently infantilising yourself to a therapist, you allow the great parent to be modelled to you as you internalise it. If the job is done well and your need to be seen as 'good enough' is sufficiently met, you will reach the end of the road; the furthest point of where your relationship with the therapist can take you. You will arrive at ambivalence.

The same goes for the other side of the split. Everyone carries rage toward a parent, no matter how good a job that person did. It is a consequence of being bound to a person of higher power who has flaws. This rage must be expressed as part of the grieving process. In therapy, the person of interest does not have to be present. The therapist usually asks the patient to designate an inanimate object to represent the person who the patient feels rage toward. This might sound odd, but by being allowed to project their loathing, the patient can channel the negative side of their split. If this is permitted without resistance or shaming, then the patient experiences a release and relaxes from their polarised state. They realise that nobody in their life is perfect or evil; each person has a capacity for good and wrong based on a complex set of circumstances. By being allowed to project their split completely without obstruction, the patient will learn to hold the good, the bad and the hard truth together. The split loses its intensity. The patient can then integrate the whole spectrum of their past experience into consciousness. They can also make rational sense of their relationship with their parents, as well as other people in their life who have harmed them.

The struggle to resolve the split occurs on three fronts:

1. A female therapist as the great mother.
2. A male therapist as the great father.
3. The True Self as the divine child.

Whether you work with a female or male therapist will depend on you. You may naturally gravitate toward someone of the opposite sex, but this does not have to be the case. Revisiting worship and infantilising oneself is a fragile process. It helps to begin with the gender you trust most, even if that trust is limited.

Keep in mind that your split will be most active at the beginning. Trust takes time. Even the slightest boundary set by the therapist can be perceived as rejection. People frequently leave therapy early because they wrongfully projected their split and convinced themselves the therapist was bad. The challenge is to figure out whether your paranoia is hijacking the process, or if you need to look further to find a better match. Ideally, you want a person who is 'good enough,' someone who can put you at ease and set firm boundaries while giving you space to express your genuine emotions — regardless of whether those feelings are hateful or loving.

Also, while it is common for a patient to project the tyrannical parent onto their therapist and then end the therapy, it is just as common to experience the great parent and idolise the therapist. Like any good 'parent,' the therapist should allow this projection without encouraging it. The point is to help you feel safe as you experience your inner world. When this has been successfully modelled, you will eventually learn to offer such parenting to yourself. The result of this process is ambivalence, and each person is unique in how quickly they reach that point. Some idolisation is expected initially, but it should pass over time. Like a good parent-child relationship, therapy is a long-term process which deepens through experience and vulnerability. There is no goal, and no 'sickness' to fix. It is about learning how to cultivate both love and hate in yourself and in relationships, as well as becoming skilled at managing your emotional space with maturity and humility.

Indeed, nobody is perfect, and working with a therapist is not reminiscent of a real-life, back-and-forth relationship. Yet neither is the child/parent bond. The idea of good parenting is for the guardian to model unconditional love and to adapt to the child's needs. A parent, like a therapist, ideally makes themselves needless for the benefit of someone else. Behind this selfless facade which demands nothing, however, the parent and the therapist have their own needs and wounds. In real life, relationships are about equal responsibility and accountability. There is nothing perfect about how we achieve connection. It is at times messy and stressful. Yet by modelling the great parent, by being as close to 'perfect' as possible, the therapist allows the patient to internalise what a calm, loving and accepting parent truly feels like. With that, the patient can apply this method of self-care to themselves.

When dialoguing with and learning about your True Self, neutral awareness will be the key. The therapist will need to model this to you by avoiding judgement or analysis as much as possible. Anger, frustration, sadness, despair, fear; it all needs space to come out. This is not the time for philosophising. In the same way someone can disturb the process by projecting their beliefs and judgements onto you, so you must train your mind to sufficiently detach.

Grounding in reality

All of us, deep down, want to be liked simply for being us. This desire to be loveable to everyone is a remnant of childhood which is amplified by trauma. Nobody likes to jump through hoops to be liked, or to admit that people might not like them — even on their best days.

Often what holds us back from forming real, vulnerable and flawed relationships is our shame anxiety. We fear being with someone flawed because such a person might leave or disappoint us. Shame is painful, either when we or the other person fall short, or when someone rejects us. We often warm to someone who is perfectly nice and unconditionally accepting. Unluckily for us, such people are usually as unreal as they seem.

A narcissist makes you feel loveable like nobody else. There seems to be something about you which lights them up. You and they are soulmates, or at least deeply compatible in an uncanny way. This, unfortunately, is a projection, and we often forget that it works both ways.

In childhood, the split is a standard way of seeing the world. Yet as our mind develops, we gain a more nuanced view of the world. People have positive and negative traits, and there is usually a reason behind it. Some of those traits work for us, others are a turn-off. Not everyone can like everyone at all times.

The hard reality is that people like each other for a reason. Maybe you're a good listener, have an interesting way of seeing the world, are intelligent, or you share common interests or values with the other person. Usually, an external structure binds two people together, such as school, work, common friends, a community or a sports team. Within this context, two people might slowly share positive experiences and develop a bond. In such a case, there is vulnerability, empathy, support and understanding. You have shared good times, bad times and mundane times. You have seen the best and worst of each other and nonetheless chose to remain in the relationship. It is by no means perfect, but it is *real*. You are grounded in reality.

A narcissist wants to avoid the hard-earned path. In the beginning, you feel like you have finally met the person who truly accepts you for who you are. The narcissist will project onto you their paradigm of 'all-good', and you do the same in return. You can do no wrong in their eyes. The narcissist will then help you channel this into a magical, shared world full of joy and potential. This world feels exclusive to you both, and you allow no one else inside. In this bubble, you can be as open as you like. Nobody is flawed or wrong in this world.

And that is why it is so hard to see it. This bubble is *the* red flag of a narcissistic relationship. When you are in a situation where anything goes, then the narcissist is free to influence and manipulate you. If it seems too good to be true, then it most certainly is. While you have on rose-coloured glasses, the narcissist will experiment with their grandiosity, checking the water temperature to see what you will tolerate. You will notice none of this during the initial phase. Because your relationship originated from such a wonderful, joyful state, you will be reluctant to resist. It is hard going from Utopia to having to tell someone: *No. I don't want this.* Negativity has no place in paradise, docs it? To return your relationship to its magical equilibrium, you will acquiesce. Before you know it, you are slowly being dragged into the narcissist's Dystopia, where they dominate and you submit. By now, you are already attached. You have invested so much into the relationship, even your pride and dignity, that you feel there is no way back.

This is why the Utopian bubble is so dangerous. It is not based on reality — it is a *trauma response.* The level of pain you carry only amplifies the illusion. Meanwhile, through the fog of the fantasy, you are vulnerable to every move in the narcissist's playbook. We all knew in our gut that these behaviours were wrong, yet we ignored them, too afraid to face the truth. We lacked the courage to challenge the fantasy. Like a warm blanket, snatching it off exposes you to the cold harshness of reality: *You are dealing with a toxic person.* Allowing this truth to set in is incredibly hard. It means coming face-to-face with gut-wrenching fear and confusion. Worst of all, it means facing the unholy heaviness and darkness of the death instinct. Anxiety, doubt, fear; we latch onto fantasy to avoid drowning it.

As a child, you learnt to believe that you could not handle such emotional storms alone, and of course, you were correct. You were not ready. The solution was to deepen your split and either surrender to your loved ones, or to cut yourself off entirely from the 'evil' people in your life. When you idealised your loved ones, you did so because you needed a safe container until your personal power sufficiently grew. As an adult, such a belief is outdated. You are now capable. You only need practice and experience as you integrate complex emotional states into your reality. When repressed trauma plagues you, fear is always at the forefront, and you may still believe that you must avoid it at all costs. When you have pledged to develop your True Self and transcend duality, you will need to challenge this thinking. The way out is *through* your repressed emotions, which your split projections distract you from.

Until we resolve our split, that is, until we embrace our True Self and others as they are, we will remain polarised, and our empathy will be reduced to a commodity for those who wish to manipulate us. However, once we can embrace the entire spectrum of emotion, we awaken from the fantasy. The process of grieving the great parent begins, and we move into Orphanhood.

Stage Two: Orphanhood

Loneliness is the absence of the other. Aloneness is the presence of oneself.

- Osho

In a narcissist regime, everyone is clinging to control. Each member holds onto their role for a sense of identity and belonging, no matter how rigid and oppressive it becomes. The underlying fear is that if the role is lost, so is the control — even when that control is based on an illusion.

Because the target's identity has fused with their role, losing it means losing oneself. A person in an abusive relationship struggles to leave partly for this reason. Without their identity to cling to, unconscious trauma surfaces, and they spiral into a dark, painful place. Hoping to maintain structure and order, the target deems *any* identity better than none.

Even if a person breaks away from a narcissistic relationship, their previous role has an uncanny way of reinstating itself in new relationships. This repeat of history happens partly unconsciously, and partly because familiarity brings comfort. The role is the path of least resistance, and anything unfamiliar is frightening. When considering shedding your role and embracing an authentic way of life, you will experience an impending sense of doom. You wonder what you will find on the other side, what will define you, and whether you can cope with the challenge and unpredictability of individuating. Looking ahead, it feels as though an unconquerable force stands between you and freedom. This wall of terror is not there by accident. The greatest fear for the target of narcissism is abandonment, which makes conformity and the repression of emotions a must for survival. Even if you conjure enough bravery to test the waters, you may not find answers, or you may meet with inner chaos and confusion, forcing you to return to the familiarity of a narcissistic relationship. However, after a lifetime of playing your role, turmoil is a normal reaction to walking away. The resulting emotions alert you that you have stripped yourself bare, and that it is time to face and release your trauma.

Reaching for a lifeline after stepping out alone will aggravate feelings of terror and helplessness, and force you to cling desperately to the familiar. When you do step out, it helps to understand that you need time alone with your True Self. You need to become acquainted with your shadow. This moment of uncertainty reveals to you who you are, in that the True Self is not a rigid construct like the ego, but rather an organism which evolves in surprising ways. Such a reality eludes the person caught in the narcissist regime. As long as they are attached, they limit themselves to a rigid role. The second they leap into the unknown, they can finally shed their old layers and undergo transformation. This subsequent journey into the wilderness is one which you and you alone must take. Fear will arise, but as already explained, fear is the ingredient behind all growth. It is how you know you are on the right track. This is crucial to remember as you take your first step.

Walking alone

The depressive position, where a child realises their parent is not omnipotent and all-knowing, is a jarring moment. Without the blanket of illusion, the child feels isolated and vulnerable. The experience is similar to when the child learns that one day they will die. What they may not understand in their despair is that now their life belongs to them, and that the clock is ticking.

When a person undertakes the path toward individuation, they find that there is a clear distinction between being alone, and being lonely. To be lonely is to crave a kind of connection and belonging that never comes, whereas being alone is to be centred within, free of outside influence and manipulation. Loneliness is crippling. Aloneness is empowering.

That is not to say that empowerment means always being alone. It is in our relationships where we feel nurtured, seen and encouraged. It is well-known that a lack of healthy social connection leads to mental illness and the degradation of one's soul. However, it is also in relationships where dysfunction and abuse occur. In such cases, it is not isolation which is detrimental to our health, but connection. Therefore, not only does isolation not work, nor does codependence and toxicity.

When our relationships grow harmful, we must have the option of separating from them to rediscover emotional balance within. Caught in the madness of crowds, it is only when we escape into solitude that we can return to ourselves. When you lose your sense of Self within your relationships, you become enmeshed and can no longer distinguish between yourself and the other. It is then time for solitude.

Yet much like shaving without a mirror, relationships reveal things about you which you could never see while alone. When you feel isolated and empty, it is time to re-engage your loved ones. This capacity to pendulate between enmeshment and solitude while maintaining a sense of Self throughout is what the narcissist regime aims to cripple. Therefore, the critical ingredient in achieving harmonious connection is to *first be comfortable being alone.* That is, if being alone without distraction terrifies you, then you have work to do. It is during this phase of your hero's journey where things get real, as you detour into the land of loneliness and despair.

The power of Orphanhood

The wounded child is either deeply enmeshed with others or utterly lonely when not. There is no reassuring middle ground for them. It is all or nothing, and in this case, nothing is excruciating. Many parents are not emotionally attuned to themselves, let alone their child. The ensuing lack of nurture is prone to leave the child feeling abandoned. The result is not the constellation of a cohesive Self, but rather of an *Orphan complex*, which keeps the child from venturing into the heart of aloneness and connecting with their True Self.

In mythology, Orphan stories describe an initially down-trodden yet gifted figure who is wounded by the loss of their parents. Feeling unwanted and unloved, they survive as best as they can in a harsh, uncaring world, where danger arises from all sides. Then, seemingly out of nowhere, the Orphan's fate takes a turn. Caught in a dire situation, the Orphan proves quick on their feet and able to find allies. They take the tremendous energy they had to conjure to survive their ordeal and channel it in creative ways. The story ends with the Orphan having transcended their abandonment and becoming their divine Self. They consequently enter a regenerative world which not only accepts them as they are, but encourages them to shine and grow.

To take the Orphan stories at face value would be to miss their underlying significance. The real world will not provide us with magical solutions, such as when Annie was adopted by a billionaire, Harry Potter was chosen to join a school for wizards, the Ugly Duckling became a beautiful swan, or when Cinderella was transformed by her fairy Godmother into a woman 'worthy' of a prince. What these stories allude to is that out of chaos and despair comes the opportunity for radical change. Out of death comes rebirth. Being isolated and left out, while deeply painful, gives the Orphan an outsider's perspective, and frees them from the confines of the social collective. Out of this seemingly nothing state comes a divine, spontaneous being who transforms the world around them. From an alchemical perspective, these stories are all accurate.

Furthermore, in every Orphan story, there is a tyrannical adult who tries to hinder the Orphan's growth. Annie dealt with the evil Miss Hannigan, Harry Potter fought against Voldemort, Cinderella had her stepmother and stepsisters, Peter Pan had Hook, and so on. These figures represent not only the narcissists in our life, but also the dysfunctional relationships which keep us embroiled in frustration and despair, and stop us from awakening our divine destiny. The Orphan stories show us that if we stay in these environments, we will get nowhere. We must find the courage to break out and face the darkness which awaits us. While magical forces may not save us, we will nonetheless open ourselves to being helped by conscious and caring people who wish to see us succeed. The universe has an uncanny way of providing what you desire — if you are brave enough to take the leap.

Another positive side-effect of Orphanhood is the ability to experiment and fool around without a judgemental eye watching over us. Much like children taking part in game-playing, we get a chance to learn about our divine capacity during these moments. As Simba and his friends Timon and Pumbaa put it in The Lion King: "Hakuna Matata; it means no worries." When we do 'find our happy thoughts' as Peter Pan did, or 'discover our magic slipper' as Cinderella did, much like the Ugly Duckling, we come to realise that our potential is great. We may not be swans, but we have all the resources needed to attain an equivalent state — if we allow ourselves to be torn apart and remade in the image of our divine Self.

Finally, we can look to the story of Jesus to put this archetype into perspective. Christ was born to a virgin mother, as though being birthed by God yet adopted by Mary and Joseph. This symbolises the spiritual separation between the child and their parent, or as Khalil Gibran puts it in his book 'The Prophet': "Your children are not your children. They are the sons and daughters of Life's longing for itself. They come through you, but not from you, and though they are with you, yet they belong not to you." Here we see how the Orphan's duty is not to their parent, but to life itself.

This urgency to break out only grows when a parent becomes possessed by the tyrant. It is the Orphan's duty, unfair as it may seem, to discover their divine essence and transcend their unfortunate situation. The human parent cannot help in this regard, and this becomes clear during the depressive position. Dysfunctional family origins or not, it is our duty to rise beyond the split and, metaphorically speaking, to slay the mother and father in our psyche. In doing so, our True Self can grow out of their ashes, and with that, we are finally able to connect with the great parent energy within ourselves. Only when this is complete can we begin our ascension.

The land of loneliness and despair

Needless to say, you do not have to lose a parent to encounter the Orphan. Feeling neglected and unseen by those you care about is enough. Furthermore, a parent does not have to be 'evil' to cause it. Many parents mean well but come up in harsh conditions, often undergoing economic hardship and conflict during their formative years. When stress is too high, a parent cannot 'be there' for their child as expected.

Yet regardless of whether the parent lashes out, emotionally closes off, or physically leaves, the Orphan wound is the same. During those moments, the child feels painfully abandoned, and the resulting feeling of loneliness cripples them. To cope with this pain, the child retreats mentally and emotionally from their parent and becomes lost in their Orphan wound, identifying with it as part of their core identity. It remains there as they grow into adulthood, as a reminder of the child they left behind, aching, howling from the depths of their soul.

The Orphan complex, when active, can have the following symptoms:

- A persistent, dull ache in the chest.
- A general feeling of sadness and despair.
- An assumption that you do not 'belong' anywhere.
- An inescapable belief that you are unlovable.
- An unbearable loneliness.
- A schizoid sense of viewing the world through a psychological window while not feeling able to 'go out there' and participate.

The Orphan complex may activate in the following situations:

- Someone you care about becomes emotionally distant.

- You find yourself alone in a foreign place.
- You get the silent treatment.
- After a breakup.
- You fail to get into the group 'flow' in a social setting, and feel like an outsider as a result.

When an abandonment wound came in the form of emotional neglect and abuse, each instance connected with the others and formed into a belief that 'I am unwanted, and therefore, I am unworthy of love.' This belief remains within us and activates after any perceived instance of neglect. Much like the chicken and egg, it can be hard to tell whether our emotional withdrawal *caused* others to retreat from us in response, or whether abandonment by others activated our Orphan complex first. The trigger itself is not necessarily important. Instead, it is crucial to notice that we have in fact been triggered, and be open to welcoming our abandonment wound and giving it space to express itself — without reacting.

When our Orphan complex activates, the ego assumes that we are isolated and want to connect and feel a sense of belonging. Therefore, it scrambles to make the pain disappear by looking for a 'family' or 'parent' to complete us. The only problem is that the ego is not attuned to the True Self, let alone the Orphan. As long as our attempts are ego-driven, we will lack the wisdom and vulnerability required to form a genuine connection. A self-fulfilling prophecy then ensues, where we feel alone and wounded, make a misguided attempt to connect with a potential 'other' or 'family,' and due to a lack of alignment with the Self, experience a breakdown in the bond. This

failure then stacks a new wound onto the existing
forcing our belief that we are unworthy of love and
belonging.

The descent

It is often when we are most desperate for connection that we fail to achieve the bonds we crave. Our neediness suffocates and pushes others away, leaving us feeling more isolated and unlovable than ever. Worse still, when our attempts do work, it is because we blindly walked into the trap of a narcissist, who upon witnessing our craving for connection, set their all-seeing eye on us and began the devouring process.

We leave such relationships having sworn off ever trying again, which as we know is futile, since a) we need connection for well-being and growth, and b) it will not solve our abandonment wound. Like Sisyphus dragging that rock up the hill only to see it fall to the bottom again, we need to try something different. It is time to slow down and pay attention to that haunting ache calling from within.

Using a combination of solitude and mindfulness, you can awaken and heal the Orphan as follows:

1. Remove distractions

Put your smartphone on aeroplane mode or leave it behind. Go to a location where you have no family or friends, where you can sever all emotional lifelines. Choose somewhere in nature, or a part of town you have never been. Go there with no agenda or goal in mind, other than disconnecting from normal life. Our smartphones and social media can create the illusion of constant connection, so even not having internet can activate the Orphan. It is one reason we hook up to WIFI immediately upon checking into a hotel.

2. Pay attention

When you have no source of external validation, the Orphan will send a signal from inside, urging you to re-engage. For now, just pay conscious attention to it and how it feels. It could be a sense of dread, a longing for someone, or an ache in your chest. It also manifests as a heavy feeling. If abandonment depression does not arise, *keep an eye out for anxiety* instead, which is a common way the psyche covers up the terrible pain of our abandonment wound.

3. Persist

The Orphan wound can seem to have no end. Nonetheless, one must be willing to move deeper into the discomfort. Create conscious space, welcome it, and invite the Orphan to come into the light. Do not identify with it, or let it convince you that you are unlovable, or that you can only feel ok if you are in familiar territory. Remain with the discomfort as long as possible, until one of several things happens:

– The pain may shift, and your senses light up. You become aware of the finer details of your environment, and your true state slowly reveals itself to you. If something uncanny does awaken, go deeper into it.

- A toxic shame attack may arise. You feel heavy and sad, and thoughts of inferiority circle in your mind because you are 'all alone.' Let this go on for a while, but try not to lose yourself in it. Toxic shame attacks are covered in detail in 'Stage Eight: Reclaiming wisdom.'
- The Orphan wound might not fade but rather continues unabated. In this case, just stay with the feeling until it gets too much. If at any time you become overwhelmed, stop the exercise and aim to try again another day.

4. Come back

Remain with whatever feelings emerge for as long as you can tolerate, then feel free to return to and re-engage your normal life. Pick up your smartphone, go somewhere familiar where you know people, or reach out to a loved one. Alternatively, go home and journal about the experience to help you better understand what came up.

Going back and forth between connection and Orphanhood will eventually give you a sense of what lies between isolation and enmeshment. Because you are actively awakening your unconscious, many uncanny changes will happen to you during this time. You might have dreams with varying themes, such as the ocean or deep water, venturing into a cave, claustrophobia, loneliness, or anything else centred around darkness and fear. There is no way to predict how this will play out, however, because each person's unconscious is unique. If you do experience nightmares or emotional flashbacks, know that this phase will pass with time.

The Orphan wound remains in place until you can shine the light of your awareness on it and welcome it into your conscious reality. The painful longing from inside is the Orphan calling for you to acknowledge it and reassure it that you are there, where 'you' is your Higher Self who is capable of 'seeing' it. When you feel ready, you can begin the journey toward this transcendental state by moving deeper into the heart of the Self.

Stage Three: Metamorphosis

Individuality is only possible if it unfolds from wholeness.

- David Bohm

A crucial step to leaving the narcissist regime's orbit for good is to establish your own point of gravity. This means being sensitive to when people pull you off centre by targeting your triggers, desires and emotions. In time, you will have an anchor point for when the temptations and emotional storms come. And they *will* come, as will the desire to surrender your centre to a source outside yourself, whether to a narcissist or other toxic person, group or movement.

By being centred, you will know yourself beyond duality. That is, you will not lose yourself in the vertigo of 'good enough' or 'not good enough,' 'loveable' or 'unlovable.' It is in this environment that a narcissist may approach you and lather on the charm. Because you will have grown accustomed to your internal centre, you will notice yourself drifting from calm to shame, from reality into fantasy. As a result, you will instinctively disengage from the narcissist's Dystopia and return to the safety of your centre. Even if you do get sucked in, you will have moments of clarity as you learn to re-centre yourself despite the narcissist's crazy-making manipulations. Leaving the situation then becomes much easier. In the wild storm of daily life, you will always have your anchor at hand.

A narcissist needs you engaged and off-centre at all times. They need you fluttering in the wind. A centred person can still share themselves, but they do so from an awakened, aligned place – not on the whims of others.

Finding gravity within

Before anything, we need to understand what a 'centre point' is. In his book 'The Sacred and The Profane,' Mircea Eliade explored the religious and spiritual practices of archaic and tribal people. One consistent theme he found in all cases was the establishment of a centre point, an *axis mundi* which represented the very centre of the world, without which the society would fall into chaos. By having a fixed pillar which connected Heaven and Earth, a people could integrate the sacred realm into their being, and therefore establish order in their world.

The axis mundi can be embodied in many ways, such as a tree, a mountain, a tower, a gathering place, a pillar, a town or city centre, an altar, and so forth. For example, the sacred centre of the Roman Empire was Rome. As long as it existed, the city energised the citizens and soldiers of the empire to fight and die in service of something greater than themselves. A place of worship is another example, where we feel ourselves filled with 'the spirit of God' when we cross the entrance into the building. Jerusalem and Mecca are classic examples of holy cities which hold enormous power as sacred religious centres.

This phenomenon also works on a personal level. That is, we can pursue transformation by directing our consciousness toward a *singular point of focus,* which consequently acts as our centre; our axis mundi. In doing so, we can a) remain anchored during intense emotional storms, and b) establish an opening in consciousness capable of conducting life energy, which lights the way toward our True Self.

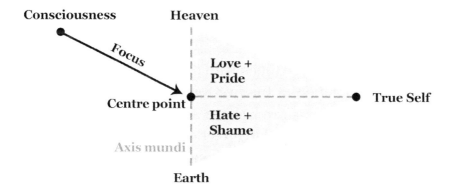

Figure 12: The art of centering. *By maintaining a point of focus, we can channel a path toward the True Self and directly experience our life energy. How we perceive ourselves is what converts this life energy into the five developmental forces.*

Naturally, a lack of focus leads to a loss of centre. Without a centre point, we lose our anchor and become susceptible to having our reality manipulated.

Losing your centre

Those who have never consciously centred themselves have no way of checking if they are uncentered. If you have ever experienced a flow state where everything seamlessly worked for you, then you were centred — even if you were unaware of it. That moment where the magic ended and the wheels fell off was either the end of the flow cycle, or someone or something knocked you off by impacting your emotional state.

If any of the five forces inundate us or we become over-identified with them, we lose touch with our inner centre. Earlier we saw how an emotion of the five forces, when consistently incited for long enough, can become a permanent state. The further we fall in a particular direction on the continuum, the easier it is to push our buttons and activate a torrent of repressed emotion which hijacks our reality.

Some examples of how we can be polarised and taken off-centre are:

1. **Fear:** 'What if' scenarios. Being threatened with abandonment or verbally or physically threatened or attacked.
2. **Love:** Being charmed, infantilised or starved of affection.
3. **Hate:** Being trolled, purposely irritated, badly treated, scapegoated or convinced to scapegoat another person or a minority.

4. **Pride:** Being fed propaganda, flattered or ridiculed.
5. **Shame:** Contemptuous stares. Being compared to others, put down, rejected, stonewalled or controlled.

The above and more can create a residual emotional hangover that can last for days, or in chronic cases, can remain a permanent fixture in one's psyche. Like a blocked drain, our consciousness becomes flooded with emotions, and a connection to our True Self is no longer possible. To clear out our inner space and restore our point of centre, we will need to observe our dominant emotions, create space for them, and then release them. In doing so, we can re-open the path toward the True Self.

The art of centering

The most potent way to explore the five forces directly is through meditation, which brings you into a state of awareness and alignment with your life energy. Yet without an 'axis mundi,' you will lose consciousness and become lost in a sea of thoughts and emotions. Your inner centre is your compass which leads you toward wholeness and mastery of the True Self. To begin with, however, we need to anchor ourselves on the *outside*, which in turn helps guide us toward our inner centre.

The centering meditation can be done as follows:

1. Setup

– Find a quiet room where you will not be distracted.

- Pick a spot on the floor and sit cross-legged with your back and neck upright. It helps to have a meditation pillow to sit on, since elevating your torso allows you to maintain good posture and makes the meditation less painful. If you have no meditation pillow, you can stack up some folded towels or clothes and even place a towel under your knees if the floor is hard. The important thing is to establish as much comfort as possible while maintaining a seated, upright position to help you remain alert.
- Set a timer. The ideal period is twenty minutes or more. At first, you may need to begin with a much shorter duration and work your way up.
- Rest your hands on each lap and let your shoulders hang back.
- You will keep your eyes open throughout the sitting. If you feel a need to close them, do so, but open them again when ready.

2. Establish a point of focus

Find a simple object or spot to focus on, such as a mandala, an item without printing on it, or a blemish or line on the floor. In this way, *wherever you focus becomes your centre.* As long as you remain focussed, life energy can redirect out of your thoughts and into consciousness. Lose focus, and the line of connection will be severed, wherein your mind will take over again.

3. Initial challenges

During the meditation, you will have difficulties. Sitting still and silent is a mode the ego does not like very much, and it will rebel. You need to prepare yourself for this. Exposing the mind to consciousness threatens its power over you. Here is a list of the most common obstacles and how to deal with them:

- **Incessant thoughts:** As you sit, the mind will keep ticking. This is perfectly fine. You may drift away and start thinking about the washing, or you could replay parts of the day like a movie, or you could even begin analysing the object on which you are focussing. The key is to catch yourself and gently bring your focus back into the present moment. A helpful way to ground yourself is to concentrate on your breath. Breathe ten slow, deep breaths, then return to a rested, natural state with regular breathing.

- **Pain and discomfort, including hot flushes:** During the meditation, repressed emotions will rise to the surface and manifest as pain, especially in your shoulders and back. Some gentle stretching after the sitting can help, but just know that it will subside in time. You may stop the meditation if the discomfort becomes too much, but the more you can tolerate, the more effective the sitting will be.

- **Doubts and impatience:** The mind will play its games. It will make you feel silly, and tell you that you could better spend your time planning your next holiday. It will think of countless other things you could be doing. It will tell you there is no point to what you are doing. This is all a ruse. The ego hates feeling exposed without something to dis-

tract it. When these doubts arise (and they will), simply acknowledge them and keep going.

- **Foggy vision:** Meditation changes your brain chemistry.
Foggy vision is a side effect of this, and will settle as you go
deeper and your focus improves over time.

4. Scattering and tension

When a thought or realisation triggers your emotions, the intensity can force the ego into creating a distraction. Also, the
more your True Self surfaces during the meditation, the more
fear you will likely experience. As energy increases, your
thoughts may speed up to create a smokescreen, or your focus
may scatter. The more the True Self reveals itself, the stronger
your concentration must be. You might also dissociate during
the meditation. The idea is to gently bring yourself back while
being simultaneously aware of your bodily sensations. It is a
balancing act, where too much focus brings too much ego,
which blocks the path to the True Self. Too little focus causes
you to become unconscious, which means the True Self will
overrun you.

Tension arising in the body is also common. Because trauma
is overwhelming, many people permanently tense the muscles
in their body from an early age to stop feeling emotions. The
longer you meditate, the more life energy will flow, and the
more pressure your body will be under to maintain this tension. Your shoulders, neck and jaw are usually the first points
of resistance you will notice, but in time you will also find that
your stomach, thighs, buttocks and even face hold tension.
During the meditation, simply continue allowing your breath-

ing and ask each body part to relax one at a time. Noticing the tension can sometimes be enough to cause it to dissipate. If that fails, then purposely tense the body part as hard as possible and then relax it again. This creates a contrast between pressure and ease, and will help you get a sense of how to let go.

5. Finding the doorway

When you stop *seeing* the object, it is time to gently restore your focus. Expect to drift in and out as often as once every few seconds. Even when your skills improve, you can probably only expect fifteen or so seconds of consistent focus at a time. This is normal.

If you succeed in concentrating on the centre point long enough, you may eventually feel intensity rising from the bottom of your spine, through your torso and up to your face and the top of your head. Stay with the pressure as long as possible. You are entering into being, and the Self is emerging.

On the other hand, if rather than intensity you only notice the presence of heavy emotions weighing you down and drawing your attention, then you have emotional residue and need to undergo releasing.

6. Releasing

For many people, the path to the Self is treacherous, swamped with unprocessed emotions and trauma. Even when a person has done the work and cleared their mind, body and spirit, a bad day can be enough to muddy the waters. When you are in the present moment, your repressed emotions will sense an opening and bubble to the surface. In this case, close your eyes and *shift your focus into the feeling instead.* Observe how it forms inside you. Ask your body to relax, and allow space for the energy to flow. Inhale and exhale using your body's natural rhythm. *See if you can establish a centre point in the middle of the feeling, as though you are staring directly into the eye of a storm.* However, be wary: this will also intensify the emotion. Courage is key.

Forms of unprocessed emotional energy which may need releasing are:

- **Toxic shame:** Anyone who has dealt with narcissistic abuse knows that shame is one of the most challenging emotions you can experience. Heaviness, an inability to think clearly, and a general sense of inferiority and hopelessness may be the first things you experience when doing this meditation. Instructions for releasing toxic shame are outlined in 'Stage Eight: Reclaiming Wisdom.'
- **Trauma:** When you open a gap in consciousness and energy flows, repressed trauma will dislodge and flood your body with fear. Withstand it for as long as you can before ending the meditation for the day. Trauma release should not be taken lightly. Easy does it. If too much fear arises, it can cripple you for the remainder of the day and numb your capacity to experience pleasure. Only process a manageable amount, then live to fight another day. One bucket at a time. Trauma is dealt with in 'Stage Four: Reclaiming security.'

- **Grief:** We can grieve the death of a loved one, emotional and physical abandonment, the loss of our childhood, or the end of a relationship. Often we do not go through this process in its entirety, and grief remains lodged inside, waiting to express itself. Grief is covered in detail in 'Stage Five: Reclaiming vitality.'

- **Sadness:** When we have been riding an emotional high for too long, sadness is the inevitable down cycle which most people avoid feeling. Permit yourself to be sad. Bask in it. Know that it is carving out room for joy to return. By accepting sadness and giving it space, you can allow it to pass, restoring you to wholeness much quicker than resisting otherwise would have.

- **Rage:** Repressed anger is extremely common when someone has gone through narcissistic abuse. Rage festers deep inside, remaining out of awareness. If you brush up against it during your meditation, be mindful, but stay calm. Often you may feel rage without any particular cause. This is repressed anger which requires space and time to express itself and be released. Simply allow it to be there by relaxing your body and breathing through it, tolerating as much as you can. Avoid mulling it over or overthinking. It will reduce in intensity over time if you allow it. Rage is covered in detail in 'Stage Six: Reclaiming tenacity.'

- **Grandiosity:** Pride is a swelling of life energy, where the body and spirit expand. As energy fills you during the meditation, you may experience a rush of power along with grandiose fantasies. Your ego may be trying to cover up underlying shame which it does not want to acknowledge. Observe this wave of grandiosity, but do not engage it. It may or may not be useful in achieving your goals, but in the context of this meditation, it only serves to keep you trapped in the realm of the ego, blocking the way to the True Self in the process.

- **Apathy:** Some days you may feel completely numb and indifferent, unable to feel anything in particular. Although it is deeply unpleasant, you should treat this state like any other. Simply focus on it and sit with it as long as possible, noting any changes that occur. Apathy passes like any other emotion.

Whatever emotional energy you encounter could merely be the tip of the iceberg. Everyone is different, and keeping the pool-cleaning analogy in mind, it helps to remember that each day represents a bucket of water cleansed. Releasing repressed emotions can take months or years, yet the benefits will show well before your work is complete. Like the weather, some days are clear while others will be cloudy or stormy. The only constant needed is your attention and focus. Amid an emotional storm, remember to maintain focus within the energy. Then ask your body: Can I let go of one percent of it? If the answer is no, sit with it a bit longer until you feel ready to ask the question again. If the answer is yes, ask: Can I let go of another one percent? *Watch out for overthinking*. The ego is trying to distract you by hijacking the emotion and creating a story about it. If you feel overwhelmed, either stop the meditation, or simply focus on your breathing. This is not an active process, but rather one of allowing, of gently guiding the body toward letting go and coming into being.

In time, the intensity of your repressed emotions will reduce. One day, regardless of how long it may take, the heaviness will pass, and you will notice raw energy rising to the surface, clearing the path toward the True Self.

7. Aligning the five developmental forces

When you have done sufficient releasing and can remain focussed for long periods, then the five forces will emerge.

This unfolding can be dealt with as follows:

- **Fear:** As raw energy flows, fear will be the first form it takes. This surge in intensity might cause a dorsal vagal shutdown, an effect similar to taking a sleeping pill. This is the body's freeze response to threat or over-arousal. Although you know there is no danger, the body reacts like this to regulate the fear energy until you are ready to handle more. As the heaviness falls over you, remain calm and stick with it as long as possible. It will become less potent with repeated meditation sessions until it goes away, as your capacity to allow more life energy to flow into consciousness increases.
- **Vitality:** If the intensity becomes a feeling of joy and hope, then vitality is flowing. Often it will create excitement in you, an urge to do something, such as getting to work on that project you have been holding off on. Enjoy the feeling, and only move into action if you truly want. It is up to you how long you remain in this state, or if you choose to end the meditation and act on your impulse. Just keep in mind that at this stage you are moving into a state of power, and it could be your fear of this which causes you to

stop. Resisting the temptation to act and continuing with the meditation brings its own rewards.

- **Tenacity:** Regardless of whether you are experiencing fear, bliss, rage or shame, the ability to maintain focus for longer than you thought possible is how you develop tenacity. Easy does it, but always move slightly beyond what seems like your limit. That leap of faith, that capacity to stick it out where others might have quit, is a key requirement of not only this meditation, but of Self-development in general. As energy flows and acts within your body, you are being forged by the fire of life. Tenacity is what allows it to do its work.

- **Divinity:** At some point, it will not be intensity that stops the meditation, but a sabotaging presence from within. Experiencing states of consciousness beyond the ego's 'norm' is deeply unsettling. A voice will whisper to you, telling you that you can spend your time doing more important things, or the urge to stop the meditation will come over you. Remain steady and tenacious, allowing the True Self to unfold, regardless of how strange you feel. Only stop when it truly gets too much. If you can push through, then divine energy will bubble to the surface. You become one with your environment, as though everything in the world is as it should be. You feel curious, satisfied and alive, with a deep sense of your potential.

- **Wisdom:** When all the previous forces are aligned, you may notice that revelations about your life and the world begin to emerge. This philosophical mindset is wisdom coming from the Self. You can simply observe these mysterious insights with your mind, voicing them in your head to give them conscious form, or you can roll off your meditation pillow and write them down if you feel that they are important enough.

Aligning the five forces makes you whole. You achieved this through absolute focus and harmony with the present moment. Your consciousness buckles at the seams, flooded with life energy, and for a fleeting moment that grim, ego-created, duality-based reality falls away. Sure, you cannot sit there forever like a Buddhist monk; you will need to return to a world dominated by ego. But for now, there is reprieve. Relief floods you. You have space to breathe — so long as you maintain focus.

Although this is a milestone worth celebrating, you are not yet done. There is one more step — one subtle shift in perspective which opens the door and reveals what you have been searching for.

The one awakens

When you focus on a specific point, your eyes capture the image via the reflection of light. Yet *who* precisely is observing this point?

Me, you might answer. *I am observing the point.*

Here we have reached a crucial moment. In claiming that you are the observer, you would not be wrong. What you may not appreciate, however, is what precisely *makes* you the observer. Like losing yourself in a movie or train of thought, the observer can quickly become immersed in what it is observing.

When this happens, there can be no consciousness, and the observer no longer belongs to you, but instead becomes a slave of the ego. When you lose yourself in your thoughts or your life situation, *you stop being yourself,* and become what you are observing. Here another form of the original question arises: who exactly is 'yourself?'

To unravel this mystery, you will need to shift your perspective. As you meditate and concentrate on a centre point, truly *seeing* it and noticing it with absolute focus, try turning that focus back toward 'the one who is observing'. In short, *observe the observer.* Notice the centre point, notice the separation between 'you' and the centre point, and finally, notice the one who is seeing the centre point.

Now ask yourself: *who* precisely is aware of this observer's existence?

By shining the light of your awareness on the observer, something uncanny lights up; a *Higher Self* which is capable of transcending mind, body and spirit. That is, the observer notices itself, and a new, higher observer emerges. This circular process can be repeated infinite times. The more you practice this, the brighter the Higher Self becomes. It is how you access your God-Self; a higher consciousness which opens you to the universal realm.

Losing awareness of the observer causes it to descend to the level of ego, a place where consciousness cannot survive. Maintaining awareness of the observer reignites the torch of the Higher Self. As a result, evolution can take place, because the True Self is seen by a presence which transcends the ego.

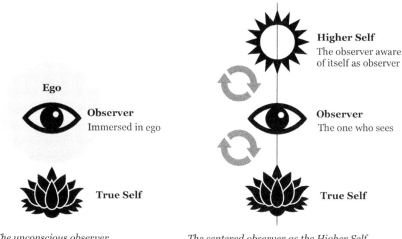

The unconscious observer   *The centered observer as the Higher Self*

Figure 13: Awakening the Self. Losing awareness of your observer causes it to descend to the level of ego, which incarcerates it within a psychological prison (left). By shining the light of your awareness on the observer, you awaken your Higher Self, and evolution becomes possible (right).

When the Higher Self awakens, the law of attraction opens to you, allowing you not only to witness reality from a transcendental point of view, but to imagine and bring about new realities without being limited by your ego. The entire spectrum of life energy opens up to you, of which duality is just a tiny slither which you can easily brush aside when needed. You transcend the ego and unite Heaven with Earth. You are finally whole.

Ascending the throne

We lost awareness of our Higher Self long ago because we believed ourselves to be what we were observing, and with that, became lost in our ego. This is what unconsciousness is. When we are in an ego-identified state, all a narcissist has to do is introduce duality into our life. By awakening our Higher Self, we finally break the spell. Our perspective widens far beyond our previous tunnel vision.

If trying to awaken this Higher Self only confuses and frustrates you, it may be that you are still immersed in ego and trying to 'figure it out' in your mind. This always fails. The observer is *beyond the mind*, and when you observe the observer, you are going beyond your perceived reality altogether. Take your time. Only a shift in perspective will reveal it, and only faith, patience and focus will get you there. When you become impatient and goal-oriented, you are back in the realm of the ego, and it is time to take a step back. Simply know that the Higher Self is there, and that you will *know* this state when you are ready. As you undergo more and more sittings, you will eventually brush up against it and, finally, welcome it into consciousness. You will arrive there when you experience absolute clarity and peace while gazing out at the world in a fully-awakened state. You feel light all over, the tension in your body slowly melts, and tingles shoot over your skin.

When the Higher Self awakens, you will notice that rather than having one Self, you have two: A Higher Self based in the realm of Heaven, and a True Self based in the realm of Earth. The Higher Self sees and accepts the True Self as it is, and self-love is born. Much like love versus hate, and pride versus shame, they are opposite halves of a unified Self. A person who lacks the True Self to ground them loses touch with their empathy and grows corrupt. Rather than accepting their True Self and 'seeing' it through their Higher Self, they instead seek to be seen from the outside, using others to get what they might otherwise be able to offer themselves. Sound familiar?

A narcissist never acknowledges their True Self, let alone yours. They never *see* you. The focus is always on their grandiose self, and so your observer loses itself in their world. The centering meditation helps you remember your true nature, and with it, who you are. It is a reminder that there is much more to you, and much more to reality than the oppressive, narrow version the narcissist programmed into you. The full spectrum which reveals itself must be experienced to be believed.

When the Higher Self awakens, you gain awareness over the entirety of your inner realm, including your previously 'unacceptable' shadow side. Your True Self finally feels *seen*. The presence of this 'other,' which is you but also beyond you, reassures and inspires you from beyond. With your Higher Self awakened, you can shine the light of awareness on the current state of your mind, body and spirit. Life makes more sense, and you gain the gift of insight and wisdom. You have assumed the throne, as all that you are comes into the light. The divine 'King' or 'Queen' has arrived, and you are now empowered to bring order and harmony to your 'realm.'

The divine presence of this Higher Self is the great parent that the Orphan has been seeking in an outside figure. The Orphan wanted to be seen, knowing it was the only way they could come into the light. Through the pangs of loneliness and despair emanating from inside you, the Orphan was calling your attention home. In childhood, it was the parent's role to not only love and care for their child, but to mirror their child's True Self. In doing so, the child would feel genuinely seen, and their Higher Self would awaken. The child who is seen from the beginning has no awareness of what happened, they merely sense the light of their divine nature shining, and they evolve and actualise from there. That reality is available to you now.

Awakening your Higher Self also weakens the grip of outside figures who try to imitate it, namely demagogues and narcissists. Just like the narcissist sees all, so does your Higher Self. By observing the observer and awakening it, you create a feedback loop which only grows brighter and goes deeper. In time, your Higher Self strengthens, and your True Self thrives as a result. So long as you remain centred through your Higher Self, your True Self becomes an impenetrable fortress. The five forces align when you are alert and relaxed in being, and they flow when you are in unity with your Higher Self. With a reassuring presence now watching over you, personal power comes within reach.

Finally, when you have sufficiently created enough distance between the observer and your inner state, you will notice a place open up beyond your emotions which is infinitely quiet and calm. This is your *inner* centre, which acts as a doorway into the True Self. The more you meditate on it, the more you will experience this place of peace, and the more effortlessly you will be able to return to it in any situation. In doing so, you will have the five developmental forces on tap, channelling them with ease as a mysterious hand guides you toward your actualisation.

Stage Four: Reclaiming security

Panic is a sudden desertion of us, and a going over to the enemy of our imagination.

- Christian Nestell Bovee

For many of us, security is an elusive unicorn prancing in the distance, daring us to catch it. We get the occasional glimpse of it. In the arms of a lover, for example, or as a sudden burst of self-confidence. Yet as we come within a whisker of it, reality rears its head, bringing with it existential angst and shattering the notion that we are anything but 'ok.'

We all know what security feels like; even the most traumatised person. It requires the mere simple act of 'checking out' and drifting into another state of mind. If one dissociates enough into fantasy, then anxiety, uncertainty and the spectre of death can all be left behind. Opioids and recreational drugs can also have this effect. So does hubris, with overinflated pride giving a person a feeling of invulnerability. Experiences like these are not security, per se, but a psychological form of sticking one's head in the sand. However, while they may not be the real thing, they do echo it. In understanding security, alternate states of consciousness can act like videos or photographs that point toward the genuine article.

What dissociation, fantasy and drug-induced states all share is a loss of *time* and *form*. Here the ego loosens its grip, and we enter a womb-like place. Where you have to be, when you have to be there, what responsibilities you have, or when tomorrow arrives become inconsequential. Yet unlike illusory states of consciousness, *true security* does not entail disengaging from reality. Instead, it transcends time and form through a connection with a power greater than itself. That is, true security does not rely on a lack of friction, but an acceptance of it, and a capacity to transcend it by awakening a Higher Self which sees and welcomes everything. Much like a child who is only reassured by the presence of a parent, a True Self which lacks a Higher Self is easily overwhelmed. Having welcomed your Higher Self during metamorphosis, you can cultivate true security by surrendering to this witness from above. The paradox of letting go as the only real form of security goes back thousands of years, calling upon us to accept that:

1. We are vulnerable, mortal beings who are nearing death with each day.
2. We can never halt the flow of life.

Upon entering into true security, we discover the following:

1. It is beyond the ego, experienced only in the present moment.
2. It welcomes all aspects of the True Self, including fear, pain and the entire spectrum of emotion.
3. It requires a state of perpetual surrender.
4. It is rooted in the Higher Self.

Dissociating through imagination or drugging ourselves does not change reality. On the other hand, if we learn to embody and awaken our Higher Self, we discover our capacity to adapt to life's challenges. With it comes mastery over reality, and slowly but surely, the feeling of precariousness transforms into one of competence and strength. As we encounter truth, rather than be crushed by it, we instead evolve to integrate more of it. In doing so, we can remain in harmony with the flow of life while in a state of personal power.

Mastering the flow

Because life energy never ceases, you cannot find security in isolation and stagnation — you need to keep moving. Like a riverbank, you are in harmony with the flow when you create a container for it. This is power in its purest form, governed not through hierarchy or tyranny, but under the benevolent eye of the Higher Self. The narcissist hijacks your Higher Self through duality, and thus gains authority over your life energy. Transcending narcissistic abuse is about reclaiming control of what belongs to you. This calls on you to break free of dissociation and fantasy, and to learn to work with the high-intensity energy states that life often demands of you.

True security is obtained by gradually moving toward active engagement with the world. For that, you must embrace the full spectrum of your emotions and be willing to face any situation — no matter how daunting or painful. Naturally, this requires you to be fully embodied. Practices and strategies for moving into the body will dominate the remainder of this chapter. But first, it is crucial to understand what keeps us from going inside to begin with. Toxic shame is one such barrier. The other, which often eludes our awareness, is complex trauma.

Perhaps the most crippling aspect of C-PTSD is the loss of Selfhood. A traumatised person is estranged from themselves, convinced that fear, shame and overwhelming emotion is the only reality they will ever know. They live an anxious life on the run, perpetually exhausted and never able to rest within themselves. Although labelled a disorder, C-PTSD should not be taken as any kind of illness. Rather, it should be seen for what it is: a hangover from a tumultuous period in one's life which needs to be processed and released.

Moving through trauma

Although freezing and body armouring played a crucial role in surviving trauma, now they only stand in the way of your development. It is time to unfreeze yourself so you can resume your actualisation.

Healing trauma can be summarised into the following three phases:

1. **Pendulating:** Consciously alternate between a 'safe' zone and the 'fear' zone. When trauma overwhelms you, take measures to soothe yourself. When you feel relatively calm again, continue the work.
2. **Releasing:** Use a combination of rhythm, breath and bodywork to release trapped energy in a safe, controlled manner.
3. **Evolving:** Channel your Higher Self to help increase your capacity to hold high energy states without dissociating.

To best understand complex trauma, we can look at it as inherited debt which carries over from generation to generation. While we might not be the cause of it, we are responsible for dealing with its consequences. If someone has a mountain of trauma, they may 'default' on their debt by dissociating from it and creating a false self. Narcissism is the perfect example of this, where the debt is passed on to the target. By employing a combination of pendulating, releasing and evolving, we aim to settle our debt and return to a 'zero balance.' This has the effect of a) restoring our natural flow of life energy, and b) allowing us to enter a state of calmness and presence.

A zero balance returns you to equilibrium, where you regain the capacity for self-reflection and rational thought. It eases the need to be doing something at all times, allowing you to 'be' without the need for escapism. It gives you a sense of well-being, so that perceived external threats no longer trigger you so easily. It allows you a good night's sleep and brings you back to the present moment, allowing you to 'see' and 'know' your life situation while making informed decisions. Rather than be controlled by fear, you learn to channel your energy toward personal growth. This ability is not magical; it is a birthright taken away by the unceasing anxiety of trauma.

Those who live under a narcissist regime lose this sense of okay-ness. They remain hyper-vigilant, which weakens their willpower and makes them susceptible to manipulation. It is true that children have a reason to be fearful due to their extreme vulnerability, and that any kind of abuse sets off their fight/flight response. As an adult, however, a person is no longer under direct threat. They can now develop defences and look after their well-being. The fight/flight response is no longer necessary. Abandonment does not equate to death, and one can deflect emotional abuse or remove themselves from a situation. The subconscious, however, has not yet realised this.

The journey toward healing C-PTSD begins with a simple truth: There is no danger. Although C-PTSD is a psychological wound which requires time and care to heal, the mantra of *I am not in danger* helps in tackling moments of irrational anxiety and panic. Paired with your Higher Self, it can act alongside the fear as a calming presence. From this mantra of safety, you have many methods at your disposal for healing C-PTSD, the first of which is pendulation.

Pendulating

Throughout the day, as you deal with difficult people and challenging situations, your trauma can be triggered in countless ways. It courses over your skin, causes your heart to start pounding, your focus to scatter, and makes it incredibly uncomfortable to be in your body. If it overwhelms your capacity to contain it, you dissociate and begin behaving erratically. If, however, your day is going well and you feel generally safe and in control, you grow calm enough to enter the flow, now able to think clearly and be yourself. The threshold between the two is the level of raw life energy which you are confident in managing.

Trauma can dislodge at any time, and we are often not present in our bodies when this happens. If we dissociate, the energy builds until the adrenaline exhausts us and our 'freeze' response takes over, making us drowsy and fatigued. That random slump in energy can often be a sign that we were checked out for too long, and our defence mechanism against fear took over in the meantime.

By becoming mindful of your body, including its emotions and sensations, you can witness the symptoms of C-PTSD in real time. Sometimes this will be within your threshold, and other times beyond it; especially during panic attacks. You *will* need to face it all eventually, although you will also need to be tactful. Trauma is serious business, and requires a careful touch. It takes many back-and-forth attempts over a long period. The foundational tool for pendulating is the centering meditation from 'Stage Three: Metamorphosis.'

In moments where you feel overwhelmed with anxiety or fear, go to a quiet place and try the following:

1. Invite your body to relax, especially your shoulders, stomach, thighs and buttocks. Direct your attention down your

body and into the Earth, visualising what it would be like to go underground into the molten centre of the planet. In imagining the core of the Earth, you instantly relax into *your* core. Take deep breaths, and surrender further into yourself, using the Earth visualisation to assist you.

2. Locate the intensity in your body.

3. Welcome the intensity.

4. Become aware of yourself as the observer of the intensity.

5. Now, observe the one who is observing, hence awakening your Higher Self.

6. Shift your focus between the intensity, your core, and the one who witnesses the intensity. Invite the energy to dissipate into your core, while expanding your Higher Self.

7. Continue to welcome the excess energy, staying with it as long as possible.

It is normal that, in the heat of the moment, the gravitational pull of fear will hinder your capacity to focus. If you do manage to persist, you will eventually notice a shift. Fear cannot kill you, even though it feels like it can. Faith leads to metamorphosis. Nonetheless, trauma is not to be trifled with. Easy does it. If you reach a point where you cannot tolerate any more, you should turn your focus back to the world and anchor yourself in an external source of safety until you feel ready to try again. This is the basic rhythm of pendulation.

Some ways in which you can anchor yourself in a feeling of safety are:

– Take a warm bath.

- Spend time with someone who makes you feel good.
- Watch a movie or TV series.
- Listen to some soothing music.
- Go for a walk.
- Do some exercise.

When you get comfortable with pendulation, you can use it as a base to move into bodywork, which takes trauma release to the next level.

Releasing and evolving

To create movement and flow, you need to take your efforts directly into the body so that trauma can be dislodged and processed. While this can sometimes be distressing, the payoff makes it all worthwhile.

The following exercises can be mixed and matched according to your taste:

Armouring release

Armouring causes the body to take on the form of a rock. The result is shoulder and back aches, a face that is too tight to express itself, a stiff neck, and stilted movement. Worst of all is the inability to experience the full spectrum of emotions or intensity of life energy. To feel secure, we need to be in harmony with the flow of life, for which we need to loosen up our bodies.

Ways to practice armouring release are:

- **Stretching:** Roll your shoulders around. Tilt your head slowly from side to side. Try to touch your toes. Twist your torso around, or lean it back. Squeeze your elbows together behind your back. Open your mouth wide like a lion. Squeeze your fingers and toes together. Squeeze your eyes shut. Press your fingers into random places that seem tense. Go on a journey around your body and consciously notice where you have tension, and gently expose it. Do this for a few minutes each day. It is as much a physical exercise as it is a dialogue between you and your body.
- **Squats:** No weights are necessary. Stand straight and pretend like you are going to sit down, lowering as far as you can but stopping when your thighs are parallel to the ground, before standing up again. Do as many repetitions as possible, and pay attention to the energy it sends from the lower to the upper body. For anyone who exercises regularly, this may be simple. For those who are heavily armoured, it can create dizziness and discomfort after only a few repetitions.
- **Yoga:** This is a great way to do bodywork in a group setting with the assistance of an instructor. Unlike solo exercises, the energy of a group can help you progress and better cope with the difficulties of bodywork. The added mindfulness practice is the cherry on top.
- **Reichian Therapy:** Originally developed by Wilhelm Reich but expanded upon by others, Reichian Therapy is an extensive program for armouring release which targets every muscle of the body, including the twenty-two or so facial muscles. The work requires a great deal of time and

dedication, but can have a profound impact. Some examples of Reichian exercises are raised-eyebrow forehead releases, eyeball rolling, jaw and tongue movements and pelvis rolls. A link to a free PDF by Jack Willis is in the resources section at the end of this book.

Testing your success in armouring release is simple: Can you stay in your body, remaining aware of the level of intensity inside you? Can you relax and breathe into it rather than tense up? If you notice that you 'disappeared' for a while, then it was too much. Remember your energy threshold and always move toward the point of scattering while remaining focussed. If you get overwhelmed, stop and try again the next day. Patience is crucial. Your level of trauma and health should be respected, but should not stop you from carefully working to awaken your body. The benefits of this practice are enormous.

Grounding in the feet

When it has nowhere to go, life energy flows upwards and becomes trapped in the head. It quickly overwhelms you and forces you to either zone out or become lost in compulsive thinking or talking. The cause of this is a loss of grounding, which can be restored over time. You can practice at home, while standing in a queue or waiting at the crossing — basically any time you are standing around.

The steps for grounding through the feet are:

313

1. Rock your body back and forth over the balls of your feet, paying particular attention to how the ground beneath you feels.

2. Begin by tensing your feet in a curling motion before releasing. Repeat this multiple times.

3. Move on to your calves, tensing and releasing them several times.

4. Now do the same to the back of your thighs, rocking on your feet again to remember the ground.

5. Finally, clench your buttocks, including the area between your legs, and release. Repeat multiple times. The term 'tuck tail and run' explains the need for this kind of releasing, since the tensing of the buttocks typically results when someone is afraid.

6. Take some deep breaths while bringing your attention into the lower half of your body. Continue down into the Earth, visualising yourself moving into its molten core. Again, this visualisation takes you into the core of your True Self by association, giving you a powerful grounding experience.

Doing this exercise daily creates space for energy to circulate rather than collecting in your head, allowing you to remain present and engaged in all conditions.

Sensory input

Music is the language of the subconscious. It bypasses our analytical mind and speaks directly to the heart of us. The endless combinations of rhythm resonate in the body and awaken life energy using frequency. For this reason, music becomes a potent tool for C-PTSD, since it converts tension into flow. For maximum effect, the music should not contain lyrics, as words can trigger the thinking mind. What kind of music works best depends on you.

Some examples of using music for C-PTSD therapy are:

- **Electronic music:** An hour-long DJ set can help regulate the mind by giving it a consistent yet slowly-changing pattern to follow. As the tempo of the music builds and falls, the listener goes on a ride through an inner dimension. When the right frequency develops, the fight/flight response reduces, and a sense of calm and flow takes over. You can find great DJ sets online on SoundCloud.
- **Classical music:** Classical music brings about a form of surrender. Like electronic music, it takes you to a new dimension and makes the mind calmer, more fluid and more receptive.
- **Healing music:** Binaural beats and Isochronic tones are gaining popularity as tools for healing. Binaural beats work by introducing two different frequencies of sound into the left and right ears. The contrast resonates with the brain and in turn, changes its frequency. The anxious mind is predominantly in a state of 'beta' brainwaves. Binaural beats allow you to introduce 'alpha' waves, which make the mind more relaxed and free-flowing. You can find a plethora of these on Youtube. Be sure to plug in your headphones.
- **Music therapy:** There is a whole field developing around the healing effects of music. A qualified music therapist can recommend creating, singing or moving to music as forms of healing C-PTSD. The benefits can be profound. When a

person feels blocked in talk therapy, they can play musical instruments in front of the music therapist to better resonate with their emotions before returning to talking.

Breath

When you observe babies peacefully sleeping, you see their stomach expanding and deflating effortlessly with each breath. Babies are not yet conditioned by the world, and as a result, they can harmonise with their body's natural breathing rhythm. As long as they are warm, well-fed and well-cared-for, they remain connected to their True Self. Only as we grow older do we adapt the state of our body to the fast-paced environment around us by altering and controlling our breathing.

Harmonious breathing means being open to all aspects of the emotional experience. When overwhelmed, we dampen our negative emotions by tightening our muscles and breathing shallow. Less air running through our body means less feeling. This coping mechanism is useful, yet dampens not only negative emotions but the full spectrum of life experience. To release C-PTSD and reclaim flow, we need to re-condition our body to hold more oxygen. Like watering a plant, effective breathing invigorates and energises the body while raising consciousness. Breathing is simple, but breathing effectively and with a natural rhythm is something you need to re-learn.

Four practices for effective breathing are:

– **Allowing the breath:** Here you are returning to the natural rhythm you see in a sleeping baby. Typically when we breathe in and out, we do it by tensing the throat, creating a rough sound. Allowing the breath is about creating space for air to enter your body, rather than trying to control its movement. Open your mouth slightly, relax your throat and allow your stomach to open via your ribs. As your upper stomach expands upwards, your diaphragm will open, and oxygen will enter. As you relax your ribs, air will push itself back out. Furthermore, at the end of the inhale, the exhale should follow instinctively. The body knows how to control this rhythm, so let it. There should be no assistance from anywhere else, especially not your chest or neck. The only movement is in your ribs. The rest of your body should be relaxed. Here you are no longer breathing, but *allowing the breath to happen.*

– **Box breathing:** This exercise is great for relaxing your nervous system and helping you feel at home in your body. Box breathing involves inhaling and exhaling through the nose at even intervals, all while holding your breath at the end of every exhale and inhale for the same interval. For example: *Inhale over a 4-second period, hold breath for 4 seconds, exhale over a 4-second period, hold breath for 4 seconds, and repeat.* Doing this for anywhere from 10-60 minutes can gradually ease off the fight/flight response. You can find guided box breathing meditations on Youtube.

– **Wim Hof Method:** Wim Hof, known as 'The Iceman' for his ability to withstand icy temperatures, is a Dutch extreme athlete who preaches cold exposure and advanced breathing to attain higher states of consciousness and healing. The basic idea behind his breathing method is to flood your body with oxygen with rapid in and out breathing,

breathing out fully at the end, then holding your breath and allowing the remaining oxygen in your blood to circulate for as long as possible. Wim Hof has a guided version of this breathing exercise on Youtube which you can follow. You can do this once or twice daily, especially when you first wake up.

— **Breath of fire:** This is one of the foundations of Kundalini Yoga, and is a great way to boost your energy. Breath of fire is a process of rapid in-and-out breathing with equal inhales and exhales. To calibrate, open your mouth and pant like a dog while focussing on your navel area. The chest should remain relatively still. Once you gain momentum, close your mouth and resume breathing through your nose. You want to aim for three breaths per second and continue for three to ten minutes in total. If you feel lightheaded, reduce your speed or stop until you can adapt. As you do the breath of fire, you should notice yourself becoming more awake, and your body becoming energised. Again, you can find guided versions of this exercise on Youtube.

Psychosomatic flu

Like a volcano erupting, you may occasionally feel flu-like symptoms without actually having the flu. This is trauma undergoing a spontaneous release. It happens especially when you are doing bodywork. The aches and anxiety are the result of 'lava,' i.e. trauma, flowing out. Remain calm during this process and avoid the temptation to distract yourself. Pendulating becomes crucial here, since an episode can last around twenty-four hours. Eventually, you will reach a new level of homeostasis and be ready to jump back into life with a slightly higher state of consciousness. Meanwhile, you can probably expect another spontaneous release of trauma to come in the future. All of these eruptions ultimately move you to a higher state of being.

Developing immunity

Threats are everywhere. If we internalised them all, we would go mad. Without knowing it, we ignore numerous risks each day. Driving a car comes with the chance of an accident. Living carries with it the threat of disease. Yet we humans are resilient. We cope. We reason potential danger away, and we learn to trust. More often than not, however, threats come to our doorstep. Not physical ones, but psychological — especially when dealing with narcissists. Fear is one of their greatest weapons. Fear *engages* us, arouses our fight/flight response, and forces us to react without first weighing up the facts.

Narcissists use many tactics to engage and emotionally trigger their targets. The extent of how much these tricks work depends on how on-edge a person already is. When the target focuses on healing their C-PTSD and calming the fight/flight response, the energy which often overwhelms them suddenly becomes manageable. Consequently, the narcissist's threats and manipulation tactics lose their punch. The fight/flight response causes many imaginary things to *feel* threatening. The mind in panic is susceptible to all kinds of manipulation. When trauma is released, imaginary threats fade into insignificance. A person approaching with a gun is a reason to act, manipulative threats and daunting situations are a matter of courage and good judgement.

Stay grounded

Trauma release must be done with care. The tightening of the ego and body is how we protected ourselves from being over-run by panic. Trauma, like a well-shaken bottle of soft drink, must be released slowly. Engaging the fight/flight response can be like playing with a hornet's nest. It helps to approach carefully yet bravely.

Working with C-PTSD is a fine art. The challenge is to be pa-tient in the face of countless stressors while allowing our core to ground us and our Higher Self to soothe us. Crowds, abra-sive and narcissistic people, even a triggering thought or a moment of intimacy can set us off. Like a car moving at high speed, healing C-PTSD involves taking the foot off the pedal and allowing yourself to slow down. The smallest trigger can force your anxiety to accelerate and take over. The process is delicate, and calls for you to become intimate with your body. It requires patience and grace. Beyond fear and panic is the river of life, flowing with empowerment and hope.

As you learn to embrace fear, be aware of how black-and-white thinking can cripple the whole process. Making a habit of remaining anchored inside allows you to cultivate strength and calmness in many situations. We usually cannot control threats. We can, however, control how present we remain and how much we allow threats to affect us. That vast, reassuring space inside you is a constant reminder that no matter how bad it gets, *you* are just fine, and you always will be. Do not let your mind - or another person — tell you otherwise.

Stage Five: Reclaiming vitality

Find a place inside where there's joy, and the joy will burn out the pain.

- Joseph Campbell

Those in a split state of mind pine for that special someone who can lift them out of despair and love them unconditionally. This 'divine' person will supposedly improve our life, soothe our fears and make us whole. This archetype is the ideal which inspires us toward a higher love. It instils in us hope, until we mature and realise that no one can be that perfect. Humans, magnificent as they are, cannot be Gods.

Although the divine being never disappears from our psyche, it intoxicates those who have not sufficiently resolved their split. As long as this ambiguous hunger controls us, the narcissist has a constant stream of narcissistic supply, able to dazzle us into lowering our boundaries. Moreover, love remains a 'thing' to be captured rather than being an agent for growth. Chasing after it in this way squanders our vitality in a Sisyphean pursuit of wanting but never quite getting. By withdrawing our energy from this pipe dream, we can a) channel it toward self-actualisation, and b) direct it into imperfect yet authentic relationships based on mutuality and growth.

Setting love free

When we love someone, the fear of losing that person can lead to us fantasising about them remaining in our lives forever. Here the ego is trying to 'freeze' our loved one in place as a form of security. That is why our heart aches when we long for someone — it is the pressure of trying to keep the feeling of love locked in place. Nowhere is this more evident than in childhood.

In their vulnerability and neediness, a child tightly grasps onto their parent. Love is their lifeline, dominating their reality and shielding them from the terror of the death instinct. We are all guilty of this, even in adulthood. The idea of a particular person as the ultimate solution for our shortcomings is compelling, yet ultimately this is not love, but limerence. It is a love based on lack, rather than abundance. Although we know it to be unrealistic, the fantasy is often too intoxicating to resist, especially for those with an anxious or fearful attachment style. Having rarely experienced love in a consistent, predictable manner, the anxiously attached learnt that they had to 'snap it up' on the rare occasion that it was made available. The fact that love was in scarce supply had nothing to do with them, but they did not know that. They found themselves in a painful cycle of intermittent reinforcement which fed their addiction. This began with the anxiety of not having a consistent connection, which led to neediness, which led to expectations beyond what reality could provide, which led to eventual disappointment, which ended in the cycle repeating as existential fear and another bout of aching for a source of love.

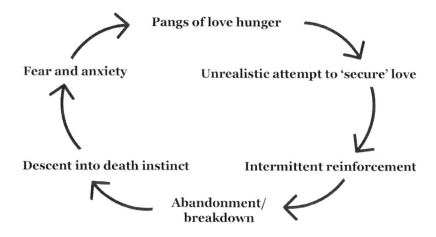

Figure 14: The cycle of grasping. *Inconsistent love creates a neediness that can never be fulfilled, and an existential terror that can never be faced. The hope that such an intermittent connection creates keeps this cycle in an endless loop.*

The cycle of grasping is the psychological equivalent of fighting to stay above water, sinking with exhaustion, then continuing the struggle for fear of drowning. This can occur many times over as we shift our divine being projection from person to person. Longing driven by fear keeps us stuck, and this false hope can be turned against us by manipulative people. Breaking this vicious cycle means letting go and having the courage to sink to the bottom. Far from 'drowning,' however, we move into a world of opportunity.

In a healthy relationship, a person learns to 'allow' love to act through them and accepts where this leads. Closeness and distance are two sides of the same coin, while conflicts and differences of opinion are welcome as part of the process. Beneath it all is a steady stream of shared love which each person bathes in like a river. The tide goes up and down, desire comes and goes and comes again, but the river remains. There is no need for grasping and controlling, since nobody is chasing an idealised picture in their mind. Each person is conscious and appreciative of the love flowing between them, and learns to work within the river's current. As the relationship matures, love becomes like the air one breathes, maintaining a natural up-and-down rhythm as it supports and nurtures the relationship. A platform for actualisation is established, and while the possibility of losing the other person remains, the relationship paradoxically *grows stronger* when it is not suffocated by rigid expectations. The unpredictable nature of relationships can be frustrating. However, if one learns to accept this, they can open themselves to higher states of love than clinging otherwise would. Love given space to roam becomes a force which enriches and transforms.

For many people, including the anxiously and fearfully attached, giving up the struggle is difficult, since it is a deeply-ingrained pattern. There is, however, a pathway out, which crosses through the valley of grief.

The grieving period

Fighting for the love and acceptance of others leads to nothing but dysfunctional and narcissistic relationships. Like trying to control the flow of a river, we only end up in a whirlpool of suffering and confusion. It is therefore time to embrace a new paradigm around love:

We need to let all relationships die.

This includes current as well as future relationships. Anyone we know or meet — we must accept that our time with them is coming to a close, and there is nothing we can do about it. The fact remains that people pass away, and people grow apart. Some evolve quicker than others, and some people are only supposed to join us for part of our journey. Most relationships die a necessary death, while a select few grow and deepen over the decades. We do not decide these outcomes. Love does. In its drive to evolve, it brings the people into our lives who we need, and not necessarily the ones we want.

The narcissist regime fights against this natural process by enforcing a rigid role. The narcissist floods the target's consciousness, charms them, shames them, terrifies them, confuses them, gaslights them, and guilts them into remaining in the relationship. The result is the entrapment of the target's natural vitality within a narcissistic framework. Shamed and starved of love, the target scurries to win the acceptance and affection of the narcissist, believing that relationships are about hierarchy and domination. The target then loses themselves in a paradigm of having to earn an elusive love, and eventually falls into the cycle of grasping.

Remembering that death is always followed by the birth of something new, we can withdraw all control from our relationships and see where the chips fall. Withdrawal in this sense means to relax into being, to awaken our Higher Self, and to engage others in a present but relaxed state. It means consciously *seeing* others without urgency or expectation. For the people in our lives used to us anxiously injecting all the vitality, this will have a dramatic effect. By giving up our grasping and instead moving into being, the space between us and others comes into focus. If love has been lacking from the other side, then we will find only emptiness, which can bring with it immense loneliness and despair. Most difficult of all can be letting go of the utopian dream for that special someone. The search itself was what distracted us from our abandonment wound. When our spirit has fallen silent, we sink down to the realm of the True Self. There is nobody to grasp onto in this state, nobody who will make it all better. The heartache which results from this can seem to have no end. It is usually at this point that we try to resume the cycle of grasping. This time, however, we will allow ourselves to 'sink to the bottom,' by finding the courage to remain with the resulting pain. There is no set time for how long this process will take. Grief passes when it is ready, and it eventually will. You may pendulate between periods of grief and clinging before finding an equilibrium. Regardless of how you handle this difficult time, the fact remains that the more you give in to it, the quicker you will emerge from it reborn.

Does this mean that we forsake and disown all the people in our lives? Naturally not. It does, however, mean forsaking our *relationship* with them *in its current state*. When we give up on the idea of having the 'right' love, our relationships gain the space to breathe and evolve. When we do this with a narcissist, they will sense our refusal to play along with their game and will double down on their strategy. Their narcissistic rage may suddenly arise, or they may withdraw and give you the silent treatment. Outside of narcissistic relationships, the right people will both remain and come into your life with ease. The 'wrong' people gain the freedom to move into relationships that better suit them, and narcissists will move on to find a new source of supply.

Letting go of all pretence is a return to ground zero, a stripping of all preconceptions we have around relationships. After the subsequent grieving period, a new state of being emerges, and vitality frees up for the development of the Self. Best of all, by focussing each day on love *as it is in the moment*, we may look back years later and be shocked at how much our relationships have grown. It was as though it happened by itself, and we only had to get out of the way. Joy, irritation, insecurity, surprise, familiarity and peace, these all come and go in waves before constellating into the bonds we have today. All of this and much more is ours if we are brave enough to allow it into our life.

Accompanying the post-grief resurgence may also be uncanny impulses to pursue things you gave up on long ago, namely your dreams and passions. There is nothing random about this shift; it is your true nature finally coming to the surface and filling the space where neediness and rigidity used to be. It is the activation of your ancestral DNA.

The descent into grief is the acceptance of the death instinct, which, due to the natural rhythm of life, is where the life instinct springs out, acting as a launching point for renewal and creativity. Without external validation and reassurance, anxiety arises. However, rather than clinging to love as the ultimate solution, you can now channel it toward your actualisation.

Fuelling vitality

Vitality undergoes a rhythm of constant ebb and flow, and remaining in touch with this tempo allows us to channel it most efficiently. When we are in a low-energy state, we can shine the awareness of our Higher Self on it and gladly move into apathy. No sooner have we done this does a burst of vitality erupt. It is equally important to shine the light of our awareness on this up-cycle. Here is where many people unwittingly stunt the process. When vitality arises, so does fear. To deal with this uncertain state, they either split and cling to an idealised person, or tense up and reject the energy, choosing to distract themselves instead.

We all fear the state of death. Many of us, however, also fear the state of life. That is, we are terrified of our own power. Reclaiming vitality is a process of not only increasing our tolerance for high-energy states, but actively pursuing them. This brings us into the land of chaos and creation.

Unleashing fire and chaos

One of the many positive side effects of trauma healing is the capacity to tolerate increased energy in the body. By reclaiming security and conquering fear, you unleash the power of the Anima. This feminine spirit exists in both men and women, manifesting as curiosity, wonder, adventurousness and passion. Yet unless we consciously cultivate it in our lives, the Anima falls dormant, and the saying 'if you don't use it, you lose it' becomes true.

Each of us carries the fire of the Anima inside. Although some people never truly become aware of its existence, most of us simply lose touch with it for a time. Our thoughts blind us to it, as the ego consumes our consciousness, and we lose ourselves in daily life. The result is a routine which has long moulded our flame into a predictable and monotonous show.

To know this truth is not enough. You must make a purposeful effort to come into contact with your inner flame *every single day*. When you wake up, you are usually already lost in your thoughts and the tasks ahead. Your life has become a predetermined stream with little space for evolution and growth. You may learn and experience new things, but you integrate little of it beyond superficial knowledge and behaviours.

Routine is the backbone of a productive life, yet it must be complemented by novelty and challenge. To shock yourself out of this monotonous spell, you need to do something which makes you acutely aware of your life energy. If your morning ritual is to have a coffee, check social media, brush your teeth, get ready and leave the house, you are still in your usual mindset. Your attention is on the activities which you have become conditioned to always do; it is not directed toward your evolution. To rouse the Anima, we need to speak her language, which is *chaos*, and we do this by putting ourselves in uncomfortable or unfamiliar situations.

Examples of Anima activation include:

— Talking to that interesting person standing near you.
— Visiting a city you have never been to before.
— Having a cold shower in the morning.
— Doing rock climbing or an extreme sport.
— Initiating touch with someone in a respectful way.
— Wearing a quirky piece of clothing.
— Making a random turn on your way somewhere and paying attention to your new surroundings.
— Doing ten squats, star jumps or push-ups at a random moment.
— Speaking or performing in public.
— Doing sprints or high-intensity interval training (HIIT).

The possibilities are endless, and the formula is simple. To light the fire of vitality, you need to a) do something different and spontaneous, or b) do something with a higher intensity than usual, or c) do something that is both novel and high intensity. That is, going for a run when you never exercise will do the trick. Going for a five-minute run every day at the same speed will eventually turn that vitality into routine. Doing things not part of your 'norm' creates cracks in the veneer that is your ego-self, and fear is what leaks through. If managed well, this energy converts into vitality and allows you to evolve and act on your feet.

The line between fear and vitality is never clearly defined. What terrifies us is often what excites us, and a feeling of dread is a given while standing on the precipice of greater things. Courage is your friend. Gradually introduce more chaos and novelty into your life, and watch as the Anima comes raging out in all her terrifying beauty, ready to carry you to a higher state of being.

Kundalini shake

Much like the prey animal's 'shaking-off instinct,' there is a simple exercise you can do at home which uses rhythmic vibration to awaken vitality.

Start with your feet shoulder-width apart, your knees slightly bent, and your arms hanging loosely at the side. Slowly release the tension from your legs and invite your body to shake from the knees. *Do not force the shaking*, but allow it to happen by directing your focus toward your knees. Relax your stomach, chest, back and shoulders, your arms, your face, and *allow the shaking to happen*. Within a minute or so, it should take on a life of its own. Now relax your pelvis. Invite energy to rise to your head from your feet and the base of your spine. If thoughts arise, gently push them aside and return your focus to the body. Continue this for as long as you feel is necessary, or set a timer if you prefer.

The Kundalini shake is similar to a snow globe effect. It creates movement which spreads life energy to every corner of the body, awakening your vitality and moving you that much closer to a state of flow. From there, you can either step into the day, or you can go deeper by moving into a form of dance or body movement exercise.

Voice and dance

In 'Stage Four: Reclaiming security,' the power of music and bodywork were introduced as tools to heal trauma. To go a step further, you can explore activities which express vitality via voice and body rhythm. You can take part in singing lessons, poetry slams, humming meditation, karaoke, or a choir. With body movement, you can take dancing lessons or participate in kundalini active meditation, or do classes at the gym.

Ecstatic dance is an especially powerful practice for vitality release. It involves 'abandoning yourself' to a drum-based rhythm or spiritual music, allowing the body and soul to guide you through the experience. Judgements, thoughts and shoes can be left at the door, and a safe container is created for you to experience your life energy in its purest and most joyful form. Ecstatic dance has existed since ancient times, where Greek women worshipping the god Dionysus were known for their 'ecstatic revelations and frenzied dancing.' It has been practiced in India, in the Middle East as 'Sufi swirling,' and in the Americas. The modern world is also experiencing a renaissance, with ecstatic dance classes being offered in most major cities.

Mindfully dancing and singing along to your favourite songs can also be done at home as a vitality-building exercise. The idea is to consciously and spontaneously channel energy through your voice and body in a rhythmic fashion. Countless frequencies of energy can awaken in this way, all of which break down the armouring in your body and throat that stops vitality from flowing.

Pay special attention to the movement of energy inside you *during* and *after* these activities. Activate your Higher Self and relax your muscles, allowing the excess vitality to flood your body. Let joy enter your daily life at random moments, and let it lead you into the flow. The NBA basketball star Stephen Curry is the quintessential example of joy channelled well. He dances and fools around with his teammates before a game to get him into the flow, and when he senses himself playing well, he rewards himself by shimmying and dancing after making a difficult shot. More joy brings him deeper into the flow, which has him firing on all cylinders as he dominates the court, seemingly five steps ahead of the rest. The success this brings him breeds more joy, which elevates him even further, hence feeding the cycle. This is what we should look for when channelling vitality.

What often gets in our way are sabotaging forces such as embarrassment, guilt, shame or the critical voice in our head. During childhood or in the schoolyard, being attacked for spontaneously expressing yourself conditioned you to make yourself small. You tensed your body and created a lump in your throat to repress these outlets for vitality. Being told repeatedly and angrily to 'keep it down' forces you to hold tension in your throat and speak softly. A person who speaks loudly challenges the power of others. If you have a soft voice, you may experience shame when raising it, which can feel uncomfortable. The alternative is to have a bottleneck for vitality in your throat. Find ways to express yourself fully through speech, and you will set your energy free. Speaking with a full voice raises your vibration and awakens flow. More vitality means more fear. Do it anyway. Make strong eye contact and be loud and clear when ordering your food or asking for what you want. Be thoughtful about what you want to say, but when you are ready to express yourself, do it without reservation. Above all, be conscious of how it makes you feel and create space for the awakened energy.

We should feel free to express ourselves through the rhythms of voice and body movement. As we adapt to higher states of energy and loosen the ego's grip, our self-esteem increases, and the barriers to the natural expression of our vitality collapse.

The art of seeing

When interacting with others, we might only see an abstraction of them. They seem like a cardboard cutout, and our focus is more on the conversation or our thoughts than on the human being before us. This is nothing more than verbal gymnastics. The back-and-forth flow does invigorate us, but something remains missing: *The Self has not been seen.* When you are sufficiently centred, approach somebody and activate your Higher Self, using it to notice the depth of their eyes. Relax the front of your body, ground yourself through your legs and feet, and allow their energy to enter you. Be conscious of their face. Be present and *let them know* that you see them. This will create some tension, but will also awaken an energised, mutual space. Your programs of interaction go on pause, and suddenly you are speaking to a real person. They come to life not only because you are paying attention, but because they know you see them. Vitality flows between both of you. It is a powerful practice for evolving your relationships.

You can also do the same when alone, drawing on the meditation practice from 'Stage Three: Metamorphosis.' Throughout the day, our observer can become lost in the happenings of our life, and vitality can fall flat in the process. When you have a spare minute to relax, allow your attention to drop into the core of the Earth. Then find a point of focus in your vicinity and take the time to truly see it. When ready, move that focus from the object to the one who is observing it. By reawakening your Higher Self, your True Self activates and feels seen again. Balance and wholeness return, and vitality flows.

Drugs and vitality

It is no secret that drugs have an enormous impact on energy. Alcohol, opioids and marijuana dampen vitality and dissolve fear, bringing us into harmony with the death instinct. Coffee and other stimulants increase vitality, bringing us into harmony with our life instinct. In significant doses, they can cause anxiety and panic. Many drugs can also change the state of our consciousness, sometimes permanently severing our connection to reality.

Experimenting with drugs can be risky business, especially for the uninitiated. Each 'high' is an exaggeration of either the death or the life instinct, or both at the same time. Drugs can be a great teacher, or they can lure you into a dangerous place. It is easy to get lost in a drug, and with that, to lose touch with your Higher Self. Once consciousness is gone, so is learning and growth. This is why one of the steps for Alcoholics Anonymous is to re-establish a higher power as an outside anchor point — it keeps a person grounded and aware of when they are slipping. Therefore, no matter what your drug of choice is, whether it is alcohol, coffee, sugar, sex, attention, or anything else, developing the Self should remain your top priority. You can enhance this process not necessarily by forgoing all drugs, but by actively practicing short periods of abstinence so that you can regain a 'sober' perspective. Anywhere from a few hours can be helpful.

When we are abstinent, we return to our body and re-experience the True Self. Because this brings us face-to-face with the death instinct, we panic and use drugs to 're-inject' ourselves with vitality, which moves us away from direct contact with the True Self and toward Heaven in the form of a high. On the other end, when trauma and intensity overwhelm us, we take something to numb the fear so we can feel grounded in Earth again. Drugs can enhance consciousness and make life more tolerable. In cases like ADHD, they can even be an indispensable tool. Yet we must never lose our natural rhythm. We must be willing to brush up against the death instinct so we may remember that we have our own source of vitality inside. With true vitality, we learn to gladly fall into the Self, trusting the cycles of death and rebirth to play out within us, knowing that life will lead us in the right direction if we allow it.

The evolution threshold

Fear can be intolerable, and surrendering our personal power to another person or to a dissociative activity is usually the path of least resistance. For example, we watch television because it gives us a sense of control while taking us through states of excitement, tension and adventure. It turns raw energy into vitality — without the risks and vulnerability that come with real life.

When we reclaim vitality, the stakes grow higher, as we open ourselves to a life of constant change and discomfort. It is not easy. Just like trust is a prerequisite for genuine connection, self-trust will be necessary to confidently experience personal growth. When we feel competent and powerful, fear morphs into vitality, and evolution can take place. When fear gets too much, we lose our nerve and seek a way out. A daunting feeling rises from the base of the spine and increases in intensity as it lifts upwards, while pressure builds in the chest and skull. Between these states of panic and competence, we find the place where actualisation happens; *the evolution threshold.*

To successfully navigate the evolution threshold, you need to maintain faith and self-trust, since you are aiming toward an unprecedented state of being. There are no certainties regarding the outcome. You can only open your heart and welcome whatever comes with every ounce of presence you can conjure. When you feel overwhelmed or cut off from your Self, focus on your chest area while relaxing and breathing into it. Allow space for life energy to flow from your lower body up to your Higher Self while your heart centre processes the intensity. Through opening this bridge, you create an environment for evolution.

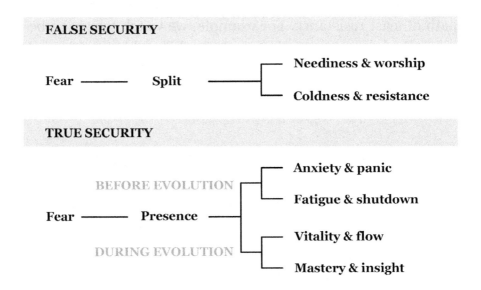

FALSE SECURITY

Fear ——— Split ┌── Neediness & worship
              └── Coldness & resistance

TRUE SECURITY

Fear ——— Presence
BEFORE EVOLUTION ┌── Anxiety & panic
                 └── Fatigue & shutdown
DURING EVOLUTION ┌── Vitality & flow
                 └── Mastery & insight

Figure 15: The importance of trust. Without consciousness, a person splits and projects their fear as neediness or emotional coldness. If, on the other hand, they can maintain presence, self-trust and an open heart, they put themselves on the path toward evolution and mastery.

In adulthood, our ego structures tend to be fixed, and the dream-like state from childhood has long been left behind.

However, this chaotic realm where our patterns were formed remains, and is where reprogramming takes place. With the courage to step into vitality, we learn to toe the line between the manifested and unmanifested worlds. The ego loathes the uncanny nature of the unconscious, but also relies on it to evolve into higher states of being. Coming out of our ego and into presence, we become acutely aware of how big a part fear plays in our life. The more we learn to dwell in the space between fear and flow, the more we evolve to contain the rising energy. This requires that we a) actively welcome and relax into fear, b) become curious about where it can take us, and c) trust that we can master it. Through this mindset, we can develop skills to manage higher states, which leads to more self-trust, which results in a stronger feeling of safety and empowerment, hence reinforcing the cycle.

Enter the vulnerable warrior

Khalil Gibran wrote in his book 'The Prophet': "The deeper that sorrow carves into your being, the more joy you can contain." Here he is alluding to the seasons of vitality, which during its summer can fill us with bliss and wonder, and in its winter can leave us in the pits of darkness and despair. To love and be open to the flow of life means that we welcome states of fullness and emptiness equally, and gladly accept the pangs of suffering which they inevitably bring. It is when we have been in Heaven too long that our True Self aches and pains for a return to the Earth, where our essence was born.

Vitality is a double-edged sword. On the one hand, being in the flow makes you more susceptible to manipulation, but it also allows you more freedom to steer the ship and make positive changes in your life. Being open to vitality without the strength to contain it or set boundaries, however, is a recipe for disaster. Like a river without a bank, all chaos must eventually be brought into a state of order, which is a task only a warrior can handle.

Stage Six: Reclaiming tenacity

It always seems impossible until it's done.

- Nelson Mandela

The tenacious are masters of surrender. Stress, chaos, despair; they handle it all. Otherwise, they surrender some more, until the pain and pressure forge them into a higher state of being. The tenacious know above all that they can expand their capacity to contain more.

The ingredients for tenacity are presence, faith and courage. A person needs to remain conscious through tense times while trusting their capacity to evolve through the challenge. Otherwise, they become easily overwhelmed by stressful situations, to which they might respond in the following ways:

1. **Dissociation:** The person will be 'not all there.' They have difficulty remaining focussed, are slow to respond to pressure, or overthink as a form of distraction from uncomfortable feelings.

2. **Ceding control:** The person looks to others for solutions or to take the lead. They cannot conceive of being the one to assume responsibility, since even the thought of it fills them with dread.

3. **Erratic behaviour:** Intensity lifts through the body and becomes trapped in the head, while the muscles tighten up. The person loses access to their intuition and grows reactive, and they begin babbling and acting abrasively. With their heart closed off, emotional intelligence is inaccessible. It is all mind.

The above are coping mechanisms we all use when overwhelmed. It takes determination to rise to a state of tenacity, and there is no way to prove yourself capable except through direct experience. In 'Stage Three: Metamorphosis,' you honed your ability to concentrate while remaining in a state of presence. In 'Stage Four: Reclaiming security' and 'Stage Five: Reclaiming vitality,' a foundation was established for dealing with high-energy states. Now these skills will be tied together for building tenacity, which we can practice in two ways:

1. **Fortification:** Overcome enmeshment by channelling healthy aggression toward establishing boundaries.

2. **Expansion:** Lean into tension as a way to grow the tenacity 'muscle.'

Fortify and expand. By alternating between the two, you establish a capacity for assertiveness as well as an outer wall against manipulation. You feel empowered and sure of who you are. Getting what you want suddenly seems possible, and those around you come to feel and appreciate your steadfastness. Narcissists will also be impacted, especially when they look into your eyes and see the soul of a warrior.

Fortification: Overcoming enmeshment

Enmeshment is an often overlooked element of narcissism, since the enmeshed are like fish in water; they have little awareness of what *not* being submerged is like. This is not a trick the narcissist plays, but a natural way of bonding which they exploit. Enmeshment is a state of intimacy; a psychological space where two or more people can share ideas, emotions and intimate desires. The concept of 'you' and 'I' fades, and those involved become a collective 'we.' Enmeshment brings a sense of belonging and mutual well-being. If used well, it can be a transformative state. For example, we can enter a shared space with somebody during a conversation. If the topic is something we value, we can drop our guard and allow the other person into our psychological space. In doing so, we internalise and integrate the other person's point of view, which in turn expands our perspective. It becomes a powerful and enriching experience.

On the other hand, enmeshment also opens you to potential manipulation and hurt. The narcissist requires enmeshment at all times to ensure consistent narcissistic supply. It is why they 'love bomb' and work to isolate their targets. They persist until the target forgets what it is like to have a separate sense of Self, and with that, loses their personal power.

In a healthy relationship, each person is allowed their boundaries, along with independent thought, feeling and action. Any attempt to influence the other person must come with their explicit consent. In a narcissist regime, nobody gets the luxury of psychological space; the narcissist must have unrestricted access. The narcissist regime must be a singular, enmeshed unit controlled by the narcissist. A person with boundaries can make their own decisions, which means that the grandiose needs of the narcissist could take a back seat. A person with boundaries is also unpredictable. They can establish their own power, and then use it to protect themselves against the narcissist's agenda. Therefore, individuality is a threat.

While the narcissist is not intimate with their target, they still expect complete vulnerability in return. They use one-sided enmeshment to gain a monopoly over their target's life, and in the process, control what the target is allowed to do. The narcissist decides what path the target's life should take. If the target has desires which do not serve the narcissist's grandiose agenda, the narcissist will discourage them at best and attack them at worst. The enmeshed state, which is seamless by now, allows the narcissist enormous influence over their target's emotions. There is no separation whatsoever, and no way to manoeuvre without interference from someone on the 'inside.' Over time, enmeshment goes from being a mild current to a rapid river which is almost impossible to break away from without enormous guilt.

The power of awareness

Recognising enmeshment is difficult, since without boundaries to provide contrast, it ends up feeling seamless. But the telltale signs are there. For example, when you get an impulse

346

to do something that does not involve the other person, do you get pangs of guilt as though you are letting them down? Do you feel a gravitational pull the second the person enters the room, as though you must do or say something? Does any sign of a person's displeasure send shockwaves of shame and anxiety through you? These all come as a result of enmeshment. When you are permanently in this state, you will feel that you can only have you to yourself when you are physically separate — if the guilt does not drag you back.

The first step is to be mindful of the emotions which arise when you wish to act independently. Where in the body do you feel resistance? The chest? The throat? In what ways does it hold you back? How strong is it on a scale of one to ten? While mindfulness will not immediately solve the problem, it will highlight the separation between you and your conditioned response, which in time will transform it and accelerate the releasing process.

Drawing new borders

Enmeshment takes away your personal and psychological space until there is nothing uniquely yours — inside or out. We all need to have aspects of our lives which only we control. We need exclusive 'property,' protected by boundaries.

Personal space includes the following realms:

- **Mind:** The right to think and decide independently of another person.

- **Heart:** The right to feel a certain way without anyone else dictating its appropriateness, and the right to not be responsible for another person's emotions.
- **Territory:** A space of complete privacy which belongs to you, where people must ask before entering. This can be as simple as a bedroom or workshop which is out of bounds to anyone but you.
- **Lifestyle:** How you spend your time and who you spend it with is for you to decide, and should not be labelled a threat because it is different to someone else's worldview.
- **Intellectual property:** Your smartphone, your diary, and mail addressed to you are for your eyes only.

This paradigm shift is simple, but after a lifetime of conditioning can feel insurmountable. Nonetheless, it is an idea which must be continuously reinforced: *It is not selfish to be separate.* The height of a beautiful relationship is free individuals who find common ground while explicitly respecting each other's boundaries. In good times, they enmesh for the purpose of sharing, and in bad times, for the purpose of problem solving and healing. But they allow space when it is needed. A relationship does not obligate you to the other person; you volunteer to participate.

In a narcissistic relationship, two fundamental truths are lost:

1. **No is allowed:** Members of a narcissist regime believe that wherever the narcissist wants you, that is where you must be. As we grow older and individuate, how we like to spend our time may diverge from those close to us — espe-

cially our family. The problem with narcissistic families is that the parents make no attempt to adapt to their children, so the children are forced to partake in the narcissist's world. The more enmeshed you are, the harder it is to act in your own interest. To be satisfied with how you spend your life, you will need to say no to other people's expectations, which sounds simpler than it is. In an enmeshed state, guilt can feel unconquerable and unquestionable.

2. **Only you know better:** The narcissist instantly assumes that they know what is right for you. They speak on your behalf or bark orders as though you belong to them. In their mind, you are like a body part. There is no difference. When you are enmeshed, the words of others can feel like gospel. When you learn to individuate, you see that another person's words are just that: Words.

With awareness of enmeshment and making the necessary paradigm shifts, transformation is inevitable. To enforce boundaries, however, you will need to channel the fuel which powers tenacity.

An unexpected ally

Elie Wiesel stated that the opposite of love is not hate, but indifference. Most people associate hate with resentment and destruction, and dismiss it as an emotion which serves no purpose. It is true that when hate is misguided, it can cause enormous damage. Yet it can be constructive; we simply need to channel it in the right way as *healthy aggression*. We also need to accept it as a necessary component of love. One cannot exist without the other.

As adults, we will never find the will to create change until we learn to express our tenacity. In doing so, we need to define an important rule: *one must never channel hate toward the narcissist.* To emotionally engage the narcissist maliciously is to fight a war you cannot win. Behind their mask of control, the narcissist is fearful and aggressive. Your hate will arouse theirs and bring up both of your childhood wounds. It will also meet their need for supply, and fuel their game. Instead, it helps to channel your hatred in productive ways which will finally give you what you most need: power of your own.

Once we reclaim our right to anger, we need to consider our motivating cause. With rage comes an addictive impulse to lash out. Anger can feel satisfying, and if we latch onto its incredible pull, can be hard to let go. Anger management classes are a testament to that. What the chronically angry usually learn the hard way is that hate breeds more hate. To direct it toward another person is to attempt to control them. The cycle of manipulation repeats.

However, when we practice welcoming and creating room for hate without acting on it, we gain the power to hone it toward setting boundaries. The rage and aggression which arises when someone pushes us too far is only a message. A firm 'no thanks,' a look of contempt, or a refusal to play along are usually more than enough to answer that call. It can often be enough to notice the feeling and take it as a sign to disengage. When rage arises due to the influence of others, we need to make space for it and then ask: *Why am I angry? What am I unwilling to accept at this moment? How can I use this feel-*

ing to reclaim my power constructively? In this regard, hate becomes a useful tool.

Permission to hate

The importance of rage cannot be stressed enough. Many people spend a lifetime without acknowledging a single shred of their repressed anger. Yet recall that a child can only express as much discontent as their parent will allow. If the guardian has not resolved their own trauma, they will have no tolerance for the child's outbursts. It is therefore entirely plausible that you have pushed the energy of your anger into your body, eventually having no awareness of its existence. Repressed rage can be frightening to discover, especially when you have grown attached to the idea that you are not hateful, and feel that anyone who experiences hate is a horrible person. You internalised this belief from people whose power was threatened by your anger.

The simplest way to release rage is creating space in solitude or therapy, and just allowing yourself to feel angry. When rage is repressed, it can come out in frightening ways. Even imagining violent acts is possible. As shocking as it can be to realise that you are capable of such aggressive impulses, it is actually a normal component of loving. Thoughts are only thoughts, and they are extreme because the emotion behind them is supercharged. When you give rage mindful space to exist without judging it as good or bad, it eventually loses its charge. The period of calm which follows is when you can decide what boundaries you need to set and what conversations you need to have. Your therapist can also help you explore this 'shadow' side of yourself while supporting you in containing the fallout.

Expansion: Leaning into tension

Tension is the result of fear and vitality increasing within the body. We feel it in the presence of someone we find attractive, when we are approached by a stranger who looks threatening, when about to step onto the field of play, when trying to solve a problem, and when we are the centre of attention. In all of these cases, our body is priming us with the necessary energy to act. How we respond to the rising pressure is paramount to our success in the world.

What the Ancient Greeks called a 'life of agon' is the perfect way to look at tenacity. Agon is the root word for agony, and points toward conflict, struggle and competition as the noblest pursuits. A student of agon sees fear, pain and all manner of uncomfortable emotions as opportunities for growth. They not only accept tension, but actively seek it out, knowing there is no limit to its depth. This simple shift in mindset turns stress from a crippling force into an agent for empowerment — and a doorway into the soul of the warrior.

Ways you can cultivate a life of agon are:

Presence

As already shown in 'Stage Three: Metamorphosis,' coming into being is often far from relaxing. The body is in a constant flow of rising energy, and leaving the comfort of your imagination exposes you to the turbulence of reality. Therefore, the mere shift in perspective from thinking to the present moment is an act of agon, a conscious step into the rapid river of life — especially for those dealing with trauma. Wherever you are, relax your body from top to bottom and direct your attention toward the outside world. Anchor yourself in a point of focus and *see* your environment. Surrender to the tension which results from your awakened state.

Eye contact

If you are out and about and lock eyes with someone, do not look away immediately. Hold it. When the tension grows, keep holding it, but smile. When ordering your coffee or food, do not just interact with an abstraction of the person before you. Make an effort to notice them, to look into their eyes and acknowledge them before you speak. People can grow threatened by another person's eye contact because of the resulting tension, which feels like a direct challenge. It should therefore be accompanied by a degree of openness and vulnerability.

As already described, narcissists use eye contact to assert dominance over others. By practicing strong eye contact yourself, when you do meet the narcissist's soulless stare, you will be accustomed to holding your own while revelling in the resulting tension. Narcissists will move on, and others will enjoy the intensity and feeling within your eyes. Everyone loves to be seen like this when you do it in good faith.

Creating a container

The presence and eye contact exercises from above can be combined in your personal and professional relationships to help you develop a leadership mindset. In any interaction, sharpen your focus onto the person you are with and use the resulting tension to create a container for their energy. Relax your body and align with that person's reality. Your calm, firm presence will help them feel secure and open to your influence.

This exercise calls on you to channel all of the five forces, especially divinity and wisdom. Through divinity you awaken your Higher Self and legitimise yourself as a worthy leader. Through wisdom you determine the right time to interject and provide insights, which helps the exchange evolve to higher levels. As the conversation builds momentum, you do not remain passive and merely nod your head in agreement. If you sense the other person behaving in a dysfunctional or manipulative way, you can adapt accordingly. You welcome the emotional intensity while identifying which thread to reinforce, which to redirect, and which to disengage from. This requires that you put your ego aside and be centred within the Self. From there, you can channel tenacity in enforcing your boundaries, which helps you disagree with and call out the other person when necessary. Discomfort does not faze a tenacious leader; they see it as an essential component of progress. If you are unskilled in creating a container, your focus will scatter, you may grow defensive and abrasive, and you will be unable to attune yourself to the other person. Leadership is about remaining calm, present and steadfast while guiding others from a place of empathy and strength, and it all begins with creating a container.

A classic example of container setting is parenthood, where an adult intuits and absorbs the child's chaotic state while supporting them as they return to a place of empowerment. Because we all have moments of chaos and crippling doubt, we can practice leadership by setting containers for each other when needed.

Raising the bar

Shame is a constructive force if channelled correctly. The narcissist shames their target by creating an unattainable standard which reinforces their grandiosity. We can turn this around by making shame *redeemable*. That is, we can pursue an attainable higher standard to which we currently do not measure up. The feeling of shame burns and irritates us, which leads us to strive for self-improvement as a way to transcend it. We start by setting a meaningful goal and then routinely reminding ourselves of the ways we are lacking. If someone tells you not to bother or that you cannot do it, all the better. Prove them wrong, or challenge them to beat you to it. Make life into a healthy competition with both yourself and others. When shame emerges, rather than criticising and defending yourself, redirect the energy into action and planning.

Examples of raising the bar include:

- Learn a new language, either for fun or as preparation for a trip to a country you have always wanted to visit. Speaking the language even when you do not feel confident is a powerful tenacity-building exercise.
- Master a martial art by moving up through the hierarchy of skill levels.
- Learn to play a musical instrument by setting specific goals. For example, learn your favourite song, play or symphony from beginning to end.
- Write a complete draft of a book or maintain a consistent writing schedule.
- Reach and beat a personal best in running, swimming or other form of exercise.
- Set an ambitious milestone for your business. Break down the goal into individual and actionable steps and stick to a regular schedule, even when you do not feel like it or have doubts about your success.
- Take part in competitive sports with one or more people.
- Ask your friends or colleagues to constructively call you out on your weaknesses. The honesty of others can hurt, but learning to humbly take on constructive criticism builds tenancy while also providing you crucial insights to grow.

The good fight

When misfortune rocks your life, turn it into a demon to slay. An investment goes awry, and you lose money. You fail to get the job you want, or lose your job. A good friend or lover turns their back on you. In any such situation, aim to welcome the uncertainty and pain, and contemplate ways to overcome them. Use these moments to strip yourself bare, to reinvent yourself and take on a new life philosophy.

A classic example is the post-breakup 'crisis,' where a person gets a make-over, goes travelling, and makes fundamental changes they held back while in the relationship. In truth, you can take on this attitude after any collapse, whether big or small. You usually cannot control when misfortune hits, but you can control whether you come out of it in a higher state of tenacity. Franklin D. Roosevelt is a quintessential example. He turned polio from a crippling disease into an obstacle to overcome, which eventually led him to the presidency of the United States. While despair and losing heart are natural human reactions, a paradigm shift may be all that is needed to instigate change. Without it, we would otherwise remain stuck in our misfortune.

Challenging the body

Undertake a resistance training program. The key to long-term success is to not overload yourself from day one, but to mindfully lean on the edge of stress on a consistent basis. Your program can be as simple as doing push-ups and squats in your bedroom, or you can get some dumbbells or a resistance band. Another option is developing a regular yoga or pilates practice. Those unaccustomed to resistance training may see it only as a vain endeavour to look attractive. A tenacious figure who embodied the advantages of resistance training for more than just appearance is Ruth Bader Ginsburg. She regularly exercised with light dumbbells, resistance bands and medicine balls. By routinely putting her body under strain, she was able to withstand the pressures of being a Justice of the Supreme Court. It was one of the many ways she welcomed tension into her life.

The antidote for procrastination

Procrastination and tenacity are two sides of the same coin. One is the down-cycle, the other is the up-cycle. Expending energy results in eventual inertia, and a period of *absolute* inactivity inevitably leads to a burst of power.

Procrastination is notorious for being a black hole of laziness. However, the mistake most people make is procrastinating in a *distracted* state. When you feel exhausted or lack the will to get anything done, the answer is to surrender completely and focus on the feeling of apathy and fatigue. If thoughts arise, gently allow them to pass by. If the urge to pick up your smartphone or put on the TV comes, acknowledge it and maintain focus on the act of surrender. Close your eyes, let your body fall slack, and welcome inaction into your entire being. Do this correctly, and the urge to get up and act will return.

When traces of energy return to you, think of yourself as a human-shaped water tank filled with sand. After a period of inaction, the sand falls to the bottom. The tiniest shake of the tank creates the smallest amount of movement in the sand particles. The next shake doubles the movement, with the momentum of the previous action merging with it. Each effort grows easier than the last until you are once again in a state of flow. It is for this reason that you should get up and act the moment you notice a sign of vitality inside you. Before you know it, tenacity is called upon to awaken.

Tenacious people are not immune to fatigue or a lack of motivation. Like anyone else, they go through phases where they lose heart and question whether they can reach their goals. During particularly dark moments, they even question the purpose of what they are trying to achieve. What sets them apart, however, is their awareness of the countless cycles of energy which go into the greater pursuit. Most people who set goals for themselves jump in with maximum motivation. Once they sense themselves losing inspiration, they wrongly believe that their window is closing and they give up, falling into shame and disappointment. The tenacious person understands that the current window might be closing, but a new one will open soon after — as long as they stick with it and maintain faith. When in doubt, the tenacious person remembers the bigger picture and reassures themselves that they are working toward a higher state. It is supposed to feel like an uphill climb.

And they lived tenaciously ever after

In a fairytale, the hero saves the maiden. These stories enchanted all of us as children. Every boy wanted to be the brave hero, every girl wished to be rescued by the courageous and righteous man. The point of these stories was not to illustrate a woman being saved from misfortune. Rather it was to direct us toward unifying the opposite forces which govern and empower the Self. The prince is our Higher Self, our yang, and the princess is our True Self, our yin. The Animus and the Anima, the masculine and the feminine. Heaven and Earth. The prince saving the princess is the discovery of independent will, a freeing of our 'feminine' life energy by the 'masculine' aspect of the Self. No matter your gender, your task is to unlock your potential by growing your tenacity and transcending the tyrannical forces which limit your potential. Cultivating this ability is crucial to standing up to narcissists.

Life is filled with fear and suffering, both of which threaten to crush your personal power. If your Higher Self can withstand this onslaught and remain present, then tenacity can be achieved, and your divine nature will rise in all its glory.

Stage Seven: Reclaiming divinity

Be yourself. The world worships the original.

- Ingrid Bergman

Those who fear the depths of their shadow will unwittingly seek out an external power to substitute for their Higher Self, hoping that a person or group will lead them to some imagined Utopia. Shamelessness, deflecting blame and refusing to be vulnerable all manipulate the target into believing that the narcissist can be their salvation. Yet the narcissist is not channelling true divinity; they are using ethos, pathos and logos to project a grandiose self, which is a counterfeit version of the real thing.

If someone hijacks your mind and gains authority over you, then your internal kingdom is lost. True divinity is the ability to maintain presence via your Higher Self along with the conviction that you are the rightful ruler of your 'realm'. This requires letting go of the hope that an outside figure will fulfil this need, and instead trying your Higher Self on for size.

Grandiosity and divinity

The narcissist's idea of divinity is being idealised, fed narcissistic supply, and never questioned. True divinity, on the other hand, is a state of alignment within the Self. It is a celebration of life. True divinity is unaffected by outside noise — it requires only focus and surrender.

A simple way to differentiate between grandiosity and divinity is in a social setting. Observe a person's body language when they are interacting with a group, followed by when they find themselves alone. Do they perk up and stand straight in the group but become sombre and hunched over when alone? Does their face dramatically change? Compare how *you* feel when speaking to others while having the attention on you, followed by how you feel immediately afterwards when you find yourself alone. If it is grandiosity propping a person up, then the withdrawal of supply will cause a dramatic collapse of pride. If the person is aligned with their Higher Self and rested in being, then the presence of their divine nature will always be enough. They can move in and out of the spotlight with minimal impact on their sense of Self. It is this state which we will aim to cultivate.

A way of being

To achieve divinity, you need to decouple your self-esteem from the outside world and bring awareness to your inner body. While having people's attention will energise you, it also goes against the natural rhythm of vitality. Happiness always transforms into sadness; a down-cycle follows every up-cycle. The death instinct continuously balances the life instinct.

The reason we get hooked on outside validation is so we can remain permanently aligned with the life instinct. Society shoulders much of the blame for this by refusing to acknowledge darker aspects of humanity, such as depression, sadness, frustration, anger and shame. Almost everywhere you go, including workplaces and social groups, you are expected to happily play along, or at the very least, to be quiet and neutral. It is no wonder we detach from our inner world and fight to keep our 'head above water,' so to speak, where the sun is shining and everything is going great. In doing so, we cut ourselves off from our True Self, which not only consists of our spontaneity and joy, but also our shadow. We remain on the treadmill, as pain and negative emotions threaten to break into consciousness while we continue to push them down. Meanwhile, our vitality continues to go through its natural cycles, and we assume we are feeling low because there is something wrong with us. Our self-esteem drops as we perceive ourselves failing to live up to society's idea of the happy, successful person. In truth, we can no more avoid shadow states than we can avoid the coming of the night.

The answer to this predicament is to accept and consciously move into the Self no matter where in the cycle it is. When happiness strikes, we welcome it wholeheartedly. When we feel sad, we move into the heaviness. During the day, make a habit of re-anchoring yourself by finding a point of focus, seeing it with all of your awareness, then turning your attention to the one who sees it. Awaken the Higher Self, and direct it toward whatever mood you find yourself in. Acknowledge that while the world has a unique state, so do you, and this is perfectly fine. To be divine is to be unique, and to be unique is to be connected to that uniqueness through your Higher Self. If you find yourself caught in negativity and doubting the existence of your divinity, then *go inside* and verify it for yourself. You will find that you are much more than what your mind tells you.

Divinity should not be mistaken for grandiosity. To manipulate a person into orbiting and validating you is narcissistic. Forsaking yourself and directing life energy toward a grandiose person is also a betrayal of the True Self. On the other hand, consolidating your awareness and directing it inwards is to be centred. When a centred person walks into the room, you notice. They are a self-contained and self-sustaining system. This person does not look around with hungry eyes or cling to someone with excessive neediness. They have everything they need, and you can tell just by looking at them.

The lion is a perfect example of divinity. It projects majesty as a matter of being, because it knows it is the king of the jungle. Babies are another. They light up a room solely with their presence, and awaken the light in even the most cynical people. They too are embodying their divine nature. This is the lost quality we must all rediscover — and we can. The key is not to seek out the light at all times, but rather to tune into the unique *rhythm* within. The more we accept the colder seasons of the Self, the quicker we can experience the inevitable up-cycle. When it peaks, our divine nature shines gloriously, much like a sunrise or a flower in full bloom. This can last for an hour or an entire day. Before long, it fades again like a sunset or the final days of summer, before later returning. Our task is to remain in step with this rhythm and to direct it constructively toward our actualisation.

The perils of being seen

The targets of narcissism, especially empaths and dependents, are used to giving their attention away and mirroring others. Yet when the focus is on them, they look down shyly at their feet and want to crawl out of their skin. Several factors cause this. Firstly, the target probably went long periods without having their True Self acknowledged. Secondly, when they were in the spotlight, they were usually being shamed or attacked. Furthermore, being seen awakens the target's Higher Self, and with it, the fear of their own power.

For all of the above reasons, the target of narcissism faces a combination of negative beliefs, toxic shame and anxiety when feeling seen or exposed. Self-doubt instantly arises when they stand before a camera, or when asked to talk about themselves or perform in some way. When they find themselves in the spotlight, the necessary vitality flows momentarily before something floods in and blunts it. Even becoming aware of themselves can stunt their flow of life energy. The cause of this is a judge and jury in their psyche who keeps them locked within a certain set of constraints. We all possess this oppressive 'other' in one form or another. It watches our every thought, feeling and instinct, and wastes no time in raining down its judgement.

The saboteur and the inner critic

Divinity gives us the green light to engage the world. Meanwhile, providing a 'sensible' structure to express our energy is what Freud called the *superego*. This internalised system of laws alerts us whenever we break an alleged social standard or behave in a way we believe will be detrimental to ourselves or others. In short, it is the blueprint we develop over time for how we *should* live our life. If we break its rules, it shocks us with an emotional spike of shame, guilt or fear. It governs us as a limiting force and a judging voice which has many messages, such as: *You could get hurt. You're not good enough for that. You'll upset so and so. You'll make a fool of yourself.*

The first superego we engaged was not our own, but our guardian's. They were the gatekeepers who indicated what was and was not allowed, and it was through them that we developed our personality. We received countless messages from our elders in the following forms:

– **Facial expressions:** A glare tells the child that they have made someone angry, a frown indicates displeasure, a blank stare communicates contempt, and sharpened eyes tell the child that they are under critical observation. These expressions can create fear, guilt, shame and nervousness in the child, and have the power to shape their behaviour moving forward.

- **Mockery:** Ridicule is a powerful way to shame someone into questioning themselves. It is a particularly cruel way to lower someone's power and force them to fall into line by communicating to them that they should be self-conscious.

- **Judgement:** More often than not, questioning someone about their choices or declaring their actions as wrong is shame-inducing. It may well seem like someone is concerned about you when they share their judgements uninvited. This is often done under the guise of 'what is best for you,' but is often a way to keep you in line.

- **Modelling behaviour:** How a parent lives and spends their time subliminally shapes the child's view of how to be in the world.

- **Granting and denying permission:** Children seek advice and permission from their parents for many life decisions, and might model their family life and careers around their parent's example. Following in your parent's footsteps can provide an empowering path through life. This is not always the case, however, since children tend to have different personalities, strengths and weaknesses compared to their parents. Not to mention children grow up in a different generation, which calls on a new approach to living in a fast-changing modern world.

- **Anger:** Children are curious and spontaneous, and they live this way without hesitation — until their behaviour threatens their parent's sense of control. The guardian might then respond with rage, and the child is forced to dampen their impulses.

These messages and more can shape how one lives in and sees the world, and it all begins with the superego of the parent. But what influenced theirs? Their parents, of course, and whatever society they lived in at the time. When it is well-informed, a superego is a powerful ally and wise consultant which allows us to navigate our world effectively. A healthy superego makes us predictable and safe to others, who in turn are more than happy to cooperate and connect with us. In short, a superego is the way toward being socialised. When it is dysfunctional or corrupted by a traumatised Self, however, the superego turns destructive. It becomes a *saboteur*; a crippling force which cuts us down and entraps us within a psychological cage, and an *inner critic*; a commentator we carry around who berates and judges us for our wants and impulses. This begins with the family and is reinforced by the people in our social circles who shame, control and judge us based on the behaviour they wish to see in us. Bullies cruelly point out our flaws, people who perceive themselves as having higher status remind us of our place in the pecking order, and those entrusted to guide us enforce their own doctrine on us based on their ideas of right living.

Some instincts must always be regulated, such as the desire to sprint through a busy road without looking, or carrying on a loud conversation in a library. The dulling of other instincts, however, can lead to chronic unhappiness and mental illness. The instinct to cry, for example, is a crucial outlet for emotional health that is often angrily attacked and stifled by parents. The desire to explore one's sexuality is often impeded by parents and religious institutions, and the results can be devastating.

The first step to exposing the saboteur is to realise that reality is subjective. That is, everyone's experience is unique, and what one person believes is a life worth living might not fit others. Life evolved to where it is today because humans gave their unique instincts and desires room to breathe. The hero's journey demonstrates this clearly. Furthermore, how one person judges us is based on what reinforces their own feeling of control and power. We should not reject ourselves because a select few rejected us first. Of course we need wise people to inform us. We need to respect our limits, accept our flaws, and lay the groundwork for a good life. However, our unique personality and life situation must be taken into context, not the idealism or cruelty of another person as dictated by their corrupted superego.

A parent can have such a wounded Self that the only way they can cope is to externalise their pain. They then tell their child that they are disgusting and worthless, and the child responds by taking on the parent's disowned feelings. Over time, the child develops their superego map based on how their parent treated them, and carries a debilitating inner critic with them wherever they go. This voice attacks the child into adulthood, replaying recordings of the parent's voice over and again throughout the day.

The saboteur and inner critic also play an enormous role in narcissistic abuse. Throughout the relationship, the narcissist's deluded, self-serving concept of 'right and wrong' dominates. By shaming, gaslighting, questioning, scapegoating and judging you, the narcissist effectively remakes your superego in their image. As you now work toward transformation, restoring your Higher Self to its rightful place becomes critical. From this state of alignment, you can shine the light of awareness on your superego's programming. The tug from within may still arise, but your conscious presence can short-circuit the forces which hold you back. As a result, the saboteur and inner critic eventually lose their power, allowing divinity to re-emerge.

Rediscovering legitimacy

The saboteur encompasses far more than the voice in your head, where your thoughts are only the tip of the iceberg. Beneath the level of consciousness are conditioned beliefs and autonomous forces which dull your expression of vitality and ensure you never go beyond your usual reality. What should be a map for navigating the world becomes a restrictive maze with no exit. Whether in a social setting, in the family home or the workplace, the saboteur reminds you to 'stay in your lane,' holding you back from claiming your rightful place in the flow of life. The saboteur assumes original sin in all situations, declaring that you are inherently invalid from the get-go. Together with the inner critic, the saboteur makes life painful and miserable.

To enjoy the ease and wonder of divinity, you need to navigate out of this psychological prison and reassert your right to elevate to higher states of being. You do this by legitimising yourself as follows:

1. Acknowledge duality

The saboteur maintains power over you through the lens of duality, where people are either valid or invalid. You, of course, are inherently invalid — according to the saboteur. In reality, those who embody divinity do so because they have momentum behind them. The people in their early life validated and encouraged them, and their pride and self-belief swelled as a result. Just like toxic shame can become a permanent state, so can divinity. While you still need to build momentum before you can embody this quality, knowing that illegitimacy is fluid is the first step. Even if you feel unworthy, you will no longer take that as gospel. It is a conditioned reflex which you can unlearn.

2. Face down the saboteur

As the dulling force of the saboteur descends, relax and welcome it. Shame may numb your mind and have you feeling like a helpless toddler. The will to act or express yourself is nowhere to be found. Heaviness holds you back, and reminds you that you have no influence. Welcome it all. Sit with it as long as possible, and encourage it to leave when it is ready. Do not try to resist or change it.

3. Awaken your Higher Self

The saboteur maintains power by clouding your Higher Self's line of sight. As you notice the saboteur coming over you, come into the present moment by observing the observer. If necessary, focus on something physical in your environment to anchor you. In doing so, you gain separation from the saboteur and create space for divinity to reassert itself.

4. Remain anchored

Those of us who habitually externalise our Higher Self typically seek out another person's validation before acting. We do this because we have not yet learned to trust ourselves, and so remain plagued by uncertainty. Maturing is about learning from our mistakes and failures. While we can seek out another person's wisdom on a particular matter, it is up to us to integrate their advice and then decide for ourselves from a centred place.

In times of revolution, a fever can sweep up the entire populace. In social settings, confident people steal our attention through the magnetism of their divinity. 'Doing you' means maintaining a sense of your own divinity even when others seem to have it better than you. This means accepting moments of low energy and remaining anchored within at all times, sticking by the Self through thick and thin.

5. Separate story from feeling

The inner critic makes judgements all day, which in turn activates feelings of shame and guilt. Observe this while paying particular attention to your emotions and sensations. We usually remain solely identified with our thoughts, which reinforces the inner critic's story and keeps us stuck in a cycle of self-sabotage. By being the observer, we remember that emotions lose momentum when they are not reinforced by a story. No matter how bad you feel, or how stuck you are, if you do this correctly, the inner critic and saboteur *will* undergo metamorphosis and lose their power. It is a matter of focus and perspective while choosing not to listen to the inner critic's crippling voice.

6. Fight back against the inner critic

The inner critic is the collective voice of all past figures in your life who judged you, ridiculed you, questioned you, yelled at you, told you what to do or expressed disgust at you. You internalised each of those instances, and it shaped your identity. Now you live with this critical voice 24/7, even when it only causes you pain and suffering.

What if rather than internalise these messages at the time, you fought back? What if you had angrily said: "Shut up!" or "Do you have any idea what kind of damage you're doing right now? Stop it!" What if you calmly but firmly had said: "I think you're disgusted in yourself," or "I'm not a bad girl/boy, but you're acting like a bad person right now."

You did not respond in such an assertive way at the time because there was a power mismatch. It was for this reason that others could offload their shadow onto you. Those days are now over, although their voices remain. On the one hand, you are being tortured by the past. On the other hand, as long as those voices remain, you have an opportunity to finally defend yourself. You do this using a technique the C-PTSD author Pete Walker called *angering at the critic.*

Whenever the inner critic attacks you, be mindful of the message. While simply noticing the thought and not engaging with it can be empowering, you also have the option of responding to it using anger. A simple "STOP IT!" can be enough, or even an "I HATE YOU!" The point of these imagined counter-attacks is to purge the inner critic from the inside. The anger is already inside you, so why not use it? Allow the rage to come up and express itself both energetically and in thought. If it helps, pick up your journal and express your anger at the critic in writing. You will find that there is a cathartic effect to this technique, and that it can lead to you finally feeling grief over the years of pain you experienced. Anger and sadness are healthy responses to emotional abuse, and they are accessible to you at any moment. There is no need to express them to the people who caused you the emotional pain.

Watch out for any psychosomatic responses to your inner angering, as you can experience a spontaneous trauma release using this technique. In the short term it may destabilise you, in the long term it will free you of the crippling weight of the inner critic.

7. Live by your own principles

Even though legitimacy is a state of mind, the consequences of your actions are still real. However, if you take any hint of resistance to your assertiveness as a sign to back down, you will get nowhere, and the saboteur will only reassert itself. Often others are critical of us because we threaten their sense of power.

Instead, it is better to establish a personal set of principles. Be critical of your own actions, but be sure to verify for yourself what others tell you is acceptable or unacceptable. Your superego is a crucial tool for navigating the world, and it is your job to keep it up-to-date while ensuring it does not unnecessarily limit you. 'Doing you' is impossible until you give 'you' permission to express itself. Between shamelessness and rigidity is a whole spectrum of experiences which could enhance your life. What you choose to do is just as important as what you choose *not* to do. Therefore, start by establishing your first and most critical principle: *It is not wrong to express or assert yourself.*

8. Reimagine who you are

The outer world reflects our inner world. We wear our emotional state and self-esteem on our sleeve, whether we like to admit it or not. The intensity and shape of our eyes, our facial expression, our energetic state, our posture — all of it informs others how we feel about ourselves.

This becomes a chicken-and-egg scenario. If you believe that you are flawed, then your eyes, face and body will communicate that belief. As a result, you will witness doubt in others, not knowing it was your own subtle displays of self-rejection which triggered it. The origin of why you saw yourself that way becomes completely lost in this cycle.

It is time to create the conditions which allow you to reimagine what you can be. Begin by grounding yourself in your body each day and creating the conditions for your divine energy to express itself. Work on establishing security and vitality in a container and see where it leads. In doing so, you enter the flow and 'stumble' onto divinity at random moments, which allows you to experience it directly. This makes the chicken and egg problem irrelevant. You get the chicken without the egg by adhering to the five forces of the Self. The 'egg' typically comes when people shine in response to the validation of others, or if they draw pride through coming from an affluent background. This is 'pre-packaged' divinity. Yet it does not have to be this way. Divinity is yours to claim at any moment. The top-down approach to the problem is to deal with your saboteur and to challenge the inner critic. The bottom-up approach is to regularly and consciously cultivate divinity.

Once you have momentum, you will *sense* the possibilities. The energy to shine becomes available, and you will notice — much to your delight — that what you imagined is finally coming true.

Embodying the monarch

The hero plays a central role in mythology, channelling the courage, strength and endurance to venture into the unknown before returning victorious with the gold. Yet the hero's journey is only a blueprint for evolving the Self into fullness. At some point, we need to put aside the adventurer and consolidate our gains in a way that helps others. That is, there must come a time when we commit to a community. For this, we will need to channel *monarch* energy, which is the embodiment of the king or queen archetype.

Monarch energy is what fully matured divinity looks like. While it comes in matriarchal and patriarchal forms, its core function remains the same, which is to provide a container for others to thrive under. The monarch is the great parent expanded beyond the borders of family, and is the foundational force behind good leaders. The monarch is a teacher, manager, spiritual guide, politician or CEO, but can also be a close friend or fellow member of your community.

The monarch is inside you, waiting to activate. It has the following qualities:

- **Centeredness:** The monarch has united their True Self with their Higher Self, and aims to maintain this state of alignment at all times. In doing so, they demonstrate divine energy purely with their presence, all while supporting others with their growth.
- **Order:** The monarch absorbs turmoil and remains calm under pressure. This is no easy feat, even though they make it seem so. The monarch does not lack emotion, but instead contains it as they hold another person's chaotic state within the embrace of their consciousness. The monarch accepts reality, no matter how challenging or painful, and creates the conditions for a healthier, more constructive approach. They do this by channelling their

own wisdom or consulting others when needed. It is not their insight, however, which makes them indispensable. Rather it is the way their divine presence reassures others by absorbing their intolerable emotions. Others can then use the monarch's state as solid ground to stand on. The monarch makes you feel as though things are right with the world. Only then can order assert itself.

- **Fortification:** The monarch does not disengage as soon as they are afraid or overwhelmed. They still protect their inner space and fortify their True Self, but they do not close it off from the world. Boundaries are intended to ensure that the monarch has sufficient energy to offer those they hope to serve. Nobody can be of service when they are burnt out or resentful. A kingdom cannot prosper if it is not sufficiently protected, and it all begins with the central figure demonstrating how that is done. The monarch tenaciously fortifies their True Self while expanding its reach, all while welcoming good-intentioned people to benefit from what it offers.

- **Shrewdness:** The monarch knows when to say "no" and "enough." They do not tolerate time-wasters or saboteurs. In such cases, which includes narcissists, the monarch has the insight to reach for the cut-off button. They know when someone is caught in a self-sabotaging cycle. Rather than be pulled under by the 'drowning' person, the monarch disengages from senseless drama. The monarch has no saviour complex; they merely light the way for others to elevate higher.

- **Blessing:** Perhaps the most potent gift a monarch can offer is their capacity to witness the best in others. The monarch *truly sees*, looking beyond the mask and into the heart of a person. The monarch then observes what is best in that person, and tells them. This is not flattery, but a blessing bestowed from one divine figure to another. There is no ego involved. While worship can be a dangerous game to play, it is still crucial in the early stages of actualisation. By generously bestowing blessings on others, the monarch legitimises that person and helps them see the best in themselves. When done with care and appreciation, it allows a person to unleash their divinity out into the world, which further benefits the greater community.

Unless we come to embody the monarch in some form, our divinity remains unactualised. Yes, channelling this energy is hard, and requires a great deal of self-sacrifice. Heavy is the head that wears the crown. Maintaining the developmental forces within oneself is difficult enough; doing it for multiple people at once requires immense strength. More difficult still is maintaining our composure without having this powerful energy corrupt and morph into the tyrant.

Embodying the truth

It is not the light but the darkness which holds truth, with light being a mere expression of that truth. For our divine purpose to play out, we need to allow a temporary collapse of our ego and welcome what comes. We need to trust that beyond the mind lies everything we need, and embracing this mysterious space is what awakens insight.

To walk the world in harmony with your divine nature is a victory in its own right. However, society requires more from you than just your presence — wonderful as it may be. It needs you to participate. Therefore, engaging the world means that you taper down and morph your energy in strategic ways that allow you to contribute. You can be gentle and a good listener to a friend, or bold and inspirational when leading your team at work. A parent can be firm with their child to maintain structure, or they can be playful and silly to grow the bond. Life energy, as we have previously established, exists in countless frequencies, from the embrace of a warm hug to the battle cry of a warrior as they prepare to defend their land. The final force which binds this all together is wisdom. It is the intelligence inherent inside all of us, which goes far, far beyond the mind.

Stage Eight: Reclaiming wisdom

Who looks outside, dreams; who looks inside, awakens.

- Carl Jung

Self-doubt is a particularly cruel side effect of narcissistic abuse. Having been excessively gaslighted and shamed, the target turns away from their True Self, finding it too painful to go inside. As a result, they stop trusting their instincts and become crippled by indecision.

There is only one road back to your inherent wisdom, and it runs through shame. Pride without a counter-force leads to delusion and ignorance. The wise sage not only tolerates shame, but immerses themselves in it, using it to ground themselves long enough to absorb the needed knowledge. This makes sense when you think about it. The grandiose person believes they know everything, so they have nothing new to learn. Shame is the emotion of limitation, which reminds you in no uncertain terms that *you do not know everything*. It may be a heavy feeling to hold, but within this mysterious emotion is the capacity to know a little more. Toxic shame is destructive because it crushes you. Facing and releasing it, however, reveals a milder and healthier form which gives the sage their power.

Shame will set you free

Put simply, narcissism is the avoidance of shame, the fear of that horrible feeling of being inferior and unworthy. When managed well by the healthy parent, shame can help raise the child into an empathic and balanced adult who is comfortable in their own skin. As a result, their growth flows organically from their True Self.

The target of narcissism, on the other hand, experiences unfathomable levels of shame. They have no choice but fight to meet the narcissist's perfectionistic standards. Otherwise, they fall into irredeemable despair. The experience is so painful that the target pushes the emotion inside and does everything possible to avoid feeling it. Addiction, compulsive work and perfectionism are all further attempts to outrun the feeling of shame. In this respect, the narcissist regime becomes an elaborate cover-up.

Because the narcissist never faces their shame, they create a blockage at the top of the hierarchy which trickles down, causing an epidemic of shamelessness to run riot. The dominant members become shameless through control; the rest rely on coping mechanisms such as fantasy, anger, care-taking and people-pleasing to keep their head above water.

The first step out of this nightmare is dropping the belief that you have to *do* something to gain a feeling of worth. When you realise that the narcissist's standards are based on grandiose delusions, the game collapses. You see that there is nothing to measure up to — it was an illusion the whole time. It has no substance in the real world, and it never did. No matter how much conviction a narcissist shows, and no matter how convincing their manipulations, the truth is never far away. One must only surrender into their body and face the emotion they have been avoiding all along.

Releasing toxic shame

For a person to 'be,' they must have the willingness to remain in touch with their shame at all times — 24/7. To sit still and dwell in the moment is by far the most liberating experience a human can have. No more showboating, no more asserting dominance, and no more needing to prove yourself. You are whole. This is the essence of being.

You cannot channel wisdom when you feel like your source of it is inherently flawed. Therefore, we set the groundwork for accessing our intuition by meditating on and releasing toxic shame.

Targets of narcissism are subjected to continuous abuse. As previously explained, these shame experiences link together before eventually consolidating as an inferiority complex. When a situation in the present resonates with shame experiences in the past, toxic shame activates and takes over, causing a shame 'episode' or 'flashback' which can last for hours, if not days. Even when the wave passes, the 'hangover' can remain in your system for some time longer.

Symptoms of a toxic shame episode include:

– Blushing and sweating.
– Uncharacteristic unease, clumsiness or uncertainty.
– Feeling like a child.
– An inability to hold eye contact.
– A desperate need to hide away from the world.
– Mind going blank, and not knowing what to say.
– Negative self-talk and a feeling of self-loathing.
– Suddenly and compulsively comparing yourself to others.
– Insomnia.
– A sense of isolation and despair.

A toxic shame episode is crippling and detrimental to self-esteem. It feels like a phantom roaming inside your soul, appearing from nowhere yet always out of reach. For those who experience it, the truth is that you *can* heal toxic shame, even though during an episode it can feel like it will never end. While these episodes are extremely painful, they also hold enormous potential for growth.

The strategy to combat a toxic shame episode is as follows:

1. **Catch it:** The first, and often most difficult challenge, is becoming aware that a toxic shame episode is happening. When it arises, it can be so overwhelming that the mind

switches off. At first, you may only become aware of it in the days following an episode. With mindfulness practice, you can reach a point of awareness when you are mid-episode. When you do catch it, say to yourself: 'I am having a toxic shame episode,' or 'I am having a flashback to childhood.' Try pinching your thumb while you do this, which creates an anchor in the present moment while you 'drown in the past.'

2. **Identify the trigger:** Toxic shame often feels like it comes from nowhere and then disappears to nowhere. It takes vigilance and patience to link an episode with its cause. Triggers can be something like a person putting you down, feeling trapped in a situation you cannot escape, feeling left out of a group, comparing yourself to someone and feeling inadequate, and so on. If you are mid-episode, you might struggle to think. If so, save this step until after the episode is over.

3. **Reach out:** The fact that toxic shame makes you want to hide away and never come out makes this step feel counter-intuitive. Yet by talking to someone, and explaining both the fact that you are having an episode and how it is affecting you, you can transform it. Shame thrives in secrecy. The loving and understanding eyes of another person carry immense healing power, and helps loosen shame's grip. For this purpose, you can visit your therapist or contact a close friend or family member who can simply hear you out without interfering or problem solving. You can also do this over the phone if a face-to-face meeting is not possible at that moment.

4. **Meditate:** The above steps are preludes to the arduous journey into shame. Once you become aware of an episode,

you also have the power to shine the light of your awareness on it. Rather than seeking a way out, go into the feeling and welcome it. Try to do this in solitude by sitting in a room alone or heading into nature. Create a point of focus and go deep inside. Do not let your thoughts interfere. Separate the story in your mind from the physical sensation of the emotion itself. Welcome the entirety of the feeling until it is ready to leave.

5. **Stop running:** The most frightening part of toxic shame is when it pulls you into a psychological void. It feels like being in a dark, suffocating space in your mind. This is terrifying, but also the moment of truth. Breathe into the feeling. By allowing the heaviness while remaining focussed on it for as long as possible, you enable it to transform. You realise that this void is not a foreign realm or a phantom; it is a part of you. That is all that shame wants. It is like an imprisoned child who needs company. To sit with it is to sit with you, and with each sitting, you become more yourself. That is, your True Self.

6. **Avoid goal setting:** Being with shame is just that; *being*. With meditation, the means is the end. Your only 'aim' is to build tolerance for experiencing shame. With each sitting, you become mentally, physically and spiritually connected to your True Self. Your goal is to stay with it as long as possible.

7. **Document:** As you observe your body and mind, watch for what comes up. Shame is usually wrapped up in acquired thought patterns and beliefs, negative messages and the impulse to self-sabotage. During the meditation, you might notice such thoughts arise as emotions are stirred up. For example, you may pick out all the ways your life is lacking,

brood about mistakes you made in the past, or remind yourself of why you will never amount to anything. Write them down during or after the meditation and, if necessary, share them with somebody later. By doing so, you can make the unconscious conscious, and therefore bring light to your shadow, which transforms and releases it.

Toxic shame is an emotional hangover from the past which can be released over time. It takes courage and patience to work through it. But the effort is well worth it, and winning this battle will bring you a long way to reclaiming your True Self. Each time you face toxic shame, it loses some of its strength. In time, it stops crushing you, and eases off to become *healthy shame*.

Tuning into destiny

When healthy shame is restored, the True Self has a clear path to express itself. You feel the pressure easing, and like a prison door left open, you dare to approach the exit. Outside, the sun is shining, and the heaviness of shame is no longer crippling. What you do with your life is now limited only by your moral compass, not by what others think. Vitality rises, and your instinct to act is no longer stifled from inside. It feels unusual to have choices, to have nothing holding you back from being more daring.

But how do you make the most of this newfound freedom? What drives you? Which decision is the right one? Should you stay on your current course, or implement dramatic change?

And what if you make the wrong choices? This is where wisdom comes into play.

Often when we are in a tight spot, we seek someone's advice, or we imitate what others are doing. If the saboteur dominates our psyche, we become plagued by indecision and stagnation. Driving to a destination with the map of another city will not work. Sadly, nobody can provide us a plan for how to live our life. The only chance we have is to allow the Self to guide us from within.

We usually only understand our decision-making process in hindsight. Trusting your instinct is to realise that the blueprint for your life is already imprinted in your True Self. Evolution has brought you this far, and has equipped you with a unique nature based on your ancestry. So no matter your ideas about who you 'should' be, who you are has already been written.

That is not to say it is all nature and no nurture. The conditions you are born into and the current zeitgeist play enormous roles. Yet beneath it all, your True Self has specific tendencies, strengths and weaknesses. Your responsibility is to let go of your social role and to allow your true nature to express itself. The critical phase comes when your unconscious reaches your conscious mind, during which your ego may interfere with the process. Your ego can question itself, defer to others, or it can be threatened by change. It is here that we usually self-sabotage by going against our true nature for the sake of security and conformity.

As they age, the wise person realises that behind the apparently random happenings in their life, there was a strange kind of *coherence* or secret plan. Even though following their instincts brought them many ups and downs, it seemed that each breakdown led them closer to a specific point. As a result, the wise are able to rest in being and trust that the intelligence within knows what it is doing. They see that purpose does not come from the outside; it finds its way to the surface and expresses itself in the world. This process can be likened to tuning into a radio station. If you stay in touch with your True Self, you will eventually find the frequency on which your actualisation occurs. While your ego makes the relevant implementation decisions, the higher plan remains with your True Self, having been there since your conception, like a seed waiting to grow. Just like scanning the radio airwaves, if you stay centred, you will spot the impulses and spikes of energy which arise when something resonates with you, or just as importantly, when something is not for you. Remaining in touch with your Self and allowing these pulses to guide you is the core practice of actualisation.

Deepening wisdom

Maintaining calm and clarity amidst emotional turmoil is crucial. If you get dragged away from your centre, then wisdom is lost. Narcissists try to throw you off by bombarding you with a combination of the five emotions. By being aware that you are more than the confusion, you can remain aligned with your Higher Self and thus maintain a direct line to your True Self.

You come to know that the infinite is always within you, and will always provide you with the answers you need.

A connecting line from the Higher Self can also be actively injected into the True Self, where discovering wisdom becomes a pursuit, much like digging for gold. This can be done top-down or bottom-up. You are using the top-down approach now by reading this book. This entails exposing yourself to a variety of novel concepts and seeing which resonate. Bottom-up, on the other hand, involves creating time and space where you can mindfully relax into your body and find ways to give shape to what arises. Top-down relies on influence; bottom-up encourages the True Self to take the wheel.

Two fundamental ways to 'mine' for wisdom are:

1. **Writing:** Putting pen to paper can give you an outlet to make the unconscious conscious. Often people hit blank page syndrome when there is no direct line to the True Self. This happens if you are unwilling to remain present with your current state or if you are dealing with unease or overwhelming emotions. As you move through the stages of Self-development, being anchored within becomes progressively easier. Establishing writing as a regular activity can be a way to deepen this anchor, and can help you give shape to unconscious and unexpressed elements of your Self. You can try storytelling, blogging, journaling, poetry or writing music lyrics. Blank page syndrome also occurs if you try to force something onto the page or screen. When writing, relax into your body, let your mind wander, and allow yourself to be receptive and observant. If an impulse to

put a word or sentence on the page arises, jot it down and see where the thread leads. Do not analyse it; simply follow the feeling. You should notice a rush of energy as you express yourself, before the wave eventually dies away. Only when flow runs out should you read and analyse the text to understand what the Self was trying to communicate. Also, remember that each flow cycle may produce a single piece of a greater puzzle, which you may need to repeat hundreds of times over many months before making sense of the whole picture.

2. **Art:** Becoming a creator is a profoundly satisfying way to enhance integrity and wholeness. Art is the opposite of narcissism, since narcissism suppresses a person's True Self, whereas art encourages the True Self to grow. Narcissism is destructive; art is creative. Narcissism is life-depleting, and art is life-enhancing. Art also personifies the beauty of personal power, because it creates a space entirely under your control while allowing you to enrich the world around you. Art can take any form; painting, music, drawing, sculpting, ceramics and so on. Art, like life, has no purpose except to realise itself through us.

Writing and art create a platform for the True Self to express itself while increasing your understanding of who you are. In all cases, you are not the doer — *the Self is acting through you.* It guides you with an intelligence that comes from beyond you. Be focussed, but receptive. Let the True Self do its work, and trust where it is leading you. Once in a while you can look back, and if you are lucky, you will grasp what has unfolded as you supported the True Self in its endeavour to burst into consciousness. It is directing you according to your true nature. You only need to be open to what it offers.

The wisdom in suffering

To grow, we must first undergo many failures. Yet we typically avoid this painful path. Making mistakes, being rejected, falling short, feeling stuck, all of it comes with a burning shot of shame and frustration. For this reason we pray for immediate success, and then give up as soon as we hit a wall.

For those of us dealing with trauma, the possibilities remain limited. We fail before we begin, because we are faced with not only the discomfort of the present moment, but the collective agony of an entire lifetime. When trauma or toxic shame are triggered, the floodgates open wide and cripple you. Therefore, the focus initially must be solely on *releasing* and *healing*. This is the part of the hero's journey where the discomfort is high, and the gratification is low.

Then, somewhere along the line, you notice a shift. A daunting situation triggers you, but rather than collapse under the weight of repressed emotion, you find you can remain present. Far from being afraid, you only *experience* fear. Instead of being shameful, you simply feel hints of it. This is a sign that releasing is working. You are now in a position to understand the purpose of suffering.

After enough releasing, shame becomes redeemable. You fail at something, and the emotion spurs you to innovate, improve and try again. The thought of taking a risk petrifies you, but you remain present and somehow come out on the other side. Some days you wake up feeling lost and full of self-pity and despair. You know you cannot stay that way, so you drag yourself through it until a minor success gives you the fuel to reach the next step. In all such cases, suffering was the benevolent force guiding you with an invisible hand.

The will to persevere, the genius to break new ground, the stubbornness to rise above difficulties, these all come about through suffering. The wise sage may appear burdened by it, but they know that within suffering are life's secrets, and by embracing it, enlightenment is their reward. Without suffering there is no feedback loop, and only hubris remains, ready to drive us into the ground before we even come close to actualisation.

The creative potential of shame

Along with the yearning to pursue our passion, we also hope to build strong relationships and have extraordinary adventures. These desires are fuelled by the id, and are as much a part of our human nature as breathing and sleeping. What we forget is the glue which binds our life together and allows us to implement what we imagined. A relationship requires that you narrow your focus so that you can relate to your loved one on the same level. Adventure sometimes requires that you slow down enough to understand the field of play. Every relationship or venture is going to challenge you at some point and test your limits. There is no avoiding this. There will be moments of exhilaration and progress, followed by frustration and disappointment. To navigate your way forward, you need to be able to shift gears. That is, you need to work with shame.

The quicker you accept that it will not all be fun and games, the sooner you can welcome the dull ache of shame. Like changing gears in a car, there will be a slight thud before you transition into a particular state of consciousness. This is healthy shame. One of the reasons that narcissists discard their target is that they do not want to deal with limiting situations. When their target cannot live up to their expectations, the narcissist looks elsewhere. They deny the limits and suffering of others and refuse to work through difficult situations. They deflect and blame rather than empathise and problem solve. Their life is a series of failed adventures. We, on the other hand, can welcome healthy shame into our lives and ground ourselves long enough to move through obstacles. If our loved one is tired or in a bad mood, we do not need to react negatively. We can simply rest in shame and love them from a distance until things change. If we plan a big party for our friends and something goes wrong, we do not need to lose heart or get angry. We can accept the situation and contemplate which direction to take to get the most out of what remains. When we consider shame in this way, we see its creative potential. Without it, we would abandon anything meaningful in our lives before it has a chance to mature to its fullest.

PART IV:
THE RETURN

Coming home

A hero is someone who understands the responsibility that comes with their freedom.

- Bob Dylan

When pursued blindly, personal development becomes an eternal pilgrimage to nowhere. A person feels incomplete and tries a new philosophy. After some effort, they find that they are still in the same place they began; insufficiency. Rather than look within, they seek out another source of salvation, and the cycle starts anew. The mistake such a person makes is failing to involve the Self. Instead, they remain caught in the dualistic realm of the ego, which spins infinitely in circles — without going deeper. This state of affairs is how we get caught in an endless loop of narcissistic relationships.

Self development takes us out of the spin cycle and puts us on the path toward wholeness, even when we have no clear picture of where it leads. This is what makes humans so fascinating; no two people bloom alike. We all have our road to take, and the hero's journey is the best blueprint we have. One leaves the familiar behind and ventures into the unknown, and with some luck, accomplishes the unimaginable. In the spiritual sense, they come of age.

Once you have awakened to this reality, you are ready to manifest it. The five developmental forces align, and remind you of the power you have within. The Self nurtures you, energises you, supports you, strengthens you, legitimises you, guides you, and awakens your creative potential. Each cycle of life energy is a brushstroke. Each instance of releasing and letting go clears the canvas and allows space for evolution.

There is no set time for how long transformation takes. You may decide to focus purely on the hero's journey for many years, even going as far as physically venturing away from home. Remaining single for an extended time can allow you to focus on your growth, or quitting the rat race and taking on your own project could be the platform for your transformation. You might integrate Self-development into your life as a daily practice, taking incremental steps as you juggle other responsibilities such as family or career. What counts is that you make a sustained and consistent effort while integrating the changes. With some luck, there will come a time — in the near or distant future — where you feel the *arrival* of the Self in its actualised form. This happens only after you have spent enough time in the wilderness, which results in vastly expanded depth and unshakeable confidence.

Upon sensing that the Self has sufficiently actualised, you will instinctively turn your attention outwards. You stand once again on a precipice, except this time, you possess the ultimate prize. You look around, and notice that not much has changed with society. People are still doing what they always did. You, however, are infinitely different. You have integrated your True Self, and as a result, your life is ready to move in unimaginable directions, nourished and informed from within. The time comes to tear up your old contract with the world.

A reason to return

Once you expose the rotten core of the narcissist regime, the reality becomes clear; narcissism is a house of cards, propped up by propaganda and manipulation. It creates a space devoid of spontaneity and authenticity, using any available tool to stop its members from differentiating. Once this truth comes out, the house of cards collapses. Then we are done. Right?

Well, not exactly. One can easily fall into the trap of believing that freedom and personal power are the ultimate solutions to our problems. Here is where people typically become addicted to self-improvement and researching narcissism without using the material to mature to a higher stage of development. According to the hero's journey, this is known as the *refusal of the return*, where the hero, having found bliss and 'enlightenment,' avoids re-engaging the ordinary world. Why risk getting caught up in further toxicity when you can stay above it?

The great teachers of history call for using wisdom not only for oneself, but for the good of mankind. The Buddha briefly considered entering the bliss of Nirvana after attaining enlightenment. Instead, he chose to stay in the world and teach people about the path toward liberation. In the Hindu Bhagavad Gita, Lord Krishna says, "I have nothing more to gain, because everything is already mine. And yet I work." The Bible does not put off waiting for the kingdom of heaven, but is full of calls for 'right' work in the world. Therefore we too should not detach ourselves from the world, because it needs us to participate in it. Deep down we know we cannot remain on the sidelines. In truth, personal power is not a destination, but the vessel for a life-long spiritual journey. It is the platform from which we are supposed to jump into life. To purge ourselves of the narcissist regime is to reach a state of equilibrium and embrace reality, terrifying as it can be. Ahead is a world full of challenges and uncertainties. We still need to support ourselves and pursue our passion, all while fostering healthy connections with others.

For those who did not experience personal power early in life, the road so far has been long. The most frustrating part of being infantilised is that one has to play catch up. Autonomy requires skill, confidence and maturity. In some ways, the road back from the hero's journey is even longer than the journey itself. Life gets harder when we embrace personal power. Before, the narcissist influenced all of our decisions. Being held in a rigid, controlling reality might not have been pleasant, but it was at least predictable. It provided structure. Now, we have freedom. We are calling the shots. But where do we invest our energy?

The long road back

When you left your 'old life' to undertake personal growth, you might have ended a relationship, or distanced yourself from certain family members. You may have cut contact with one or more friends, or given up a career that left you feeling empty and used. To actualise is to awaken, and with that, to see one's life clearly. In doing so, you may notice that you cannot return to how things were. You know and have seen too much. Furthermore, after a lifetime of suffering, freedom can be intoxicating. As personal power grows in their life, the actualised person will want to take time to enjoy what life has to offer.

Many people refuse to undergo a hero's journey due to its extreme difficulty, not to mention the existential fear it brings. One has to shed their identity and surrender their fantasy of perfect love. You have to grieve the death of illusion, as you come face-to-face with the painful reality behind the fantasy. The hero's path leads through immense challenges, and finding the way home is not guaranteed. It is no game; the hero risks all for the prize.

Even if you undergo enough Self-development, what kind of world do you come back to? Returning is often far more difficult than beginning the hero's journey. There is always the risk of falling into old habits, or you may feel you have nowhere to go, since everything you knew has revealed itself to be dysfunctional or empty of meaning. A common mistake that many people make after undergoing personal development is to return to their place of origin and attempting to 'fix' their loved ones. This form of god complex never works, since each person is responsible for their own awakening. The hero's journey was not intended to forge the world in your vision, but rather to be an *influence* on others after the journey is complete. Wherever you go, the gift of your actualised Self will shine through. Those who wish to cooperate with you will do so of their own accord.

A further stage of the hero's journey is called the *rescue from without*, wherein a person you meet entices you to settle down or commit yourself to a place, a cause or a relationship. People from your past may come calling, or you may find yourself feeling more connected to someone in the present who encourages you to grow and contribute. As you develop the forces of the Self, you become more whole, and the impulse to share those gifts with others will arise naturally. This calls on you to demonstrate patience, humility and healthy shame. It requires you to accept the flaws of others and be brave enough to expose yours. The challenge, you come to realise, is how to move back into day-to-day life without losing what you have gained.

Master of both worlds

The monarch awakens within us as the embodiment of the King/Queen archetype. This divine presence is the integration of our Higher Self. It makes peace with what happened in our past, and welcomes our present reality for what it is. It is aware of our wounds, our shadow and our strengths and weaknesses — and accepts it all. It looks toward the future with hope, channelling its energy into enabling our evolution.

By embodying the monarch, we are far less likely to enmesh with others and fall into fantasy. When the monarch shines bright in us, we know that the only legitimate reality is and always will be our own. The monarch ensures that our emotional state is balanced, that our needs are met, and that our life is in order. In short, the monarch ensures what is best for us.

In presenting the second last stage of the hero's journey, Joseph Campbell described being the *master of both worlds* as 'achieving a balance between the material and spiritual.' In short, the monarch is comfortable and competent in both the inner world and the outer, maintaining order between both. No matter what influences we meet in the world, and no matter what we choose to commit to, our connection within must never be broken. A spiritual practice entails waking up each day and creating space for the True Self. As long as we remain connected, the Higher Self can do its work. Only then are we ready to cultivate empowered relationships free of narcissistic manipulation.

Enlightened relationships

When an inner situation is not made conscious, it happens outside as fate.

- Carl Jung

During the hero's journey, you discover many aspects of yourself, including your core wounds, emotional patterns, fantasies, beliefs and self-perception. You learn to process and regulate your emotions and take ownership of your inner space, establishing healthy habits which align you with who you truly are.

It is nonetheless possible to make enormous strides, and upon re-engaging the world, to fall straight back into a dysfunctional relationship. This is because personal growth does not fully resolve our blueprint for relating. Our complexes and programming remain intact, and can only be transformed when they are directly experienced, understood and worked through. That means you will need to get your hands dirty by entering into potentially damaging relationships. This time, however, you will have a heightened consciousness and fully-developed Self to guide and support you.

The past haunting the present

We all desire love. What differs from person to person is in *how* they love, and their belief of what love means. In childhood, we love openly and without question. As our experiences pile up, we begin to form a blueprint for how to be in a relationship. When dealing with a narcissist, love means sacrificing yourself on the altar of the false self. For those who grow up in abusive environments, love means losing sanity and control. An emotionally unavailable person leaves us believing that love means fighting for scraps. Over time, these blueprints solidify and invade every budding relationship in our lives. Sigmund Freud referred to this as *transference*.

Transference is a repeating life drama, wherein we cast people in our present into the roles of key people from our past. Anyone who looks, behaves or sounds like someone from the past can awaken our transference. We get lured in by a person's posture, facial expression, voice tone or the shape of their eyes. How they treat us might draw us in, as well as how they see us. Their demeanour or emotional coldness could resonate. As a result, your dynamics with a close friend may echo those of a sibling or cousin. You could notice yourself looking for approval from your yoga teacher as though he were a father figure. You might find your girlfriend or wife scolding you as though she were your mother.

Transference fuels the split. Someone in our present resonates with our past, and we find ourselves either hopelessly attracted to or intensely repulsed by them. Instances of transference usually come with associated feelings, needs, expectations, triggers, fears or fantasies. If you find yourself giving someone more meaning in your life than they might otherwise deserve, your relationship with them might be one long flashback to the past.

What you might not realise is that the culprit for all of this drama is C-PTSD. Humans respond to trauma in peculiar ways. Firstly, trauma has a way of leaving a person frozen in time, unable to move beyond what happened to them. For example, war veterans often flash back to battle, randomly finding themselves teleported to the moment they suffered the trauma. Secondly, in order to move beyond the traumatic event, humans feel a need to *re-experience* it. This time around, however, rather than being powerless and out of control, they need to feel empowered and in control. That is, they need to renegotiate their relationship to the trauma from higher ground.

For those plagued by C-PTSD, transference is an attempt to re-experience those relationships that first created their complex trauma. However, relationship trauma is not based on a singular event, but rather a long web of interactions, including anything from abandonment, neglect, abuse, humiliation, deception or betrayal. To relive years-long relational trauma, you will need to create a real-life 'stage show,' and cast characters into their required roles. Mother, father, brother, sister, cousin, uncle, ex-friend, ex-boyfriend or ex-girlfriend, any of them could become tied to the core trauma, and anyone you meet is susceptible to being cast into one of their roles.

Furthermore, to achieve this seemingly impossible feat, you will need to mould the people in your life to behave like the original person. That is, the dynamics between you and the new person will need to resemble the original relationship. If you experienced deception, betrayal, abuse or emotional neglect with the original person, you will generally gravitate toward people who treat you the same way. If someone does not behave as you had hoped, you will unconsciously *make them* behave that way. This leads to what Freud called *repetition compulsion*, which is a pattern resulting from transference. If you experienced abuse in childhood, you will attract and tolerate abuse in adulthood because a) it feels familiar, b) you believe you can achieve a different outcome this time, and c) you believe it is the only way to be in relationships.

Transference is why some people repeatedly find themselves in relationships with narcissists. They want something healthier, but only feel attracted to a specific type of person. In truth, they have unfinished business. The person in the present can remind you of a narcissist who left their terrible mark on you. By re-casting people in old roles, we follow the path of least resistance. We remain stuck because outgrowing transference means re-socialising ourselves to authentically and vulnerably develop a different way of relating. If emotional neglect or abuse is all you knew in your past, then being loved, seen and treated fairly now will terrify you.

Trauma can dominate and disrupt our lives beyond imagination. However, trying to resolve it using other people is counter-productive and destructive. Allowing the past to act through us without addressing it only leads to us deceiving not only others, but ourselves.

Exploring your relationship blueprint

We cannot change our past, but we can safeguard against repeating it. We begin by documenting our most painful relationships — both past and present — and exploring their dynamics.

The following can help you analyse your past relationships:

1. **Limerence:** If you felt complete when you first met that person, ask yourself: What was missing before they came along? Let limerence shine a light on what is lacking in your life, and take on the responsibility of fulfilling it yourself. If that person was bright and bubbly, maybe you need to inject more joy into your life. If that person was hyper-successful and disciplined, it might be that you need more structure and stability.

2. **Fantasy:** Do you immediately gravitate toward deep connections which have little or no boundaries? Does this shared space feel womb-like, frictionless and full of wonder? Do you have a grand idea of how your relationships should look, but have yet to find proof of it in the real world? Are you especially impressionable toward the 'perfect' relationships on display on social media?

3. **Transference:** Do your relationships come with a feeling of déjà vu? Do they begin and end the same way? Do you get caught up in other people's drama, feeling it changing you over time? Does the shadow of betrayal, neglect, humiliation and pain follow you wherever you go?

Seeing your relationship patterns with a bird's-eye view helps you determine what needs a closer look. Therein lies the final frontier; *the unexamined shadow.*

Shadow work

While asking the difficult questions about your relationship patterns, look for the underlying pain. This is your shadow. Even the thought of having a 'shadow' can cause discomfort to emanate from within you. *Stay out*, this feeling tells you. *Going inside is dangerous.*

More dangerous, however, is *not* going inside.

The unexamined shadow can catch you off guard. Your core wounds and unmet needs lurk within, ready to pounce and take you over. Sometimes this can tip you off-balance and thrust you into a years-long toxic relationship. If we want to regain control of our life, we need to dare to venture inside.

Start by looking at which of the C-PTSD symptoms you resonate with. Study the protector personality map and consider which ones you seem to attract. These likely reflect the fantasies you harbour *covertly* in yourself. A voice whispers about how desirable, blessed, prosperous or loveable you can be, if you just found the right person.

Now ask yourself, which of the *core wounds* could your desires and addictive behaviours be covering up? Bring these hidden parts of yourself out into the light. Embrace them. Validate them. Negotiate with them. Ask what parts of your shadow you need to release, and which you need to integrate. You were once forced to repress and reject your core needs. Shine your awareness on them, and consider how useful they can be in your actualisation.

Consider the following protector personalities and how they can be integrated in healthy ways:

- **Borderline:** Do you look to a 'saviour' to regulate your emotions and be the answer to your problems? Consider if a DBT therapist could help you make sense of your emotions and develop tools to regulate them yourself.
- **Histrionic:** Do you gravitate toward superficial attractiveness? Do you feel unseen and unwanted? Can you never get enough validation or attention? Learn to embrace and express your energetic beauty, and understand that you can be seen without resorting to manipulation or drama — it only takes cultivating the right relationships with the right people.
- **Narcissist:** Does a person's apparent 'perfection' or confidence make them seem like the ideal partner? Dare to accept imperfection while rejecting those who act shamelessly and mistreat you.

- **Psychopath:** Do you feel drawn to people with an 'I don't give a damn' attitude? Learn to confidently pursue your goals through cooperation and mutually-beneficial arrangements. Be willing to vulnerably express to others when you feel betrayed or humiliated by them. Cut people out who do not respect you.
- **Perfectionist:** Stop waiting for the right moment to act. Embrace failure, and learn to use it for feedback and growth. Be tenacious in the face of challenge, and embrace the energetic cycles it takes to achieve long-term goals and healthy relationships.

Your shadow is fertile ground for self-discovery and growth. Explore this space, and invite the pain to surface. Your bad moods, your addictions, your dark desires and unhealthy habits; everything can potentially be traced back to your shadow. Hold it in your presence. Embrace your woundedness, and remain with it until wholeness permeates every cell of your being. As you grow, you learn that many of your coping mechanisms are only covering up pain, and creating space for that pain leads to maturity. The more of your shadow you bring into the light, the more of your True Self you can birth into existence, and the more your understanding of yourself and others can grow. A resource on working with and healing core wounds is the Personal Development School's channel on Youtube.

Attachment is destiny

Attachment trauma profoundly impacts the power distribution in relationships. Therefore, be sure to keep the attachment style of yourself and others in mind. There are no black-and-white answers, but you should remember the following:

- Narcissists tend to lean avoidant, although avoidance does not necessarily mean a person is narcissistic.
- A narcissist remains avoidant when in control, but can switch to their borderline protector and become anxious when their false self is challenged.
- Anxiously-and-fearfully attached people are often targeted by narcissists due to their intoxicating need for love and acceptance, making them vulnerable to manipulation.
- Fearful people lean avoidant with an anxiously-attached person. They can then experience a role reversal with an avoidant person, which causes their anxiety to awaken.
- Attachment style adapts to the people we are with, as we swing from one type to the other depending on the situation and the other person's style.

If you do not heal your attachment trauma, you remain at risk of falling into dysfunctional and narcissistic relationships. You may fight hard to form equal and fair relationships, only to have that progress slowly slip through your fingers as you grow insecure and surrender your personal power. You may also sabotage nurturing relationships without being aware of the attachment dynamics at play. Coupled with transference, attachment can turn a perfectly-adapted person into an insecure child who lacks meaning and direction. It is therefore crucial to undergo reprogramming. An excellent resource for healing your attachment style is Briana MacWilliam's Youtube channel.

The fear of love

Love is one of the most transcendental experiences a person can have. Along with shame, it is the glue holding society together. For many of us, however, love represents not bliss, nurture and harmony, but suffering, suffocation and disempowerment. This puts us in a terrible predicament, since what we desire above all is the thing we fear the most.

Some of us cannot love except through a split state of mind, wherein we idealise the other so absolutely that we lose ourselves and tolerate their abuse. As our hero's journey progresses, we slowly sober up. We expose duality, face our abandonment wound and evolve the Self, and begin seeing our past as it really was. The rose-coloured glasses fall off. What remain are the painful imprints of dysfunctional love. Above all, our fear of love is exposed, lifted out from the depths of our shadow.

We notice that vulnerability and authenticity terrify us, and that we would rather fall into fantasy than expose ourselves to the full weight of loving. We come to see how we lean avoidant to protect ourselves, which leads to us feeling isolated from the outside world. When we do open up to someone, we attach far too quickly and strongly. Over time, we lose heart and come to question whether we truly do want love. Maybe we are fooling ourselves, we say. We then settle for less because we think we cannot do better, or we sabotage healthy unions because we believe we *can* do better. Behind these extremes is the fear of love. In both cases, we are robbing ourselves of the possibility of a healthy and nurturing relationship.

That fear will never go away. To love is to be vulnerable in the scariest way. In an enlightened relationship, we see the other person not through the lens of the past or an imagined future, but as they are in the present. To love is an act of courage which exposes us to our darkest impulses and most painful memories. We know that the other person is as wounded as us. There is every possibility that the relationship will not end well. However, the enlightened lover also sees that every relationship brings the opportunity to learn about oneself. Every experience of loving is another piece of the puzzle which we had not previously considered. Through healthy communication and mutual respect, you can make progress.

The hero's journey is our responsibility, and the most profound way we can actualise. Yet we can never truly know ourselves except in the eyes of those we love. The hero's journey requires immense courage, and loving openly requires even more. If we enter into love with the heart of a hero, we will always stand a chance of making it to the other side, where much like the ugly duckling, our rightful 'flock' awaits us. As we form enlightened relationships, we can then take flight with people who resonate with and care for us.

The company you keep

Shame arises through relationships, while toxic shame emerges in the wrong relationships. Once you leave the narcissist regime behind, you will continue to meet new people. Some of them will look to form grounded, mutual relationships, while others will encourage you to create a fantasy where they can have their way without accountability. As a result, who you attach to could make or break your growth. Everyone is unique, but relationships tend to funnel into the following three categories:

– **Allies:** These are the people who take a genuine interest in your growth without needing reciprocity. They see your humanity, and derive joy from your presence. We thrive in such relationships because the other person mirrors and supports us while respecting our individuality. They love without agenda, simply for the sake of loving. There is little ego involved. Through loving you, they love life. Like a flower being watered and left in the sun, we bloom effortlessly under such love.

– **Companions:** Companions are people with whom you can pursue a given activity or project, or who belong to the same community. They assist your growth through sharing and mirroring — as long as both of your interests are aligned. There may come a time when one of you decides to change direction, and so your paths will diverge. The longer you are a companion to somebody, the more blurred the line between ally and companion becomes. It is often through shared interests and experiences that two people bond enough to genuinely care about each other's well-being separate from any external arrangement.

– **Regime Leaders:** These are people who will try to charm you for their own ends. They are compelling but shallow, and will accommodate you as long as you are loyal and submissive. Their support is superficial, intended to win you over with an ego boost. They never *see* you, only relating to the idea of what you can offer them. Ultimately, they do not want you aligned with your true purpose. They distract you from what is in your best interest to ensure that you can provide narcissistic supply.

Deciding whose company you will keep is not about classifying people as good or bad, but about determining who best serves your growth. Above all, it is about prioritising your actualisation and cultivating relationships where both parties can thrive. When people focus on their personal power, they create doorways which inspire those around them. When people focus on having power over others, they stunt that person's growth to serve their ego. Control creates backlogs of shame, whereas influence inspires. Seeking to actively impact somebody is how influence turns into control. The focus on power must always be inside. When a narcissist has someone look up to them, they see a chance for narcissistic supply. In reality, we look up to people to give us a hand, and the only way they can help us is by showing us how we can help ourselves. That is the true purpose of power.

The end of manipulation

O, what a tangled web we weave, when first we practice to deceive.

- Walter Scott

Fantasy is a sparkling, gilded cage. While it offers the illusion of perfection, the promise of salvation, and temporary pain relief, it is ultimately fertile ground for manipulation. Fantasy always comes at a price. To maintain the illusion, the people involved have to not only defend against reality, but actively manipulate it. Each person is trying to cope with an *inner Dystopia* while desperately trying to maintain a carefully-balanced *outer Utopia*. The more these two realms are at odds, the more loathing and madness enter the relationship.

The True Self knows all. Beneath the fantasy, we sense what is *really* going on. Yet we brush it all aside. We ignore the red flags, especially when we idealise someone. Denial and fiction help us maintain the status quo, and keep us from facing the dark truth. We sense the other person being dishonest. What they say sounds logical enough, but something feels off. Yet we ignore it all and continue to play along with the 'story' — the perfect love or inevitable success, the long-awaited saviour, the amazing future. We fall in love with the promise of perfection, and resist anything that goes against it. Any alternative seems unbearable.

Those days are over. The unbearable is now bearable. Rather than sacrifice our dignity, identity and resources for a toxic love, we need to call out manipulation, abuse and pointless drama for what they are. We need to take off the rose-coloured glasses and accept the pain of seeing the truth.

As your work with the Self deepens, healthy relationships will gradually pop up in your life like budding plants. Rather than being magical, burning unions, you find that it takes diligence, empathy and mutual respect to develop the bond. Meanwhile, you might experience lapses in judgement, as a narcissistic or toxic person sweeps you up again. Yet your awareness has grown, and your tolerance for insanity is at an all-time low. Inner peace and alignment is a hard-earned state you do not want to lose. Your main task as you transition toward a new life is fortifying and protecting it at all costs.

The one way to deal with drama

Toxicity often catches you off guard. Out of the blue, you find yourself on the back foot, questioning yourself or arguing a point which makes no sense. You end up confused, furious and indignant. You have been viciously called out, dressed down, or attacked with full fury. Other times you end up feeling horrible and shame-riddled for what you did 'wrong.'

Somehow you have become the perpetrator, while standing shocked with the pain of a thousand cuts. What just happened?

The mind of a narcissist is beyond understanding. There is no logic to or reason for these episodes. Gaslighting and drama are merely symptoms of the narcissist's need to shape reality to suit their fractured inner state. Depending on the protector personality, the hidden motive will vary. Avoiding shame, needing attention, misdirection, boredom, grandiosity, or simply wanting their way; the reasons for drama are numerous. You could rack your brain trying to work it out, or opt for another option: *Disengage, and choose sanity.*

Sanity means taking a deep breath, aligning with your Higher Self, and grounding yourself in your inner truth. Insanity involves remaining in the washing machine of madness. It is a fine line between the two. Regardless of their true intention, when a person is constantly hurting you, not playing fair, or not respecting reality, then you have every right to reach for the cut-off switch.

Transcending triangulation

Triangulation can leave you feeling insignificant and unwanted. Yet regardless of what you might believe, you do have a say in the matter. Even when the narcissist weaponises someone else against you, the control remains with you. That is, triangulation has no power without the thoughts, meanings and emotions you apply to the situation. Triangulation, above all, says less about the other person than it does about you. This is a difficult pill to swallow, but is also a doorway to enlightenment. Dealt with correctly, triangulation becomes an opportunity to break codependent habits, learn the art of detachment, and above all, deepen your connection with your True Self. Yes, a triangle has three points, but every single one leads directly back to you. By shifting your paradigms, perspectives and beliefs, you can free yourself for good.

Triangulation can be a great teacher, helping you understand that:

1. **We are born alone, and we die alone:** Accepting and leaning into this reality can help diminish the power of the triangle by bringing your focus deep into your greatest fear.
2. **Enmeshment stunts growth:** If we are to evolve, we must constantly let go of the other person and relate to them from a healthy distance. They will do or say what they must. What is it that you must attend to?
3. **Control is an illusion:** You cannot make the other person 'yours'. You cannot make them give up anyone. You can only make sure you do not give yourself up in the panic, shame, jealousy and anger of triangulation.
4. **The triangle is in your head:** Triangulation only poisons you if you let it. Reject it, call that person out, or see it for what it is. Divest your emotions away from it and into Self-development instead.

We should compare our current Self to our previous Self, and not to others. Every day is an opportunity to connect deeply with our True Self and let it guide us toward growth. Triangulation distracts us from this accessible reality by drawing us into the ego-based duality realm. Less than, more than. Special, not special. Mine, not mine.

We all have an unhealthy desire to be the 'special' one. This comes from childhood, where having the focus of your parent meant life and death. Now you are an adult with countless resources. You can always develop more, both within and without. Your relationships are important, but your survival does not depend on them. Those existential feelings come from the past. You are inherently special, but you do not need another person to access it.

Inner freedom from narcissistic triangulation

Overcoming narcissistic triangulation begins within. A spiritual approach to breaking the triangle includes the following:

- **Self-Remembrance:** Orient yourself with your world, and notice the details around you. What objects are there in the room or the surroundings? What can you hear, feel and smell? Shift your focus out of your mind, where duality rules. Stop analysing, and start being. From this place of neutral observation, you will notice your emotional state. Allow those feelings to arise. Sadness, shame, anger; regardless of what you feel, allow it all. Now ask yourself: Who is feeling these emotions? In this awareness you will remember your Self. There is no more triangle in your mind. There is simply you and your feeling Self, i.e. Your True Self. And by asking the question of who is feeling and noticing, you introduce your Higher Self into the fold. A new triangle emerges, one that serves you rather than crushing you.

- **Centering:** Bring your focus inside your body. Allow your muscles to relax, breathe deeply into your belly, and let the exhale centre you. Keep repeating this until you get a sense of anchoring and calm.

- **Self-Comparison:** Stop comparing yourself to the other person in the triangle, and start comparing your Self to your past Self. What growth have you noticed since a month ago? A year ago? Five years ago? Practice this often. Whenever you feel inferior to or threatened by another person, bring your focus back within and celebrate where you are and where you have come from.

- **Die before you die:** Reflect on death. What might it be like? How do you feel about it? Does it terrify you? Intrigue you? Inspire you to live fully? Think about it. Visualise it. Surrender to it. All reaction to triangulation is a desperate clinging to escape death. Death of a relationship. Death of your self-worth. Death of your specialness. Transcend it all by meditating on and accepting death.

Outer freedom from narcissistic triangulation

Everyone has the freedom to do what they want. You cannot control them, and you cannot control every outcome. However, freedom is not free. It comes with consequences. A person can find someone else 'more special.' A significant other can cheat and leave you behind. A person can be 'better' or 'more desirable' than you. Someone could replace you. Yet if you drop the triangle regardless, then you have a chance to live on your own terms. You are no longer being crippled and controlled by another person's manipulation or circumstances.

With narcissistic triangulation, you have two options:

1. **Codependency:** You control each other, and limit your relationships to each other. You use triangulation as a tool for control. You lash out whenever you feel insecure or threatened. You panic, grow anxious, and try to snoop around on the other person to feel secure again. You feel terrible about yourself and fight for the acceptance and approval of the other person.

2. **Freedom:** There is another way: You let go, and accept the consequences. Your parent might yap on about how great your sibling or cousin is. Your partner might have feelings for others, or have awkward close encounters before deciding to pull away. They might cheat. You might be left for someone else. Your boss might favour your colleague. Others might appear better than you. Ultimately, you need to accept that you have no control over such things, and nor do you need it. You can live with this reality while trusting and hoping for the best. This is the nature of freedom.

The end of narcissistic triangulation

Until you have done the inner work, you are always susceptible to manipulation. If you let it, triangulation will bash you around and gradually wear down your sense of security, serenity and agency. When you have done the work, however, it will cease to impact you. You can speak out firmly when a narcissist introduces another person into the relationship dynamic in a manipulative way. You can bask in your own serenity while they do what they have to. From this place of power, you can then look over what is left of the relationship calmly, and simply act, rather than react.

Walking away is always an option. Either the person is being grossly manipulative, or the situation is untenable for you — or both. But first, ask yourself: What inner work can you do? Can you truly be fine alone? If not, then why? Can you tolerate the presence of 'outsiders' in your intimate space? If not, then why? Can you feel sufficient and worthy, even when others enter your relationship dynamic? Why do you need to be 'special,' i.e. the only one? Is it possible that such a rigid two-person world can grow stale, and become a breeding ground for resentment? Do you not think that some flexibility and trust in yourself and others can create space for wonder and growth to enter into your life?

Regardless of whether you are alone or in a romantic relationship, in a narcissistic triangle or out of it, ask yourself: Can I direct my focus within every single day, and grow from that place? Do that, and you will discover the greatest triangle: You, your True Self, and your Higher Self. There is no more empowering dynamic.

The personal power 'doctrine'

We must be willing to get rid of the life we've planned, so as to have the life that is waiting for us.

- Joseph Campbell

When we stop looking outside for meaning, we can finally access the wisdom of our True Self. This is not about denying reality, but enriching it through living out of our core. The True Self makes life meaningful because it contains the blueprint of who we are, and by allowing it to express itself, everything we do merges with our essence. From there, life evolves naturally. Our task as we embrace personal power is to listen to and accommodate the True Self, one day at a time. Conditioned behaviour will continue to hinder you, negative thought patterns will muddy your mind, and people will continue their attempts to influence and manipulate you. Moments of frustration and confusion will arise. In such cases, when you experience a loss of grounding and control, the best step you can take is to focus inside and reacquaint yourself with your centre. Solitude and a period of releasing may be necessary before you can think straight again and restore your intuition.

Rediscovering trust

Personal power is a spiritual practice which you can cultivate at any time. This involves taking responsibility for your life and making a habit of remaining present. Once you have centred yourself through metamorphosis, you can return to and re-engage the world. In doing so, remember the five emotional forces. When expressing love, be aware of how other people use the power you have given them. When expressing hate, question your endgame. Are you setting constructive boundaries or just offloading frustration and pain? The strains of hate are there to balance power, not to rupture your relationships or assert dominance. Furthermore, when somebody is overly grandiose, and you feel the warm flush of shame come over you, it is time to act, detach, or at least to explore new ways to empower yourself.

The cliche goes: Before you can love others, you need to love yourself. To be more specific: Before you can experience love, you need to be aligned with your True Self. A time came when we stopped being present and had to abandon the Orphan. Deepening our relationship with the True Self is a lifetime process which flowers as we grow and mature. If we hope to succeed in this endeavour, we need to restore inner trust, and the only way to do that is to prove that our Higher Self can stick it out during the ups and downs of our daily experience. Like having a loving parent, the True Self will only flower when it is sure that your Higher Self is consistently there to witness and support it. You will never be able to tolerate the shadow of others unless you have sufficiently embraced yours. Days will come when your inner experience is unbearable. Proving that you can handle the worst is a painstaking process as you cycle between turning away with fear and shame and turning inward with curiosity and hope.

The power of values

To ensure healthy, sustainable relationships, we need to live by a moral blueprint. Coping mechanisms and corrupted protector personalities always serve one value at the expense of all others. Narcissistic supply, getting your way, desirability, acceptance, control; when these are a person's only values, then they are doomed to act immorally. Worse still, they are also doomed to be *acted immorally upon*.

Our values protect us against manipulation and keep us grounded in reality. When dealing with people, we must decide what is in our best interest. That is, we need to set a blueprint for what will and will not fly — and firmly enforce it. If someone acts against our values, there must be consequences.

Furthermore, when judging if someone crosses our values, we should not focus on what they say, but rather *how they behave*. The spoken word is the narcissist's favourite tool for manipulation. A narcissist can be a staunch social justice warrior, screaming from the rooftops that a particular minority deserves rights and fairness. Then, with their next breath, they can put down their loved one, treat them like dirt, and manipulate them into doing what they want.

When we idealise, we cannot set and enforce values. As long as the fantasy is in place, we will see values only as a hindrance. This is why they are so crucial to ending emotional abuse for good; they provide us with a compass in the treacherous waters of a narcissistic relationship. When we lose our way, our values get us back on track.

Some values you can integrate into daily life are:

– Loyalty
– Humility
– Honesty
– Mutuality
– Fairness
– Kindness
– Integrity
– Respect
– Tolerance
– Trustworthiness
– Empathy

When someone *acts* against your values, you will need to push back tenaciously and decisively. The other person must feel your conviction, and eventually, must face real-world consequences. Again, *never* take someone's words as proof of their values. Any value can be faked. For example, a narcissist might declare many times how loyal they are, then follow this up by triangulating. They can feign honesty and respect, but then be quick to gaslight and attack you.

We all *feel* when our values are crossed; this is one of the greatest gifts the True Self offers us. But how many of us are willing to act on that feeling and risk losing someone? Enforcing values takes discipline, strength and a willingness to suffer. It often means standing alone. Those with dependent and anxious styles of relating will find this practice extremely difficult. The cost can be high, but so too can the reward. By filtering out people who do not adhere to our values, we also filter out the people we most want to be done with; narcissists.

Take some time to consider all the ways a narcissist has hurt you. Then ask yourself; what values did they break? Write them down. Search up examples of values online, and see which resonate with you. Add them to the list, then use it each day to determine which behaviours go against your values. Stand firm, communicate your boundaries, and if need be, walk away. Those who share your values will respect you, those who do not will leave you alone, and those who remain will determine your destiny.

There is no room for hypocrisy with this way of life; you also have to hold *yourself* accountable to your values. If you want honesty, do not lie. If you want loyalty, act in the other person's best interests. To maintain your values, you need to have sufficiently explored and integrated your shadow. You need to know your core wounds intimately. Under the watchful eye of your Higher Self, you can catch yourself when your protector personalities act up. It is crucial to find healthier ways to defend the integrity of our True Self without abusing our values.

For values to hold, *everyone* must adhere to them. If you cannot stay true to your values, then you can never trust yourself. If others do not honour your values, then you cannot trust them. Narcissists have a way of corrupting others through their behaviour, since to maintain sanity in such a relationship, a person often has to adjust their behaviour to match. The people in your life are your tribe, and a tribe can only thrive if it has shared values which all parties honour and withhold.

Finding your tribe

What is right living? It is not a given that your family or society has the right script. Your family might be caught up in addiction, denial, perfectionism and dysfunction. Modern capitalist society often wants you to be a good consumer and obedient employee. Social media wants you to feed the attention machine. Narcissist regimes want narcissistic supply. Are these the values we want to rule over us?

Without accountability, psychopathy and narcissism flourish. If your tribe has the right values, then enforcing them in your life becomes far easier. Narcissists isolate you in fantasy because it makes you easier to manipulate. Whether it is family, friends, your therapist, your club or your support groups, your tribe can help ground you in reality. Above all, it can keep you aligned with your morals.

Modern society has not only alienated us from our communities and tribes, it has also contaminated their values. As you move forward, consider your values and those of the people in your life, and finally, work to harmonise them. Invite people who share your values to come together, or seek out groups whose values align with yours. This is the crucial step toward a connected, harmonious and happy life. Nothing protects you from narcissistic abuse more than a loving community of people who care about you, respect you, and see you for who you truly are.

We cannot shine alone. We need to share our masculine and feminine gifts with others, much like a tree offering its fruit. Our human nature compels us to be useful members of our tribe. There is no way around this. Fragmentation and alienation will not work. When you have undergone your hero's journey and discovered your gifts, you will work toward bringing them forth. Create. Teach. Support. Enlighten. Inspire. Lead. Your prosperity becomes your community's prosperity, and vice versa. You do not need to be the master of the hill. You only need to feel constant movement and growth, as well as connection with others. Your tribe is your destiny, for better or worse. So choose wisely.

Finding meaning

Exploring the True Self is a never-ending process; it only goes deeper. While enlightenment can be a catalyst for growth, it can also lead you into an existential void, leaving you with questions such as: "What is the point of all this absurdity?" and: "What is my purpose?" This is the most dangerous aspect of personal power. Being trapped in the narcissist regime shields you from life's challenges like being imprisoned protects you from the outside world.

When you embrace the unknown, you will come face to face with the emptiness inside you. Zen Buddhists refer to this as 'dying before you die.' Beyond rock bottom is the source of all things. You can visit this state any time you like. Yet each time you do, you are faced with life's fundamental questions. This can be the moment you lose your nerve, or the moment your life truly begins. From this state of nothingness, you re-emerge with renewed vitality, and a desire to explore the unimaginable. This is the final step in the hero's journey, known as the 'freedom to live.' Within all of us is the desire for greatness, along with the accompanying fear of our own power. Between these two opposite instincts is where the search for meaning plays out.

Ikigai: A reason for being

Meaning is not a goal, but a state of being. The Japanese call it *Ikigai*, which translates to 'a reason for being.' It is abstract but also provides a powerful framework for actualisation.

Ikigai consists of four components, each of which needs to be integrated:

Figure 16: Ikigai. *Rather than committing yourself to a role based on security and familiarity, you can pursue a path which allows you to cultivate the four traits of a meaningful existence: Passion, Mission, Profession and Vocation.*

1. Passion (Doing what you love)

Some of us find our passion early and pursue it into adult life. Many of us leave it behind as our parents pile on the pressure to do something more 'realistic,' which often comes from their inherited concept of success.

As a child, finding passion is not hard. A child is oblivious to the world's expectations, and is usually still in a state of oneness with their True Self. When considering what your passion is, it helps to think back on what moved you early in life. Was it painting, business, media, fashion, arts and crafts, writing or serving others? If you run short on ideas, the best strategy is to feel around in the dark. Find groups to join or establish a space where you can fool around with an idea that arouses your interest. In a state of openness and curiosity, passion finds its way to you. You only need to be ready to receive it.

Finding things you are passionate about should be done in isolation from the other three elements of Ikigai. Passion is the building block. It is about allowing aspects of the real world to resonate with your True Self; nothing more and nothing less.

2. Profession (Mastering what you do)

Once you establish an activity which feels right, maintain a space where you can practice it daily. Having passion is great, but having confidence and skill makes it much more pleasurable and enriching. If you have been practicing sitting with shame, then the initial phase of lacking skill will be less painful. A bit of awkwardness is expected at the beginning, and if you accept shame, then it becomes a driving force for you to improve.

One hack you can use is bringing someone on board who can work in tandem with you. This has numerous advantages, such as:

- Having someone to support you through moments of doubt.
- You no longer work in a vacuum, and so you have someone to point out any mistakes you make, which saves you a lot of time.
- The accountability to another person keeps you on track when your motivation drops.
- Through sharing and mirroring each other, you both grow exponentially. A thought from you triggers an idea in them, which they combine to create something new, which inspires you further, and so on.

Teamwork makes you both better at what you do, and can be the difference between success and failure as you live out Ikigai.

3. Mission (Providing what the world needs)

Having mission is about finding a target audience with which to share your passion. You can seek out established markets or work toward creating a new one. Opening a dialogue with others about what appeals to them is also useful. It helps to experiment with various ideas and see which ones stick. Having mission in what you do bridges the gap between your True Self and the world. The trickiest part is remaining true to yourself while still providing value to others in a way that resonates with them. This stage is where most people become stuck, being either unable or unwilling to compromise and educate themselves about the market. A certain level of humility is needed to bring your passion to others.

4. Vocation (Being paid)

Being paid for what you love completes the process, where your target audience is what sustains you financially. It is not uncommon for people to abandon their quest for Ikigai at this stage. Whether through influence from outside or due to financial pressure, many of us accept jobs far removed from our passion. It takes perseverance, creativity and a willingness to embrace risk and failure to complete the process.

A life worth living

Establishing and maintaining Ikigai is a challenging, lifelong process fraught with frustration, but is also the backbone of a fulfilling life. Some people split Ikigai up by working a decent job with great people and practicing their passion after hours. Others take risks and invest time and money into finding ways to combine the four elements into their career. Some are more willing to make sacrifices than others. It all depends on your life situation. Again, there is no one 'doctrine.' You will need to be creative with your resources and find ways to draw inspiration and support from those around you. Even when it feels insurmountable, and your life situation is weighing you down, you can always find space to practice the fundamentals of personal power. With more growth comes more resourcefulness, from which comes more capacity to pursue your passion, improve your life and make meaningful contributions to the world around you.

Viva la revolución

Don't walk behind me; I may not lead. Don't walk in front of me; I may not follow. Just walk beside me and be my friend.

- Albert Camus

The label 'narcissist' has become synonymous with exploitation and malevolence. Pigeonholing like this helps the targets of narcissism identify the source of their misery, but in the process threatens to rob them of personal responsibility. As we explored the origins of narcissism in this book, it became apparent that a narcissist was the product of a system beyond their control. The people who controlled that system were also powerless at one point, themselves earlier creations of the same kind of system. This inevitably leads us to the question: Who do we point the finger at? In asking this, we are again reverting to our tendency to split, to find a villain to label as 'bad.'

The short answer is: Nobody is to blame. The problem is *systemic*. This is tough to accept. Rage needs an outlet. *Rage must be acknowledged!* In a narcissistic family, the solution is to hand the trauma down to the next generation. To end this cycle of passing on the hot potato, we need a different approach. The answer is not to seek out a source of salvation or a source of blame, but to look inside. We need to reclaim our hate for the purpose of healthy boundaries, and reclaim our love for the purpose of actualisation. We need each other to thrive, but we are useless to each other if we interact through a false self. If we embrace narcissism as a solution, life becomes a crazy-making drama detached from reality, which in time grows despairing and destructive. The power grab which distracts us from our shame and trauma keeps us from developing genuine connection, and our reluctance to own our shadow keeps us caught in this madness.

Worship, with all of its potential, should only ever be a temporary measure. The one true worship is that which we give to God, and we practice it by connecting deeply to our True Self. Anything else is false worship. Our place as human beings is to grow our personal power and to help others discover theirs. We are born alone, we stand alone, and then we die alone. But that should not hold us back from connecting and sharing with one another. That does not need to stop us from living out our purpose. There is nothing more beautiful than human beings relating deeply and authentically, tethered through mutual sharing and love. Beyond the fear and suffering of existence, life is a beautiful unfolding, and our responsibility is to ensure that all can bloom in their own way. Like flowers in a field, we need to allow others space to grow, and resist the urge to exploit their love. Flowers cannot bloom in each other's shadow.

To love and to actualise is your divine purpose. You can lean on others when times get tough, and you can look outside for inspiration, but you must never forget the truth: power and fulfilment are within, waiting for you to claim them. You only need to give up the fantasy and shift your focus inside, and then fall. Will anything catch you? If you're brave enough to take the leap, you may just find out.

Resources

The Drama of the Gifted Child: The Search for the True Self (Alice Miller)

https://www.goodreads.com/book/show/4887

Healing The Shame That Binds You (John Bradshaw)

https://www.goodreads.com/book/show/98399

The Hero With a Thousand Faces: The hero's journey (Joseph Campbell)

https://www.goodreads.com/book/show/588138

When the Past Is Present: Healing the Emotional Wounds that Sabotage our Relationships (David Richo)

https://www.goodreads.com/book/show/2725658

The Body Keeps The Score: Brain, Mind, and Body in the Healing of Trauma (Bessel A. van der Kolk)

https://www.goodreads.com/book/show/18693771

The Wisdom of Insecurity: A Message for an Age of Anxiety (Alan Watts)

https://www.goodreads.com/book/show/551520

The Narcissistic Family: Diagnosis and Treatment (Stephanie Donaldson-Pressman, Robert M. Pressman)

https://www.goodreads.com/book/show/197874

Waking the Tiger (Peter A. Levine)

https://www.goodreads.com/book/show/384924

Complex PTSD: From Surviving to Thriving (Pete Walker)

https://www.goodreads.com/book/show/20556323

The Sacred and the Profane (Mircea Eliade)

https://www.goodreads.com/book/show/28024

Beyond The Pleasure Principle And Other Writings (Sigmund Freud)

https://www.goodreads.com/book/show/85416

Character Analysis (Wilhelm Reich)

https://www.goodreads.com/book/show/339384

Letting Go: The Pathway To Surrender (David R. Hawkins)

https://www.goodreads.com/book/show/16098910

Malignant Self-Love: Narcissism Revisited (Sam Vaknin)

https://www.goodreads.com/book/show/651943

Reichian Therapy, The Technique for Home Use (Dr. Jack Willis)

https://reichiantherapy.info

Printed in Great Britain
by Amazon

26666691R00253